Prentice Hall
is an imprint of

PEARSON

Harlow, England • London • New York • ... g
Tokyo • Seoul • Taipei • New Delhi • Ca... n

PEARSON EDUCATION LIMITED

Edinburgh Gate
Harlow CM20 2JE
Tel: +44 (0)1279 623623
Fax: +44 (0)1279 431059
Website: www.pearsoned.co.uk

First published in Great Britain in 2011

ISBN: 978-0-273-74413-9

British Library Cataloguing-in-Publication Data
A catalogue record for this book is available from the British Library

Library of Congress Cataloging-in-Publication Data
Bluttman, Ken.
iPad in simple steps / Ken Bluttman.
p. cm.
ISBN 978-0-273-74413-9 (pbk.)
1. iPad (Computer) 2. Tablet computers. I. Title.

QA76.8.I863B63 2011
004.16--dc22

2010040970

10 9 8 7 6 5 4 3 2 1
14 13 12 11 10

Typeset in 11/14 pt ITC Stone Sans by 3
Printed and bound in Great Britain by Scotprint, Haddington

Ken Bluttman

Use your iPad with confidence

Get to grips with practical iPad tasks with minimal time, fuss and bother.

In Simple Steps guides guarantee immediate results. They tell you everything you need to know on a specific application; from the most essential tasks to master, to every activity you'll want to accomplish, through to solving the most common problems you'll encounter.

Helpful features

To build your confidence and help you to get the most out of your iPad, practical hints, tips and shortcuts feature on every page:

ALERT: Explains and provides practical solutions to the most commonly encountered problems

HOT TIP: Time and effort saving shortcuts

SEE ALSO: Points you to other related tasks and information

DID YOU KNOW? Additional features to explore

WHAT DOES THIS MEAN?

Jargon and technical terms explained in plain English

Practical. Simple. Fast.

Ken Bluttman is the author of several books, including *Brilliant JavaScript, Photoshop Elements 8 in Simple Steps, Excel Formulas and Functions for Dummies* and the *Access Data Analysis Cookbook*. Ken develops and maintains several websites. Visit Ken's site at www.kenbluttman.com.

Dedication:

To my precious wife, Gayla. Even as we approach 20 years of marriage, the best is yet to come.

Acknowledgements:

Numerous talented individuals contributed to building and perfecting this book. Special thanks to Katy Robinson and Steve Temblett for their patience and care. Thanks to Natasha Whelan, Sue Gard, the production staff, copy editor and anyone else behind the scenes I am forgetting. Thanks to Neil Salkind for his long-term friendship and support. Thanks to Apple for making the iPad. I'm loving it!

Contents at a glance

9 Reading on the go – iBooks for ebooks

10 Pinning down the map

11 Caring for your contacts

12 Stay organised with Calendar

13 Taking notes

14 Accessibility

15 More about Settings

Top 10 iPad problems solved

Contents

Top 10 iPad tips

1 Hello iPad!

2 iPad basics

3 The iTunes store and the Apps store

4 Web surfing with Safari

5 Staying in touch with Mail

6 Photos on the iPad

7 Watching videos and YouTube movies on your iPad

8 Sound advice – using the iPod app

9 Reading on the go – iBooks for ebooks

10 Pinning down the map

11 Caring for your contacts

12 Staying organised with Calendar

13 Taking notes

Top 10 iPad tips

Tip 1: Create a home page

The Safari web browser in the iPad does not allow you to set a home page. However, it does let you create an icon that leads to a web page of your choice. This icon is placed on the Home screen and tapping it brings you to that particular web page – in much the same way as having a home page.

1. Tap Safari to open it and then navigate to your chosen web page (see Chapter 4).
2. When you are on the web page, tap the plus (+) sign at the top of the browser.
3. A list opens, of which one choice is Add to Home Screen. Tap it.

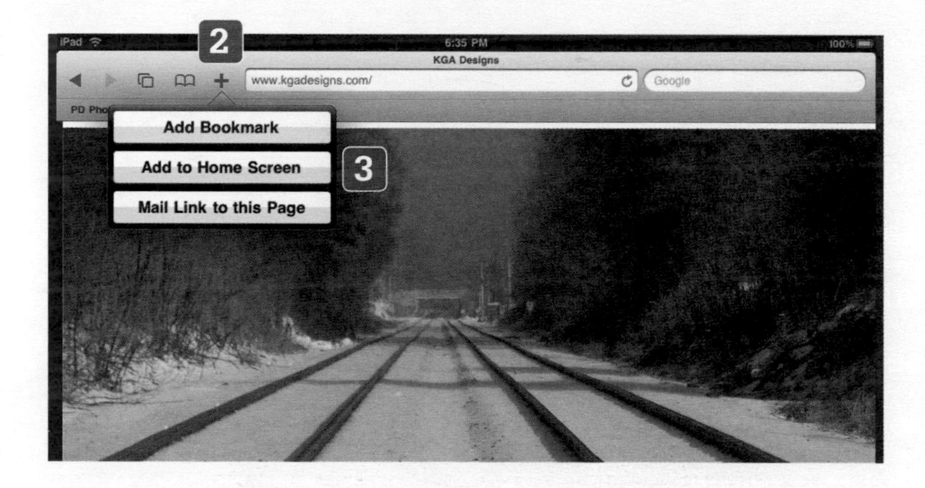

4. An icon is placed on the Home screen. Tapping it will bring you directly to the web page.

HOT TIP: You can set up as many direct to web page icons as you like.

Tip 2: Set an event to repeat

The Calendar app acts as an appointment/schedule book. If you attend an event that occurs at the same time every day, week, two weeks, month or year, you can set it up as a repeating event. This way it will appear throughout the calendar.

1. Set up a new event (see Chapter 12).
2. Tap the Repeat button.

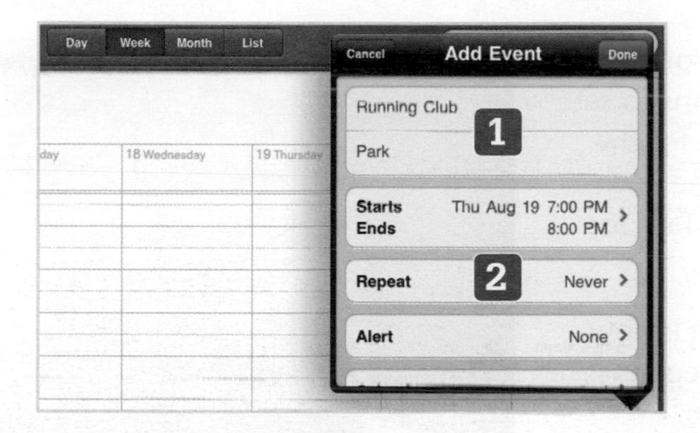

3. A list of repetition options is presented for you to make your choice.
4. Tap Done when you've finished.

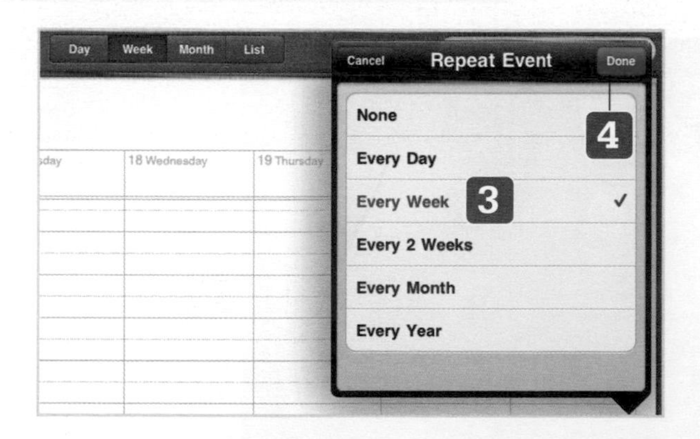

HOT TIP: After tapping Done you will see a button captioned End Repeat. Tapping this lets you set a date on which the repeating event should stop – or lets it repeat indefinitely.

Tip 3: Change the wallpaper

The wallpaper is the background image you see on the iPad. You can change it to a photograph of your choice.

1. Tap Settings, then tap Brightness and Wallpaper on the left. On the right is a button that leads to available photo albums on the iPad.
2. Tap into an available album, then tap a photograph you would like to use for the wallpaper.
3. At the top right of the screen are buttons to set the photograph for the Home screen, the Lock screen or both. Tap one of these buttons.
4. The photograph is now the wallpaper, seen behind the icons.

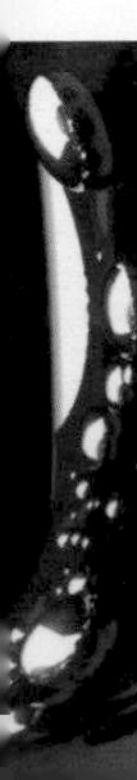

Tip 4: Change how the Home button works

Tapping the Home button once brings the iPad to the Home screen. However, there are options for what a double tap (two quick taps) does.

1. Tap Settings, then tap General on the left side. On the right side, tap Home.
2. Select one of Home, Search or iPod (for music).

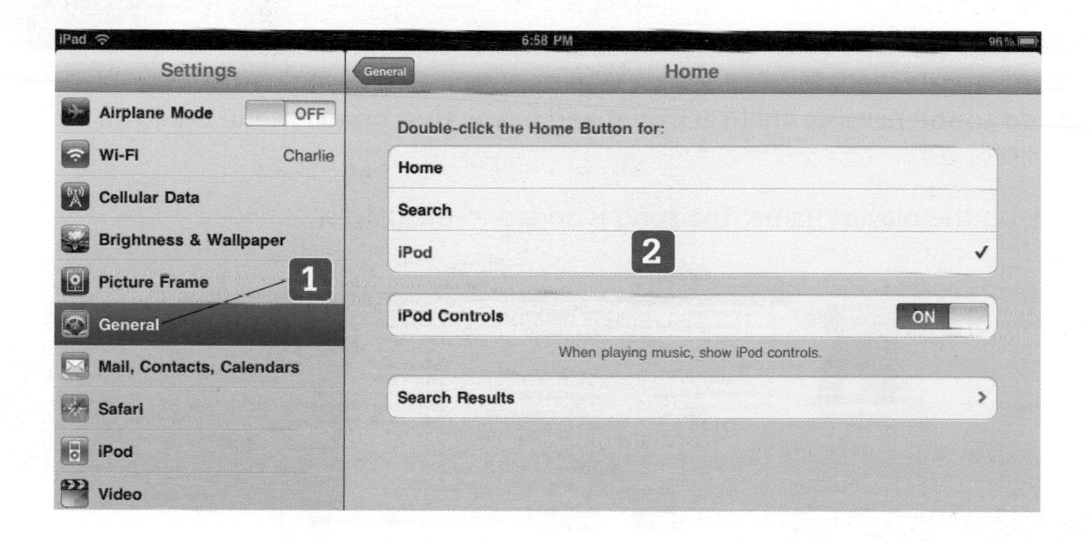

? DID YOU KNOW?

The Lock screen is the one you see when you press the Home button to exit the iPad's Sleep mode.

Tip 5: Make a playlist

A playlist is great for assembling your favourite songs. A common approach is to set up multiple playlists, usually centred around a type of music. A playlist is made in iTunes on your computer and is transferred to the iPad the next time you sync.

1. On your computer, start up iTunes (see Chapter 3).
2. On the menu, click New, then click New Playlist. A playlist is created and needs to be named. Enter a name. Here, a playlist named Morning Music has been created.
3. Near the top, in the Library section, click Music. Then click on albums to see the individual songs. When you see a song you wish to add to the playlist, right-click on it and follow the context menu until you see the playlist.
4. Click on the playlist name. The song is added to the playlist.

PLAYLISTS
iTunes DJ
60's Music
Classical Music
Music Videos
My Top Rated
Recently Played
Top 25 Most Played
Aaron's Favorites
Mellow Songs
Morning Music
2

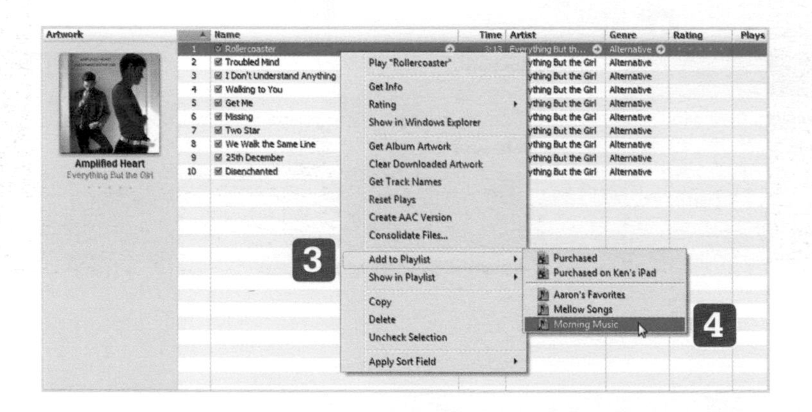

HOT TIP: Instead of adding individual songs to the playlist, add an entire album. From the view that shows album covers, right-click on the album cover, then click to add to the playlist. All the songs are added.

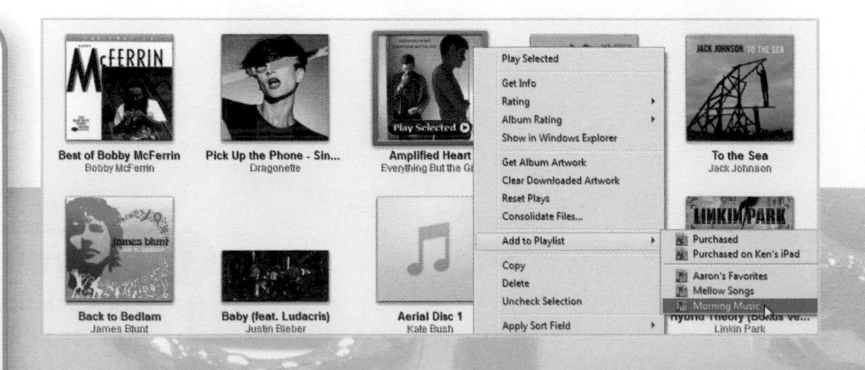

Tip 6: Use international lettering

Although we use an English keyboard, there are occasions where international lettering is needed. No problem! The iPad has this feature.

In any app that uses the virtual keyboard, if you hold your finger on a key, variations of the letter appear. While keeping your finger on the screen, move it to the variation, then remove your finger.

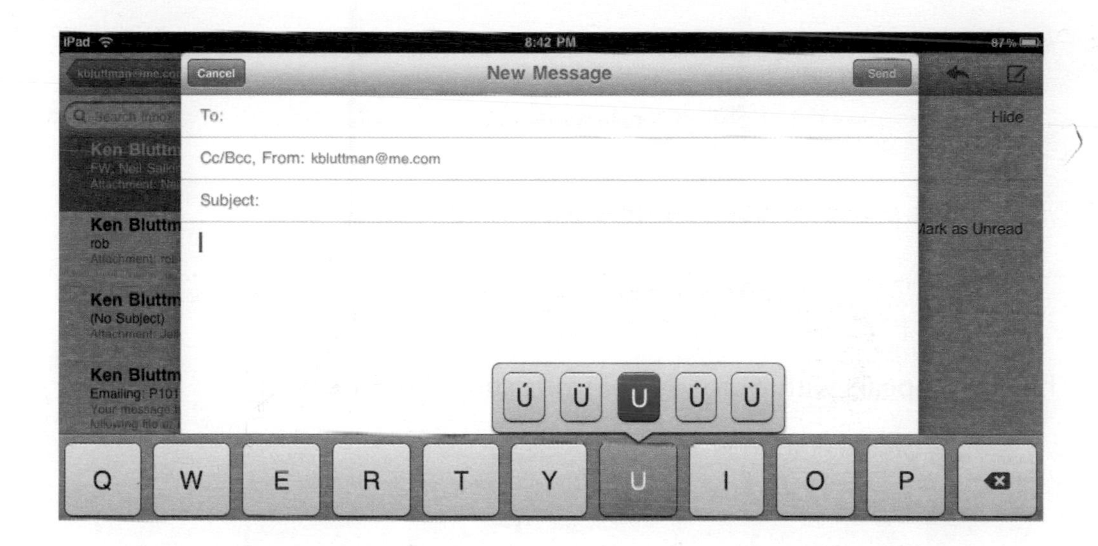

DID YOU KNOW?

The technique is to tap and hold your finger on the base letter. In a moment the variations appear. To use a variation, you have to slide your finger over it, without lifting your finger. Lift your finger only when the required variation is under your finger.

Tip 7: See where a contact is on the map

From your contact list, you can tap on a person's address and the map will open with a location marker of their address.

1. Select a contact from the Contacts app (see Chapter 11).
2. Tap on their address.

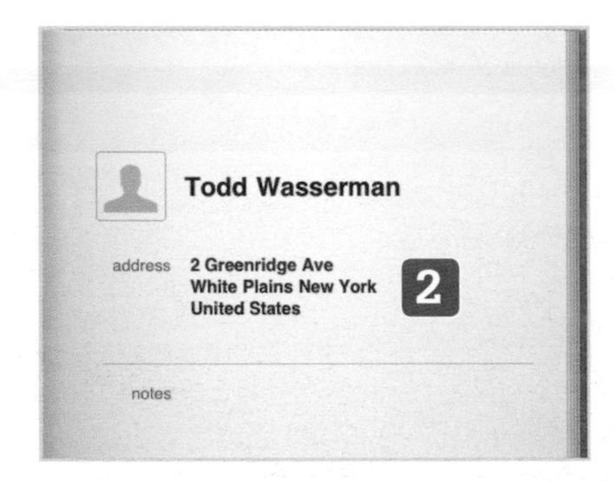

3. The map appears with a dropped pin indicating their address.

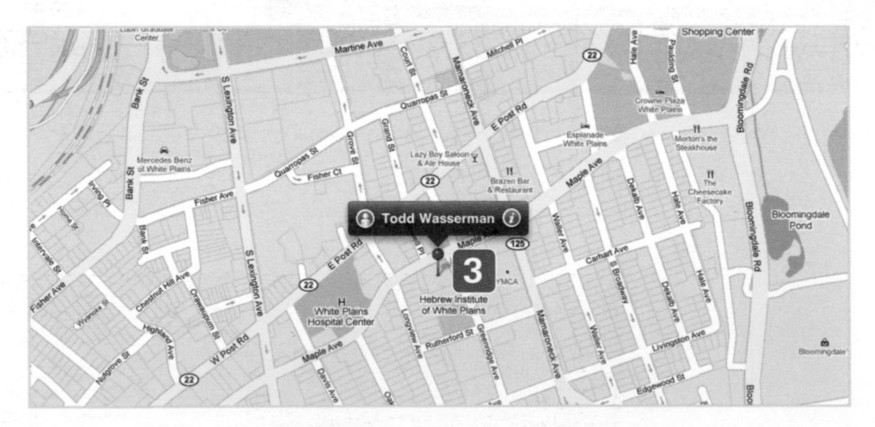

Tip 8: Read the news

There are many news apps in the App store.

1. Tap the App store icon. The App store opens. Search for news (see Chapter 3).
2. Select a news app of your choice. Tap the Free button, or if there is a cost, tap the button that displays the cost.
3. Log in to your account. The app will download and install. A new icon for the app will be on your Home screen.
4. Tap the icon and the app will start.

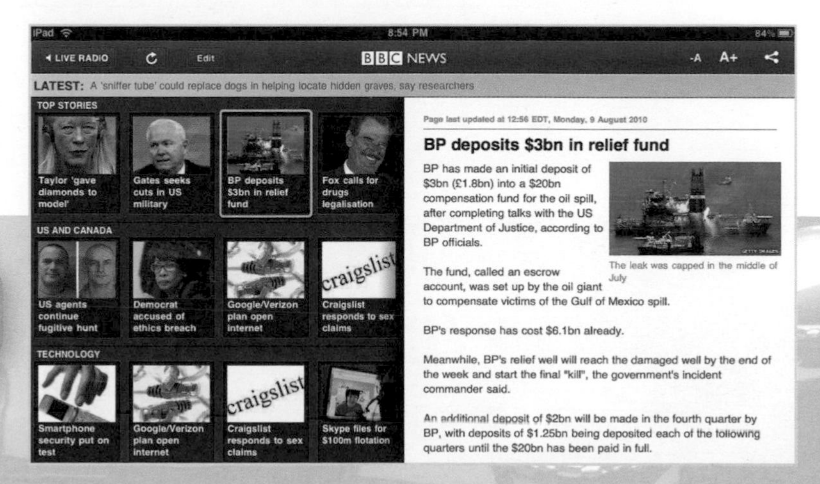

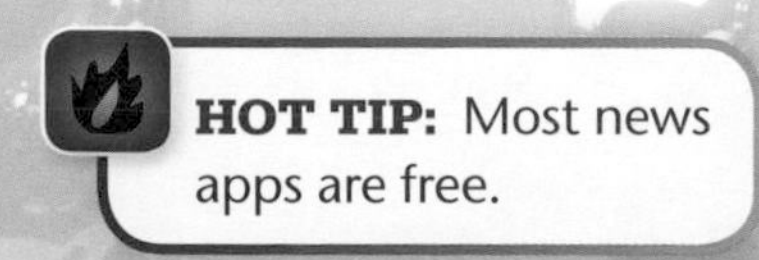
HOT TIP: Most news apps are free.

Tip 9: Use a word processor

The iPad does not come with a word processor. The popular Apple iWorks suite is available in the App store. The suite is not available as a comprehensive package. Instead you can buy the individual apps – Pages, Numbers and Keynote. Pages is the word processor.

1. Tap the App store icon to enter the store.
2. Search for iWorks and tap it in the search results. The individual apps will be shown.
3. Purchase Pages. Once it downloads and is installed there is an icon on the Home screen to start it.

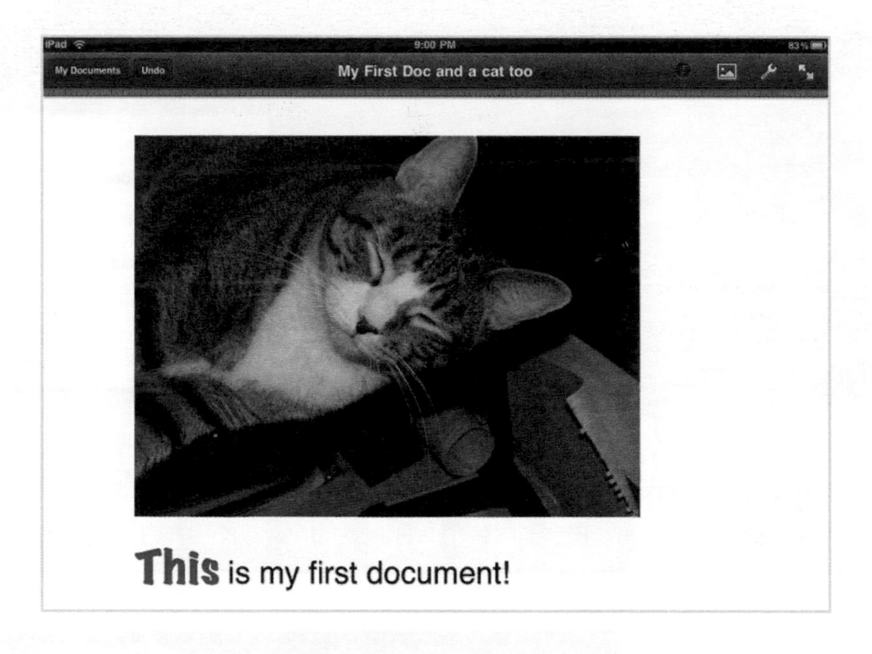

Tip 10: Use a spreadsheet

The Apple spreadsheet program – Numbers – can be purchased in the App store. Numbers is part of the iWorks productivity suite.

1. Tap the App store icon to enter the store.
2. Search for iWorks and tap it in the search results. The individual apps will be shown.
3. Purchase Numbers. Once it downloads and is installed there is an icon on the Home screen to start it.

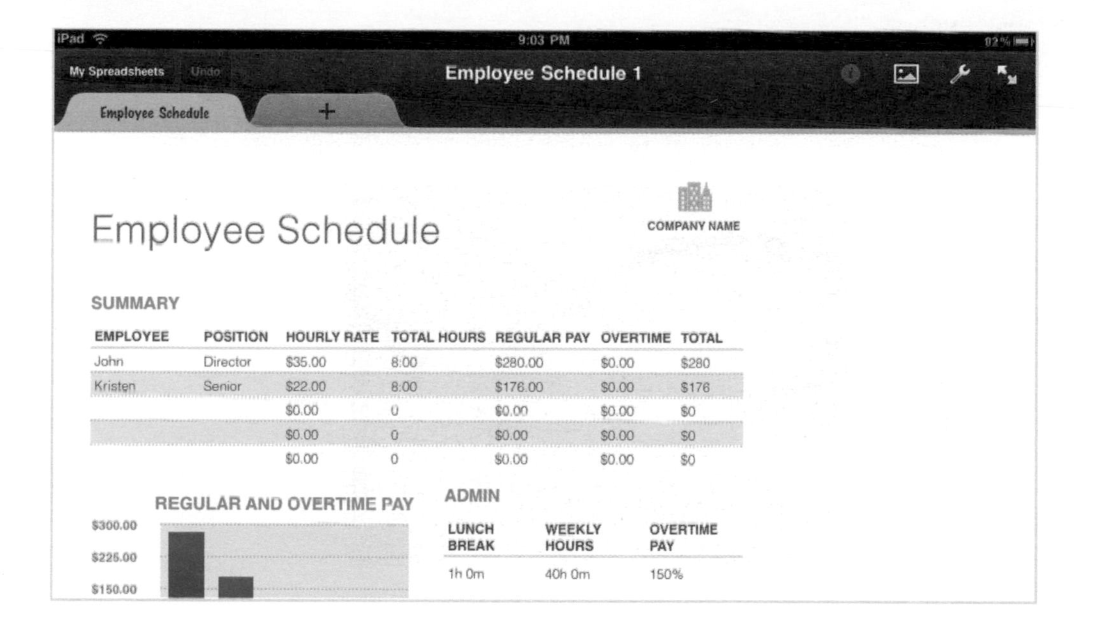

1 Hello iPad!

Introduction

The iPad is a marvel of engineering. There are very few controls on the unit, as most settings and actions are handled through the screen. Around the rim of the iPad are:

- a headphone jack
- a microphone
- the On/Off, Sleep/Wake button
- the screen rotation lock button
- the volume control
- a speaker
- the dock connector
- optionally, the sim card holder.

On the front of the iPad is the Home button and the screen. The screen is touch sensitive and various finger motions, such as tap, swipe, squeeze or stretch, make changes occur to what you are doing with the iPad at that time. These finger movements are collectively known as 'gestures'.

The iPad comes loaded with a number of applications:

- Spotlight Search
- Calendar
- Contacts
- Notes
- Maps
- Videos
- YouTube
- iTunes (the iTunes store)
- App Store
- Settings
- Safari (for web browsing)
- Mail
- Photos
- iPod.

Each of these is described in detail in this book. Some of the applications require a connection to the internet. The iPad can connect to the internet through either Wi-Fi or a 3G account.

Turn your iPad on

Assuming your iPad is off (not just in Sleep mode):

1. Press down and hold the On/Off, Sleep/Wake button until the Apple logo (a picture of an apple) appears.
2. The Apple logo stays present on the screen until the iPad is ready for use. This takes a few moments.

HOT TIP: If the Apple logo disappears and the screen is just dark, it is actually ready for use. Press the Home button to get started.

Turn your iPad off

To turn the iPad off:

1. Press and hold the On/Off, Sleep/Wake button until a slider appears on the screen to confirm your wish to turn off the iPad.
2. Move the slider to the right. The iPad will turn off.

HOT TIP: If you press the On/Off, Sleep/Wake button quickly without holding it down, the iPad will enter its Sleep mode. This turns the screen dark – the iPad is still on. To bring the screen back to life, press the Home button.

Connect to a computer

With your iPad you received a cable. One end connects to the iPad dock connector and the other connects to a USB (universal serial bus) port on a computer. It should be obvious which end is used for the connection to the iPad (the multiple pin configuration) and which end is a standard USB connection.

1. Connect the cable to the iPad dock connector.
2. Plug the other end of the cable into the computer.

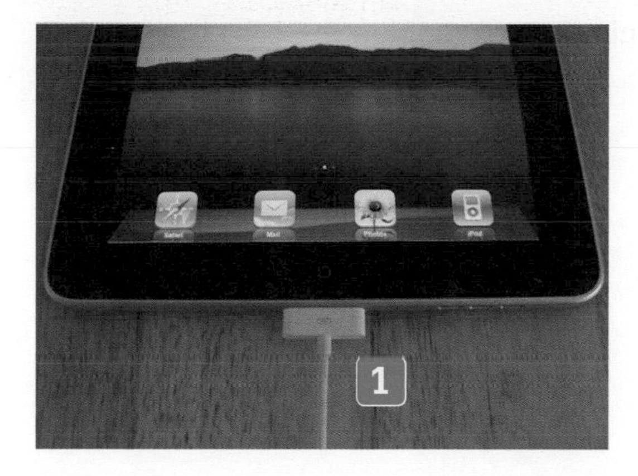

Connecting the iPad to a computer is useful for a variety of activities:

- syncing the information on the iPad and the computer
- syncing purchases and downloads from the iTunes store and the App store
- copying photographs (this is not done using iTunes).

DID YOU KNOW?

Photographs can be copied to your computer by accessing the iPad as a device connected to the computer, in the same way you would work with a memory stick or memory card.

WHAT DOES THIS MEAN?

Syncing: The action of having data and applications replicated between the iPad and the computer, essentially like a mirror image.

Disconnect from a computer

Once the iPad is connected to a computer it is seen as an external device from the computer's perspective. To properly remove the connection, one of two methods should be followed:

1. If iTunes is running on the computer, it recognises the iPad and has an eject button. Click on the eject button before pulling the cable out of the computer. Nothing is physically ejected so don't expect to see something come flying out of the computer!
2. If iTunes is not running, simply unplug the cable.

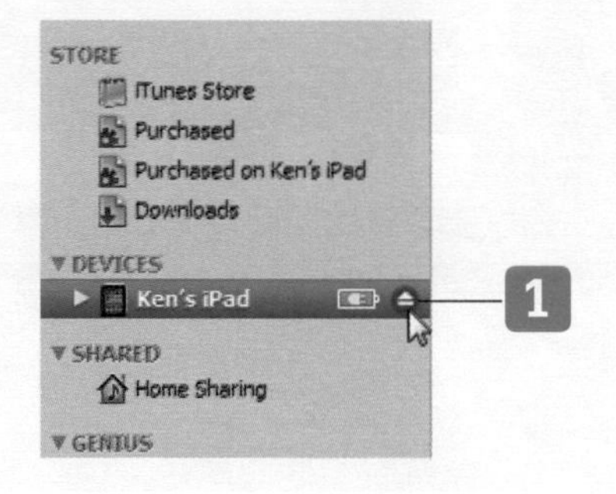

ALERT: Do not disconnect from the computer while the iPad and the computer are syncing. The iPad's screen will tell you that a sync is active or iTunes on the computer will alert you.

Charge the battery via a USB connection

In theory, having the iPad connected to a computer should charge the iPad's battery. In reality, often the USB connection does not carry enough power to charge the battery. Probably you will see a status note that the iPad is *not* charging, as shown here.

HOT TIP: Even though it appears the iPad is not being charged through the USB connection, it still may be. You can tell when you disconnect from the computer and see on the iPad screen how much charge is available.

Charge the battery with the AC adaptor

The iPad comes with an AC adaptor for recharging the battery from an electric socket.

1. Connect the cable to the dock connector on the iPad.
2. Plug the USB end of the cable into the AC adaptor.
3. Plug the adaptor into an electric socket.

On the iPad screen the amount of battery charge is seen in the upper right corner.

DID YOU KNOW?

The cable is used for charging and also for connecting the iPad to a computer.

Install iTunes on your computer

Some clarification is helpful here. iTunes is an application (app). The iTunes store is where you purchase items that will run on your iPad. The iTunes app on the iPad connects with the iTunes store. The iTunes application that runs on the computer provides access to the store as well as to other features such as syncing. You need to install it. To do so:

1. On your computer, browse to www.apple.com/itunes. You will see the free download button. Click it and download the application into a folder of your choice.

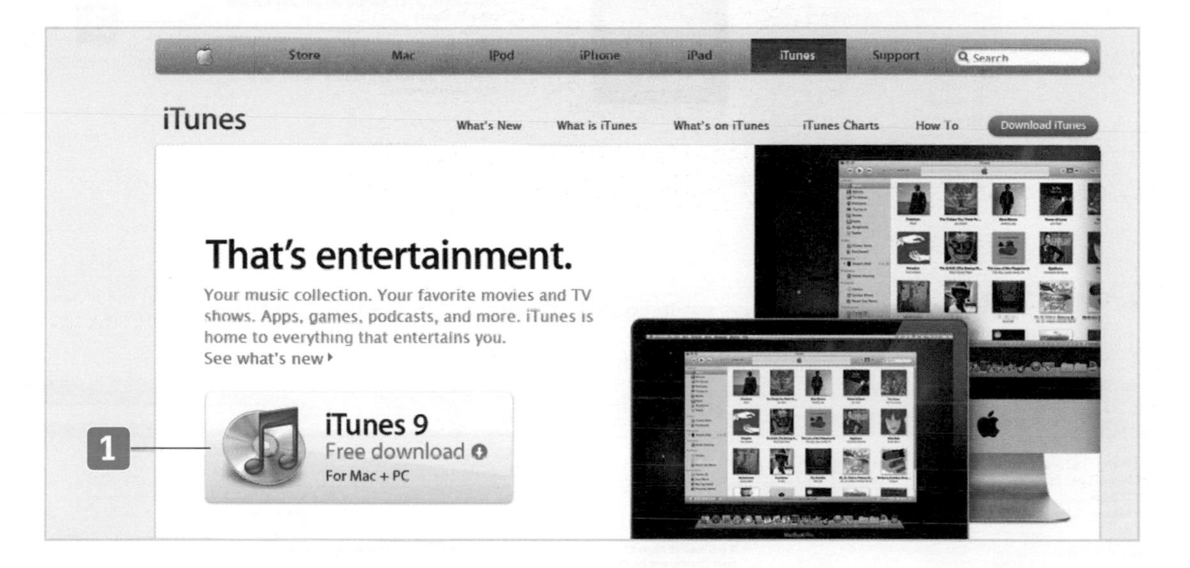

2. Once the download is complete, browse to the folder where you have saved the downloaded file. Double-click it to start the installation.

DID YOU KNOW?

You can make purchases from the iTunes store from your computer or directly from the iPad using the iTunes app. In either case you will need to log in to make a purchase, so make sure your login information is easy to find.

3 Connect your iPad to your computer by using the supplied cable. A couple of screens will appear so that you can register your iPad and set up an account with the iTunes store.

Sync the iPad with iTunes

When iTunes is running on the computer and the iPad is connected to the computer, syncing will occur. Syncing simply means that anything new on the iPad (such as new apps, movies and so on) will be copied from the iPad onto the computer. This essentially serves as a backup. Not a bad thing to have!

Syncing works in both directions. Any new items bought or downloaded from iTunes onto the computer will be copied over to the iPad. At the end of the sync process the computer and the iPad will have identical data, media and apps.

When the sync process is active, iTunes on the computer and the iPad itself both indicate the sync is in progress. The two images here show the iPad indicating it is syncing and a status bar that appears in the iTunes app on the computer.

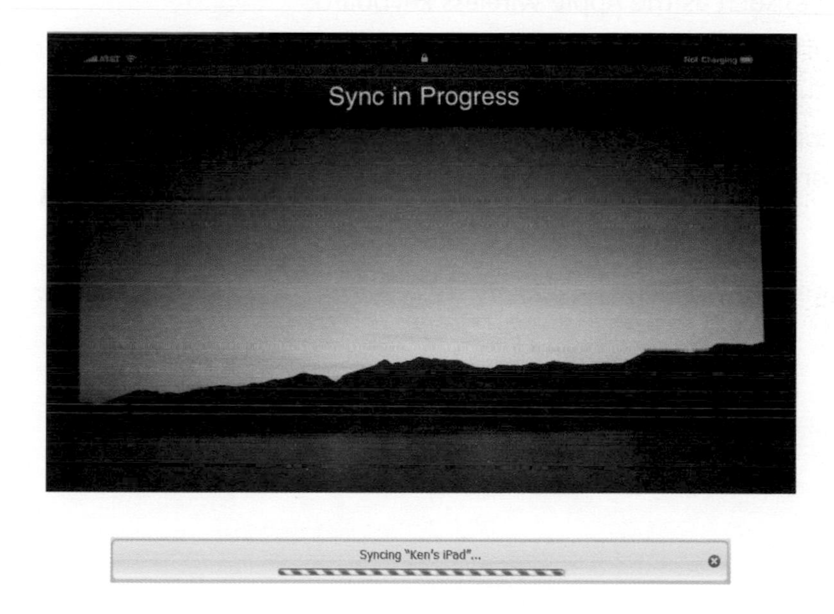

Syncing "Ken's iPad"...

1. Connect the iPad to the computer. The sync process starts automatically.
2. If iTunes does not start up automatically, start it manually.

Understand status icons

There are numerous small icons that appear when needed, or are always present, that give you feedback about the iPad.

Some of these are as follows:

- Airplane mode: the icon is of an airplane. In Airplane mode, the iPad turns off all wireless capabilities.
- Battery: the icon is of a battery, with a percentage next to it. The percentage shows how much battery power remains.
- Bluetooth: this icon is of the standard Bluetooth symbol. This indicates the iPad has its Bluetooth feature on – and that it can connect wirelessly with other Bluetooth components, such as the Apple wireless keyboard.
- Wi-Fi: this icon is of the standard Wi-Fi symbol. This shows the iPad has Wi-Fi capability turned on. The iPad is able to connect to available Wi-Fi hotspots.
- 3G: This icon literally says 3G. This means the iPad is able to connect with the internet from anywhere a 3G cellular signal is present.

Change the view from landscape to portrait or portrait to landscape

The iPad screen can show its presentations to you no matter which way you orient (or hold) the iPad. By simply turning the iPad sideways, relative to which way you are holding it in the first place, the screen will re-orient itself.

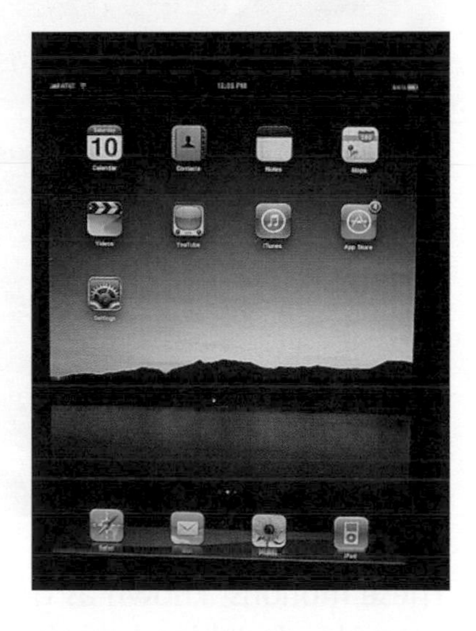

HOT TIP: Along the edge of the iPad is the screen rotation lock button. When this is engaged the iPad will not change orientation – it will stay in whichever orientation it was in when you engaged the lock.

Use the multi-touch screen

The iPad's screen is, of course, touch sensitive. Given this fact, there is a variety of actions available: tap, tap with two or three fingers simultaneously, flick, tap and hold, stretch (similar to zooming in) and squeeze (similar to zooming out). The two images here show how a photograph looks in its initial state on the iPad and then how it looks zoomed in using a stretch motion done with two fingers (the fingers are placed on top of the screen and then moved away from each other).

These motions, known as gestures, are used where it makes sense to the activity. For example, stretching is useful when you wish to zoom in on a picture or map. Tapping and holding down your finger leads to select, cut, copy, paste and other functions that are used with text.

The virtual keyboard

Depending on the activity, you may need a way to enter alpha-numeric text into the iPad. For example, when composing an email this is clearly necessary. Luckily, the iPad is smart and knows when to present a keyboard for your use.

The design of the keyboard is quite similar to an external one, but with a few particulars. Notice that in the initial view of the keyboard there are no numbers and most punctuation characters are not displayed. As you type, when numbers or other characters are needed, you press the key in the bottom left corner of the keyboard. This changes the keys to show numbers, punctuation and symbols.

To revert to the first display showing the alpha characters, press the key in the lower left again.

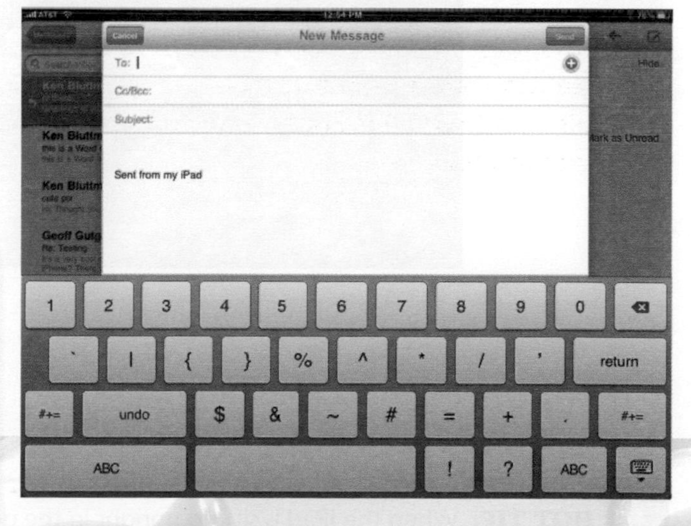

HOT TIP: If you wish the keyboard to disappear from the screen, press the key on the lower right of the keyboard. Tap the screen to make the keyboard return. In particular you need to tap in a place that is related to keyboard use. For example, the keyboard will return in the image here only if you tap somewhere in the heading area or body of the email.

Connect to a dock

An accessory item is the dock. This is a small stand that holds up the iPad so your hands are free. Note, the iPad connects to the dock via the dock connector on the iPad. This therefore limits the iPad to be in portrait orientation when using the dock. The dock is useful for watching a movie or some other activity that does not require you to touch the screen too often.

The dock is constructed in such a way that while the iPad is connected, the cable can run from the back of the dock to facilitate charging. In other words, the dock not only makes it easier to use the iPad, it can charge the iPad's battery at the same time.

1. Connect the iPad to the dock by placing its dock connector over the connector on the front of the dock.
2. Optionally, connect the cable to the back of the dock and then into a computer or an AC outlet to charge the iPad.

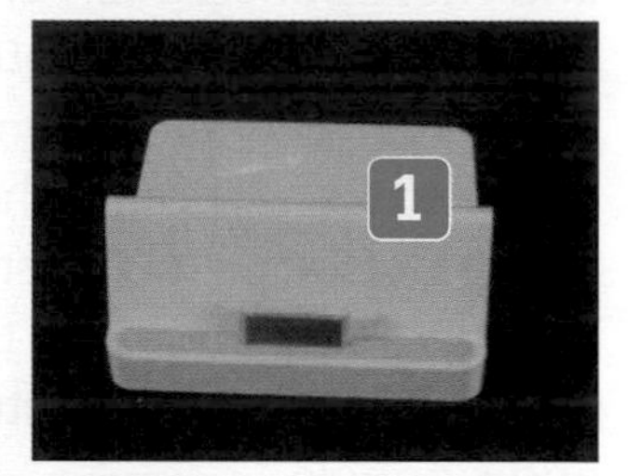

HOT TIP: When the iPad is sitting upright in the dock it is difficult to do any significant amount of typing on the virtual keyboard. An alternative is to have a wireless keyboard paired with the iPad via a Bluetooth connection. Then you can type on the keyboard without disturbing the iPad sitting on the dock.

Use wired headphones

Want to listen to something but need to keep the sound down? Consider using headphones. There is an external headphone jack on the top of the iPad.

1. Connect headphones to the iPad.
2. Listen to music, a movie, YouTube or some other media method that has sound or music.
3. Control the volume using the volume switch on the side of the iPad.

Connect Bluetooth devices

Bluetooth technology allows enabled devices to communicate wirelessly. Typically, the devices have to be within a few metres of each other. To use Bluetooth on the iPad it has to be turned on and then a compatible Bluetooth device is paired with the iPad. The process then begins with the iPad's 'discovery' of the Bluetooth device.

A popular Bluetooth device used with the iPad is Apple's wireless keyboard. These steps show how the two devices are paired, making it possible to use the wireless keyboard to type so that the text appears on the iPad.

1. Place a Bluetooth device near the iPad and turn it on if necessary.
2. On the iPad, tap Settings.
3. Tap the General category on the left.
4. On the right, you should see Bluetooth. Tap it.
5. Turn Bluetooth on by tapping the On/Off button. The Bluetooth device will be listed, but not yet connected.
6. Tap on its listing and it will connect.

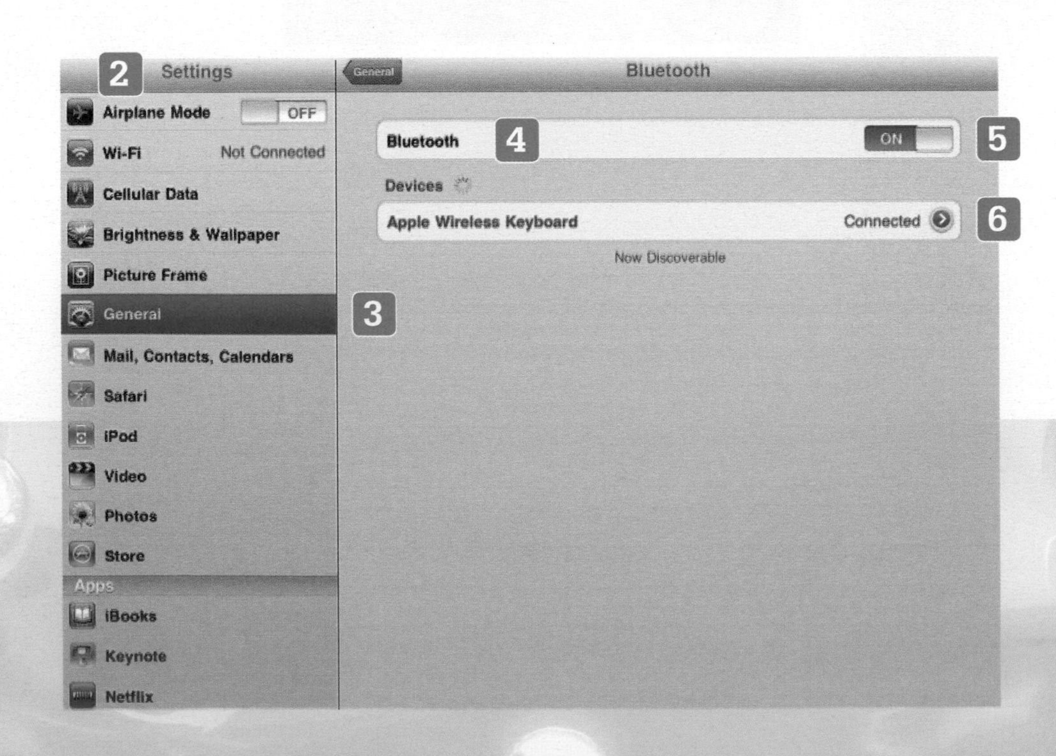

2 iPad basics

Introduction

Chapter 1 provided an introduction to the most vital things you need to know about the iPad – such as turning it on! This chapter continues with basic iPad goodies – more things you need to know about to make the best use of the iPad.

Learn about Settings

The iPad is a sophisticated device with much power and flexibility. In order to make the best use of the variety of features, you have choices of how these features work. Many of the selections you make are found in Settings. You enter Settings by tapping the Settings icon.

Once you are in Settings, the next actions you take depend on what you are making selections about. For example, you might be setting up email options, selecting the brightness of the screen, connecting to a Wi-Fi source or any other number of things.

1. Tap the Settings icon.
2. On the left, tap the area you wish to access.
3. Make your selections on the right side of the screen. Depending on what you tapped on the left, the choices on the right may require 'drilling down' to make selections. This means you may need to tap something on the right to open further choices.

HOT TIP: Apps that you download from the Apps store may have selections that are made in Settings. If so, you will see the apps on the left. Tap an app's icon to make selections on the right side of the screen.

Join a Wi-Fi network

In Settings is an option to set up Wi-Fi. The iPad senses available wireless networks and then presents them in a list.

Some Wi-Fi networks are open, while others are password protected. In the list of found networks, any that have a picture of a lock require a password to get connected. This is sometimes referred to as the WEP identifier.

1. In Settings, tap Wi-Fi.
2. On the right, if W-Fi is set to off, tap the On/Off button to turn Wi-Fi on.
3. Select a Wi-Fi source to connect to.
4. If a password is required, a box will pop up for you to enter the password.

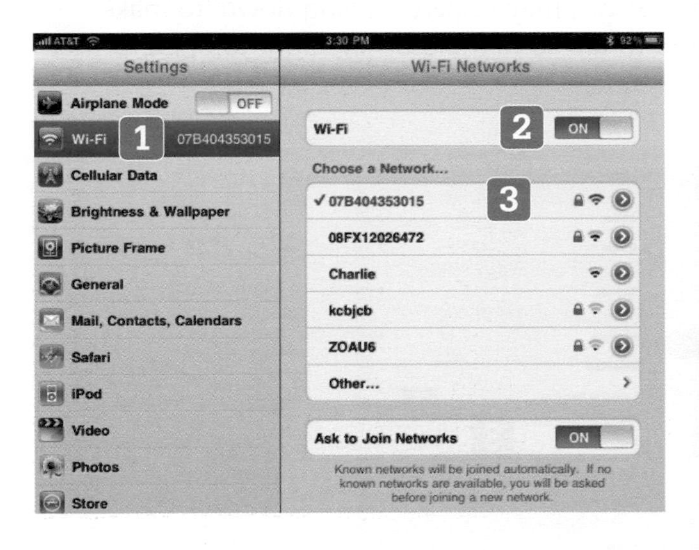

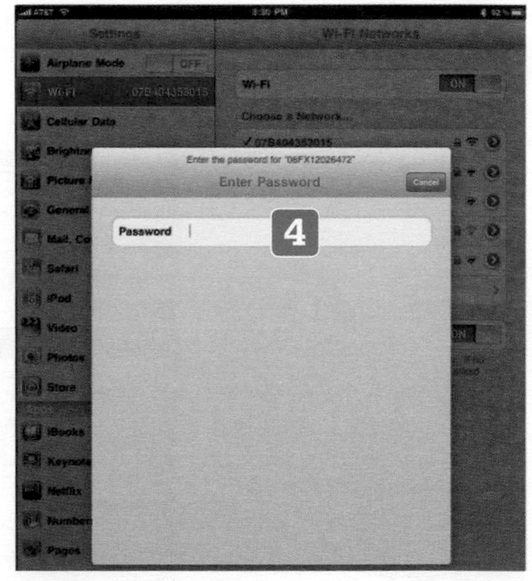

? DID YOU KNOW?

A wireless network is found only when you are near a source that provides one. They are not available everywhere in the same manner that telephone cellular service is. For that convenience you need to sign up for 3G service. Not all iPads come with this option.

WHAT DOES THIS MEAN?

Hotspot: Where a wireless network is found.

Join a cellular data (3G) network

Signing up for 3G service provides the iPad with the same wireless connectivity as a mobile phone. This option is available on certain iPad models.

1. In Settings, tap Cellular Data.
2. On the right, if Cellular Data is off, tap the On/Off button to turn it on.
3. Tap View Account. A box will pop up asking for information to set up an account.
4. Make the appropriate selections and enter all required personal and payment method information.
5. Tap the Next button if and when it appears. Agree to any presented service agreement (assuming you are in agreement!).
6. After all the information has been entered, the account will be set up. This may take a few minutes. When finished, you will see a message that the process is complete and the account is active.

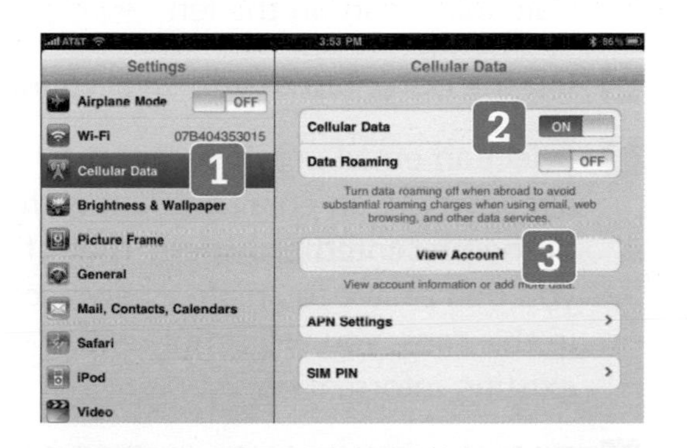

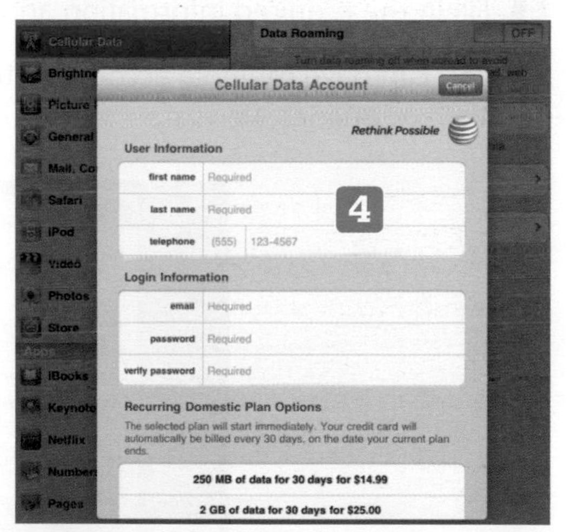

ALERT: Depending on where you are, you may be presented with a choice of provider and one or more screens to make appropriate choices.

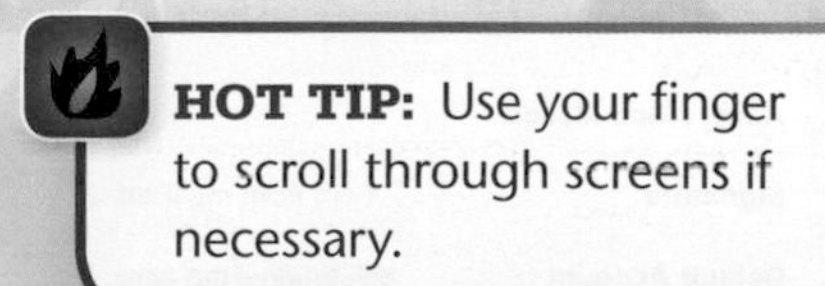

HOT TIP: Use your finger to scroll through screens if necessary.

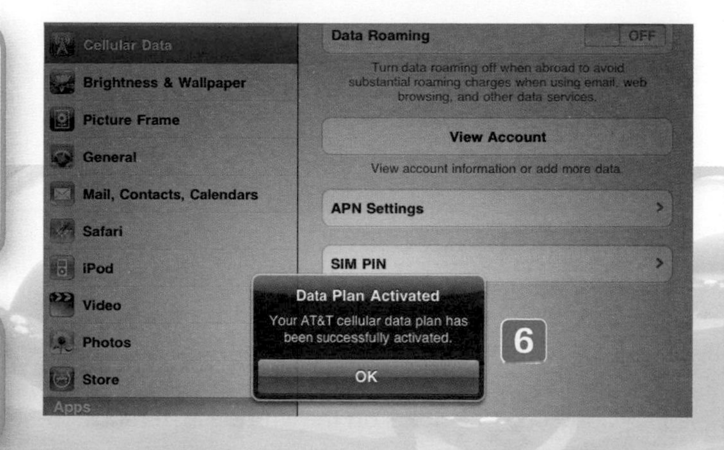

Set up an email account

Of course, you'll want to use the iPad for email. You can even have multiple email accounts. One account will be the primary account. This is seen in Settings.

1. In Settings, tap the Mail, Contacts, Calendars icon on the left.
2. On the right, tap to add an account.
3. Select an email provider. You may already have an email account with one of the presented providers. That's fine – you don't have to create a new account in this case, you will simply enter your existing information.

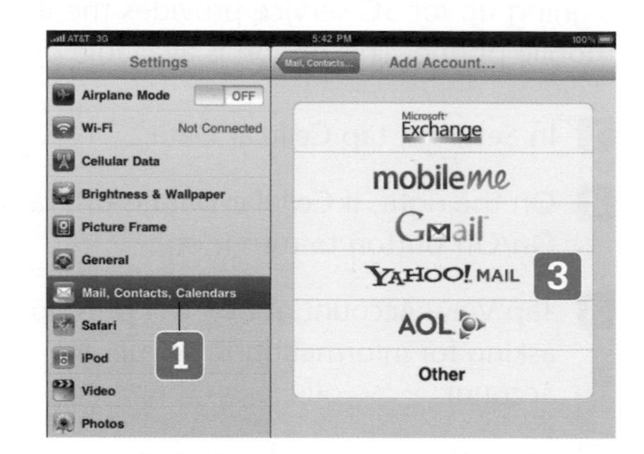

4. Fill in the required information and tap the Save button.
5. You can have multiple accounts – these can be email accounts and other services such as online calendars.

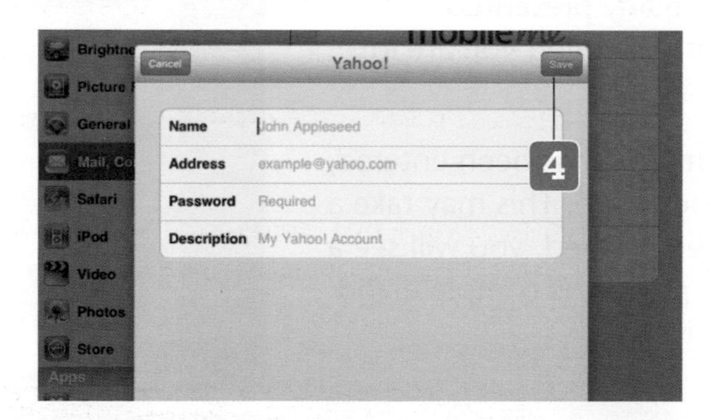

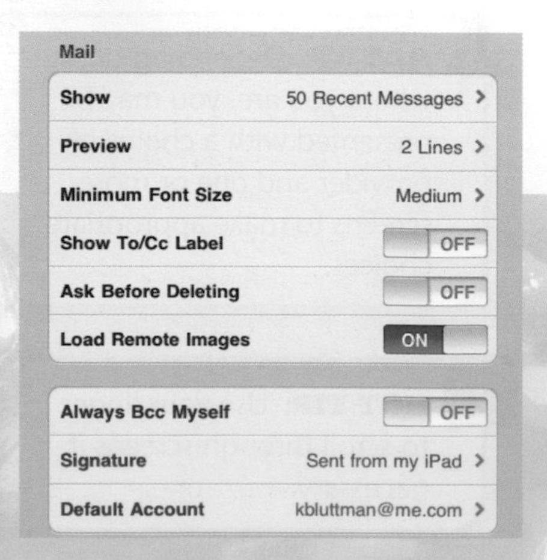

DID YOU KNOW?

There are several options you can set for email use, such as how many messages to show in your inbox, creating a custom signature line and more. These settings are available when you first tap Mail, Contacts, Calendars on the left side in Settings.

Rearrange icons

The core icons (Contacts, YouTube, Settings, etc.) sit on the Home screen. Then, any new apps that you download will also put an icon on the screen.

When there are enough icons they will appear on a second (third, fourth, etc.) view of the screen. You see these extra screen views by scrolling them into view by swiping your finger on the screen. On the screen, a small series of dots shows how many views of the screen are available.

You may find it advantageous to rearrange the icons to suit the way you use the iPad. To do so:

1. Tap and hold your finger on any icon. All the icons will begin to shake. This indicates they are ready to be moved.
2. Tap and hold your finger on the icon you wish to move. This does not have to be the icon you first tapped to prepare the icons for moving.
3. Keeping your finger on the icon, drag it to another place on the screen. You can even drag the icon onto one of the other views of the screen by dragging it to the edge of the screen. The screen will update to the next view of additional icons.
4. When you remove your finger from the screen the icon will situate itself where you dropped it off.
5. When you have finished rearranging icons, press the Home button to stop the icons from shaking and thus returning the screen to its default state.

? DID YOU KNOW?

You can move but not delete the core icons, however you can delete other icons. When the icons are shaking, the non-core icons show a small delete button in the upper left corner (looks like a lower-case x). Tap the delete button on an icon and the icon will disappear.

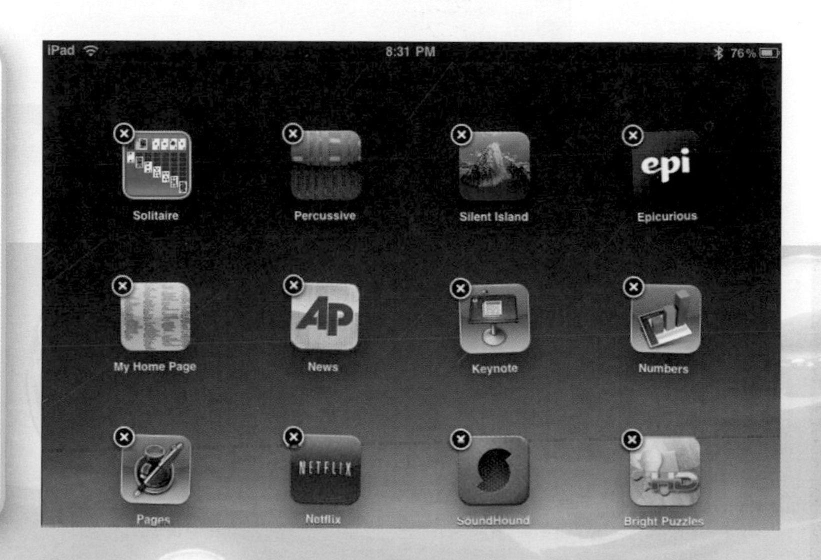

Customise the Home screen wallpaper

The background picture on the screen can be changed. You can use one of the default pictures that come with the iPad or a picture of your own (see Chapter 6 for how to get photographs onto the iPad).

1. Enter Settings and tap the Brightness & Wallpaper icon on the left.
2. On the right side of the screen are images of the current background and locked screen Wallpaper. Tap either of these, or tap the arrow to the right of them.
3. Tap either the Wallpaper button or on a photo album of your choice.
4. When the selected album opens (or if you tapped the Wallpaper button) there are thumbnail pictures of the photographs in the album. Tap on one to select it to become the wallpaper.
5. A preview of the picture is shown. You can choose to have the picture as the background for the Home screen, the locked screen or both.

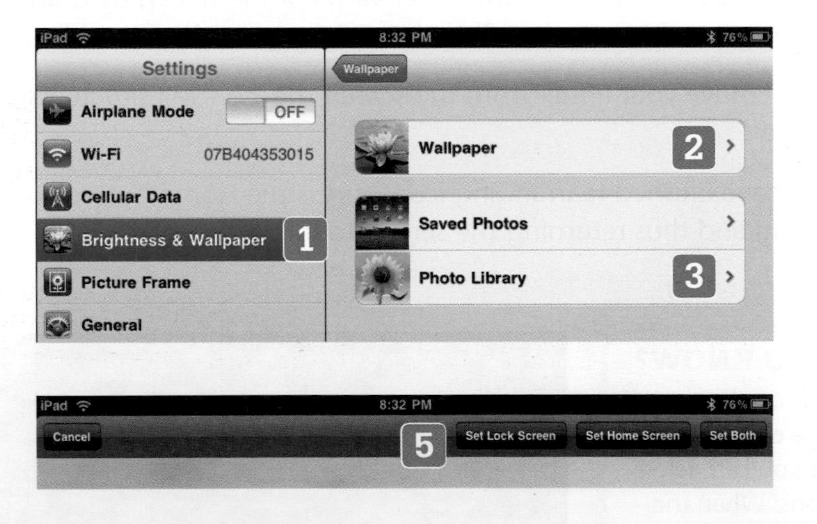

HOT TIP: You can take a picture of what is shown on the iPad. This is known as a screenshot. To do this, press the On/Off, Sleep Wake button and the Home button at the same time. A screenshot is made and is automatically stored in the Saved Photos library.

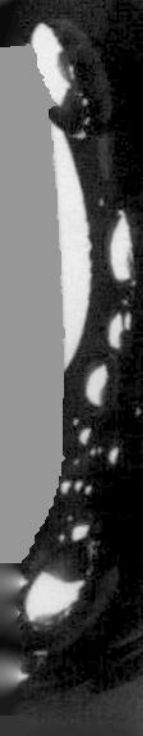

Cut, copy and paste

The first step in any cut/paste or copy/paste operation is to select the text you want to work on. To be able to do this you must have the cursor in the correct place in the text. On the iPad you can do this in two ways:

1. Use the arrow keys to move through the text.
2. Tap and hold your finger on the text. A bubble will appear with a magnified view of the text underneath. You can then drag your finger to position the cursor precisely where you need it.
3. When you release your finger, a bar appears with Select and other options. This example will select some text, cut and paste it in a different location.
4. Tap Select. The word to the right (orange in this example) will be selected.
5. Tap and hold one of the small balls that appear at the selected word. Then you can drag the selection to make it smaller or larger. Here, it is extended to include lemon and kiwi.
6. Tap Cut to remove the selected words. They are now available to paste elsewhere.
7. Tap elsewhere in the text. Here, the cursor is positioned in front of the word apple.
8. Tap Paste. The words are rearranged as planned.

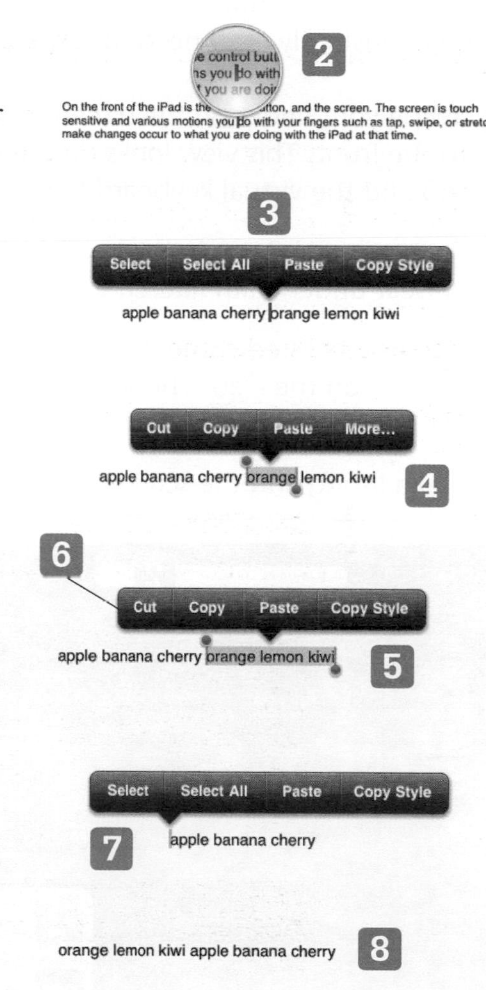

HOT TIP: After you have selected some text, you will see a place on the Cut Copy Paste bar to tap for 'More...' options. This leads to dictionary-type functions, such as getting the definition of a word or selecting from a list of replacement words.

Search your iPad

As time goes on and you enjoy productive sessions with your iPad, it will fill up with email, media and other data. Wouldn't it be great if you could search through all of that for something pertinent. Well, you can!

The left-most view of the screen is actually a search feature (known as Spotlight Search). It is a friendly and intuitive search feature. As you type into the search box, results are displayed instantly – no need to tap a button to start the search.

1. Swipe your finger on the screen to the right, which pulls the left view of the screen to the front. This view looks different – there are no icons, just the search bar at the top and the virtual keyboard (not displayed in the image here).
2. Enter a search term in the box. You'll notice that as you type each letter the results appear underneath filtered to what you have typed in.
3. The results listed come from email, media, contacts, the calendar and any other data sources on the iPad. The search result listings are categorised by type, identified by the icons on the left side.
4. Tap a listing and the screen will display the source of what Search found.

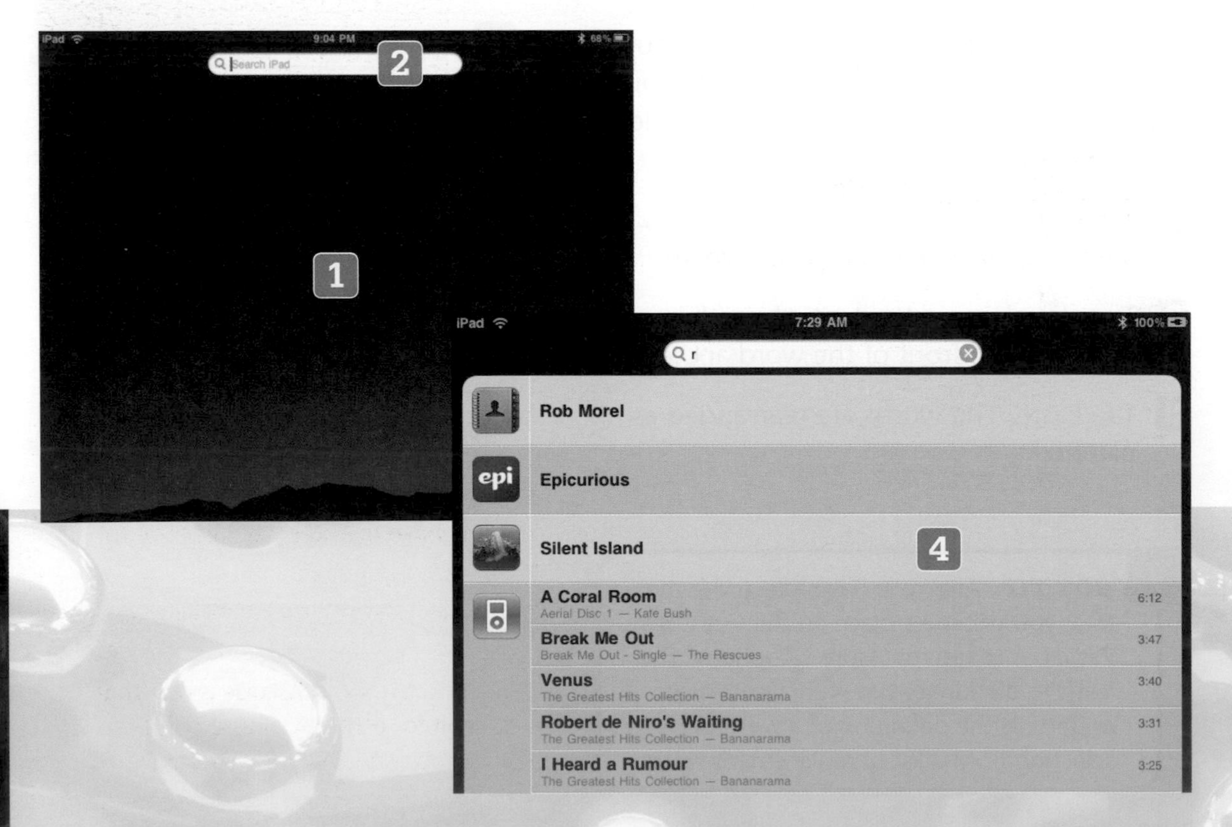

Lock your iPad

Your iPad may contain sensitive information, so luckily the iPad offers a password option to keep information confidential. The password is something you devise – it is a sequence of four numbers of your choosing.

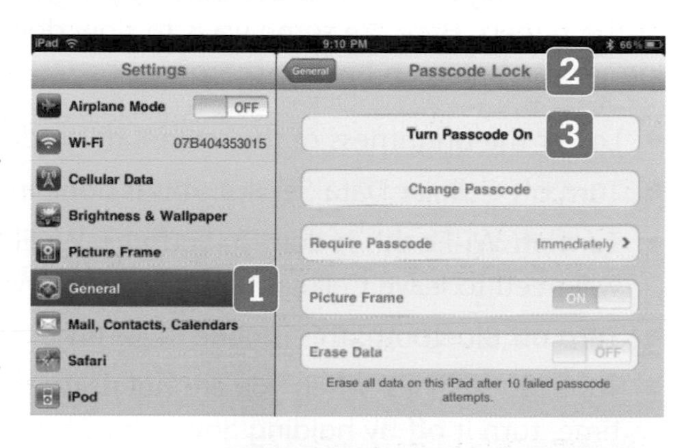

1. Enter Settings and tap General on the left.
2. On the right side, tap Passcode Lock.
3. Tap Turn Passcode On.
4. A box will open in which you set up the passcode. Enter a passcode by tapping the number keys. As soon as the set of four numbers is entered, the box will ask you to enter it again.

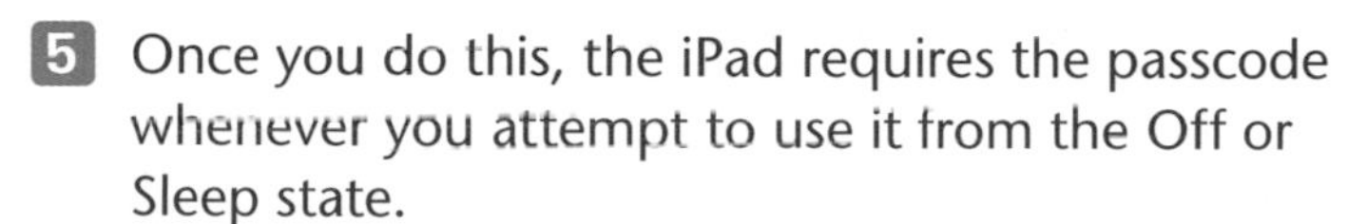

5. Once you do this, the iPad requires the passcode whenever you attempt to use it from the Off or Sleep state.

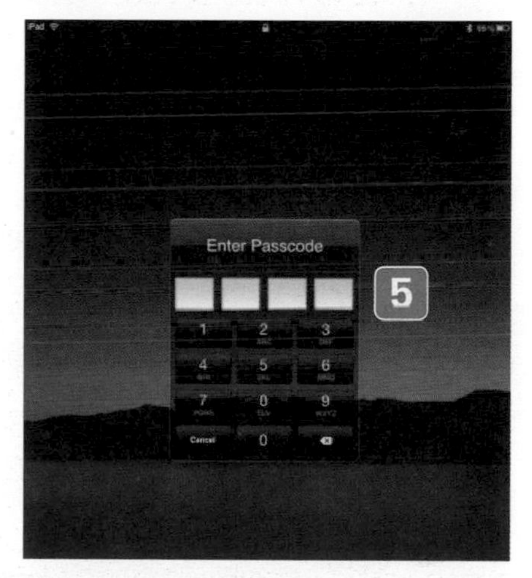

HOT TIP: To turn the passcode off, enter Settings, tap General on the left, then tap Turn Passcode Off on the right. You will have to enter the passcode to turn it off.

ALERT: A good passcode is one that is difficult for others to figure out. For example, don't use your birthday.

Maximise battery life

The iPad can be run while recharging, but for those times that you are mobile and using the battery to run the iPad, you'll want to make the battery power last.

You can always see how much battery power is left by looking in the upper right corner of the screen. Here are some ways to slow down the drain on the battery and achieve longer use between battery charging:

- Lower the brightness of the screen: this is done in Settings, Brightness & Wallpaper.
- Turn off Cellular Data Service: this is done in Settings, Cellular Data.
- Turn off Wi-Fi: this is done in Settings, Wi-Fi. Note – if you need internet access you will need to leave Cellular Data Service or Wi-Fi on.
- Turn off Bluetooth: this is done in Settings, General.
- Turn off the iPad: when you are not using the iPad for any significant length of time, turn it off by holding down the On/Off, Sleep/Wake button until the red slider appears.

Back up your iPad

When the iPad is connected to your computer and iTunes is started, a backup takes place. This can be seen in the iTunes status notice running on the computer.

A backup is great, but especially useful if you need to restore the iPad with the backup. To do this, right-click on the device in iTunes and select Restore from Backup... from the context menu.

3 The iTunes store and the Apps store

Introduction

As packed as the iPad is with powerful, ready-to-use apps, such as the Map and the Calendar, other apps require media (audio or visual) to be useful. Videos and music (or other audio) have to be purchased or downloaded for free from the iTunes store.

There is a world of other apps that developers create and Apple hosts in the App store. There are many types of apps – everything from the highly educational to the downright silly. Some apps are so popular they might as well have been included with the iPad. One of these is iBooks to which Chapter 9 of this book is devoted.

Overview of the iTunes store

The iTunes store is where you preview and purchase music, movies, TV shows, podcasts and audiobooks. There is a vast amount of media available in each format. You can filter offerings by what is featured, by what is selling best (Top Charts) and by genre or category.

1. From the Home screen, tap the iTunes icon to connect to the store. Internet connectivity must be on to do so.
2. The interface to the store fills the screen. Along the bottom are small icons to tap to access the type of media – music, movies and so forth. The image here shows featured music.
3. At the top, tap Top Charts. The view updates to allow fast access to the best-selling media.

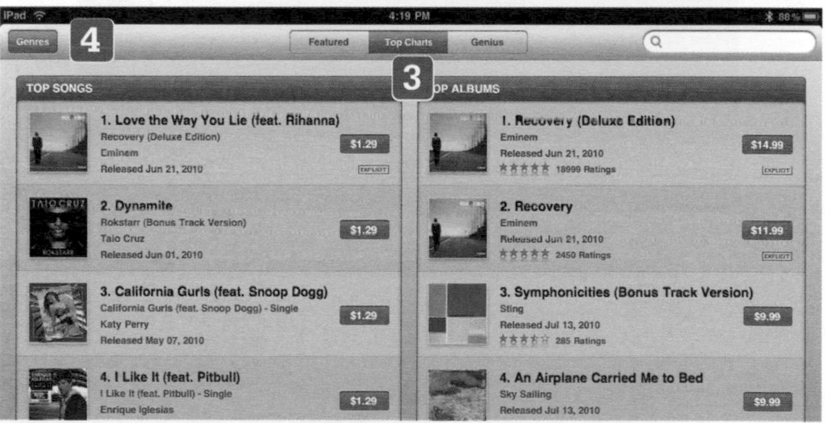

4. Alternatively, you can tap the Genres (or Category) button to filter available selections.
5. Tap the genre of your choice and the screen updates to show selections of that genre.

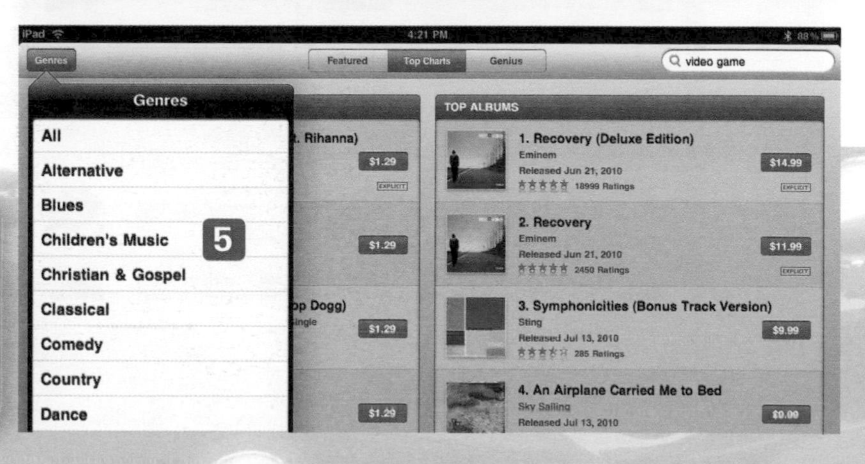

HOT TIP: Using the Featured, Top Charts and Genres buttons, you can browse the store's selections.

Search the iTunes store

When you know what you want, or to see whether an artist has a new release, or whether a new movie is available for purchase, the search feature is just what you need.

1. In the upper right is a search box. Enter the name of an artist, a title or a subject. Suggestions will be presented as you type into the search box.
2. Tap the desired item in the search results.
3. The store will filter and present items related to the selected search listing.

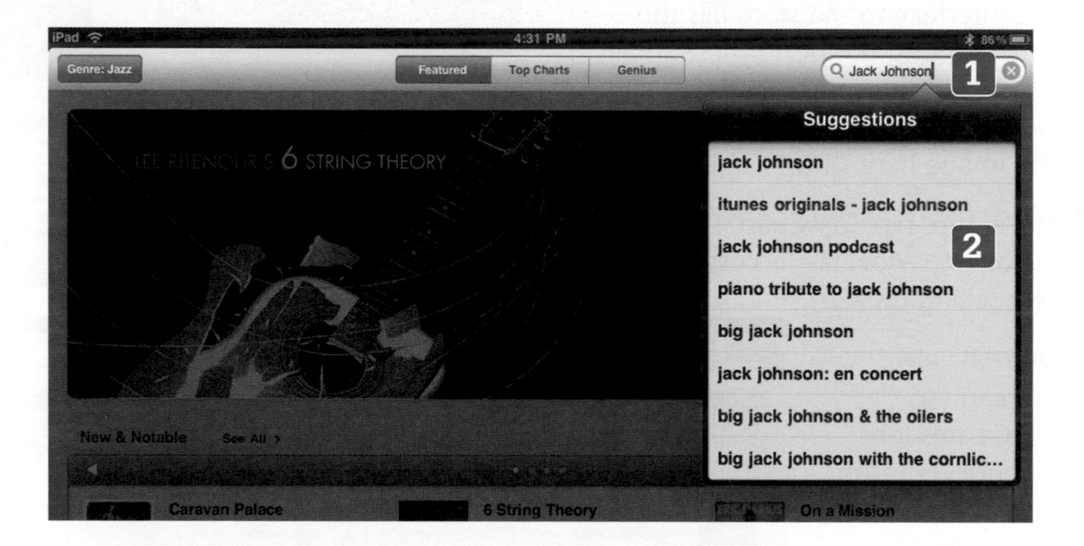

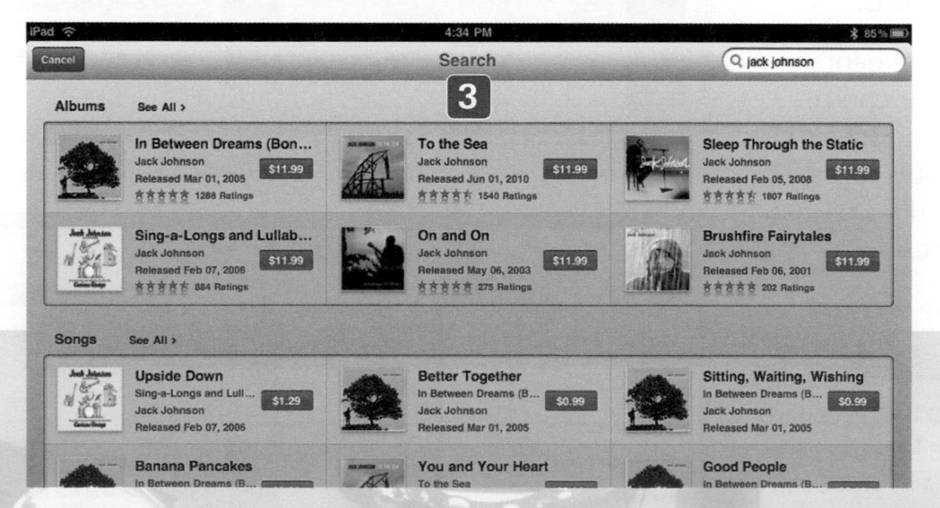

Preview media

In a bricks-and-mortar store you would pick up and look at an item before purchasing. In the iTunes store you do the equivalent by tapping an item. Depending on the media type, this offers a way to sample the media.

1. Tap on a desired item. In this example a music CD is selected.
2. Tap on a song to play a preview of that song.

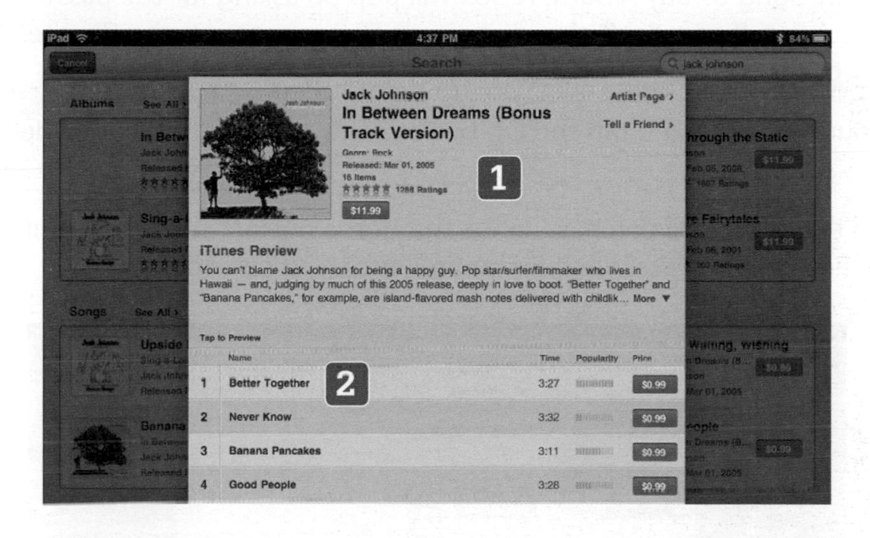

> **? DID YOU KNOW?**
>
> For other media types, such as movies, you will be able to preview a section of the movie. Note that when a movie is in preview, it may appear full screen. Tap the screen to show the media controls, such as Pause, Stop or changing the volume.

Purchase music

When purchasing music you often have a choice of buying entire CDs or individual songs.

1. Tap on the price. If it's an individual song, tap on the price associated with the song. If it's a CD, tap on the price for the CD. The price will change to a confirmation message, such as Buy Song or Buy Album.
2. Tap on Buy Song or Buy Album. A box will pop up asking for the password for your iTunes account. If you don't already have an iTunes account, see Chapter 1 to find out how to set one up.
3. Enter your password and tap the OK button. The purchase is downloaded into your iPad.
4. To listen to your music purchase, press the Home button, then tap the iPod icon. You will find your musical purchase in the Purchased category.

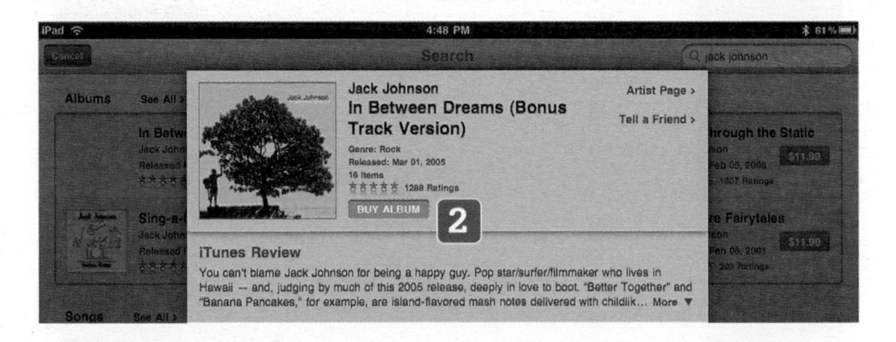

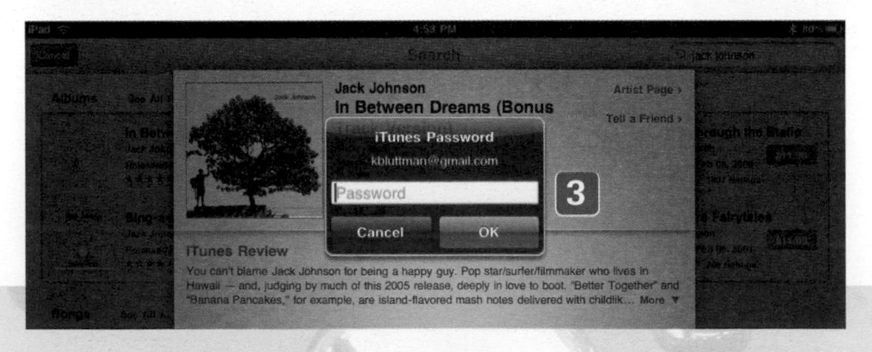

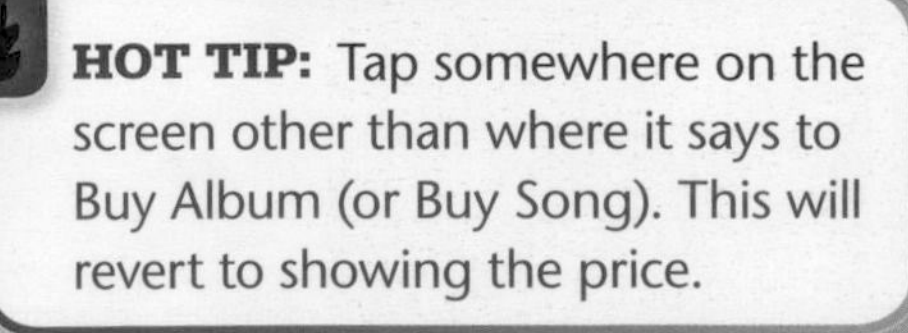

HOT TIP: Tap somewhere on the screen other than where it says to Buy Album (or Buy Song). This will revert to showing the price.

Rent a movie

Quite a number of movies are available for rental. Generally, you do not have to watch a rented movie immediately, but once you start it, you have 24 hours to view it. As with other media, you can preview the movie before renting it.

1. In the iTunes store, tap Movies at the bottom. The store presents movies that can be sorted by release date, bestsellers, and so on. Select a movie by tapping it.
2. A pop-up box presents the movie, with details such as run time and ratings. There is a Rent button that shows the price for the rental.
3. Tap the Rent Movie button, then tap it again. You will be prompted to enter the password for your iTunes account.
4. When you have finished, press the Home button. Tap the Videos icon and tap Movies along the top. Your movie will be there ready for you to view.

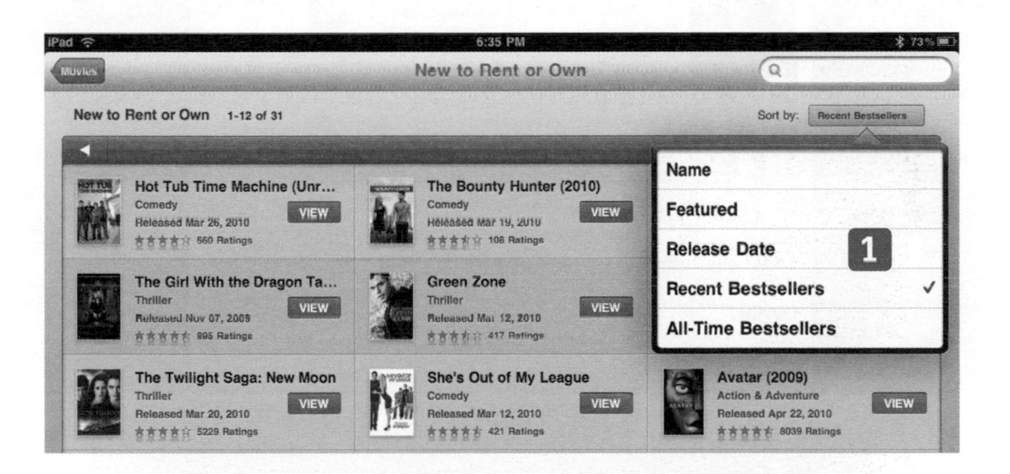

Purchase a movie

Many movies are available to rent. A smaller selection of movies can be purchased.

1. In the iTunes store, tap Movies at the bottom. Browse or search for a movie.
2. Tap the movie to show the details of the movie, including the Purchase button.
3. Tap the Buy button, then tap again when the button says Buy Movie.
4. Enter your iTunes password to purchase the movie.
5. The movie will be available to watch after it downloads. From the Home screen tap the Videos icon, then tap Movies.

HOT TIP: You can purchase music videos and TV shows in the same manner that movies are purchased.

WHAT DOES THIS MEAN?

HD: Acronym for high definition. Many movies are offered in both standard definition and HD. HD is better quality; however, standard definition looks fine on the iPad.

Listen to or watch a podcast

A podcast can be an audio-only or an audio-visual presentation. The purpose of a podcast is usually to cater to a niche group of followers. Some podcasts are long, lasting more than an hour. There are many podcasts to select from in the iTunes store and they are all free.

1. Tap the iTunes icon to open the iTunes store.
2. On the bottom tap on Podcasts. At the time of writing, there were more than 200,000 podcasts to enjoy. You can give the suggested ones a try, although searching for something of interest is a sensible approach.
3. Tap on a Podcast listing. Often it turns out that the Podcast is actually a series of several episodes (or lessons, etc.).

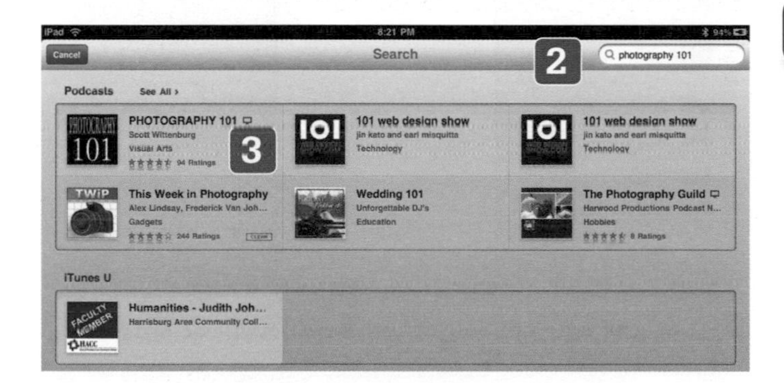

HOT TIP: Note that when a small caption icon is shown to the right of the podcast, it is visual. If none is present, it is just audio. In the image shown here, the first podcast, PHOTOGRAPHY 101, has the icon. The second podcast, 101 web design show, does not.

4. Tap on one of the listings to start listening or viewing.
5. Tap the Free button to download. Some long podcasts can take several minutes to download.
6. Once a podcast has completed its download it will appear in either iPod or Videos, depending on whether it is an audio-visual or an audio-only podcast.

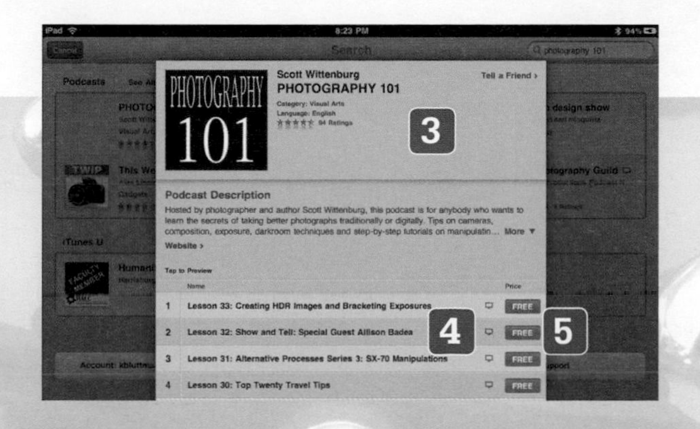

Use an iTunes gift card

As any decent merchant would do, Apple has gift cards that can be purchased and then redeemed in the iTunes store. These iTunes gift cards come in several denominations. Maybe you will be lucky enough to receive one as a gift.

But how do you use it? These steps tell you what to do.

1. In the iTunes store, scroll down to the bottom of the screen until you see the Redeem button. Swipe the screen with your finger to scroll. Tap the Redeem button.
2. Enter the code found on your iTunes gift card, then tap the small Redeem button in the upper right of the Redeem box.
3. Enter your iTunes password.
4. The amount of the gift card is credited to your account. Now it's time to shop!
5. Select the media you wish to purchase. Tap Buy Movie.
6. When the download is complete, the media can be found in the appropriate app – iPod or Videos. Enjoy!

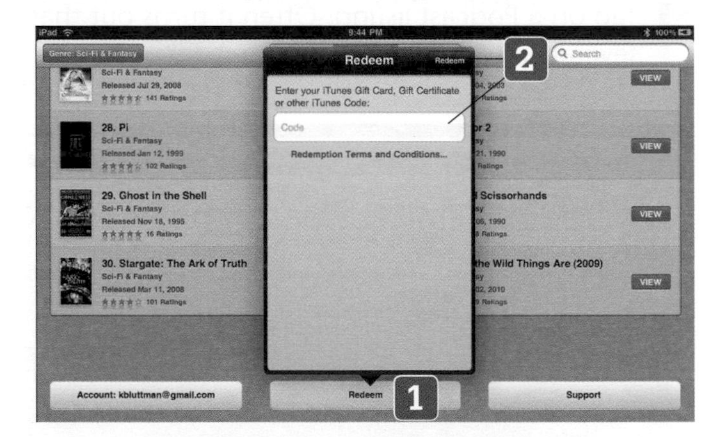

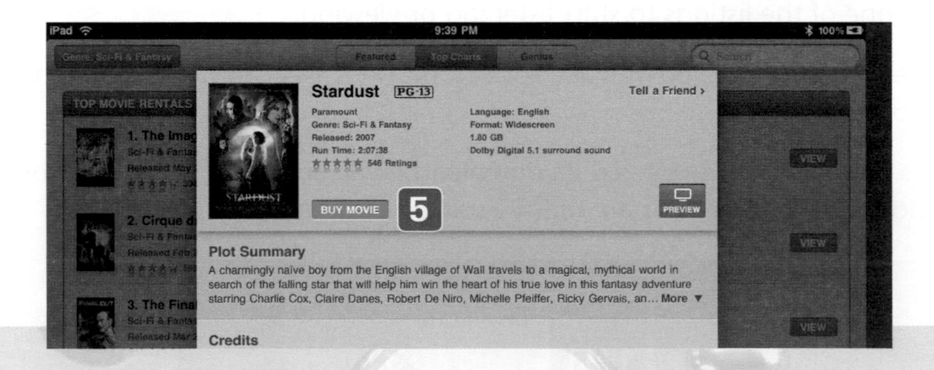

Check the status of a download

When making a purchase or simply accessing something free from the iTunes store, a download occurs from the store into your iPad. The length of time it takes to download depends on the size of the file – a single song will download much faster than a full-length movie.

If you are interested in the progress of a download, you can bring a progress bar to view by tapping Downloads in the lower right corner of the store. If there is a number next to the Downloads icon, then a download is in progress, as shown here.

The screen changes to show the progress of the download.

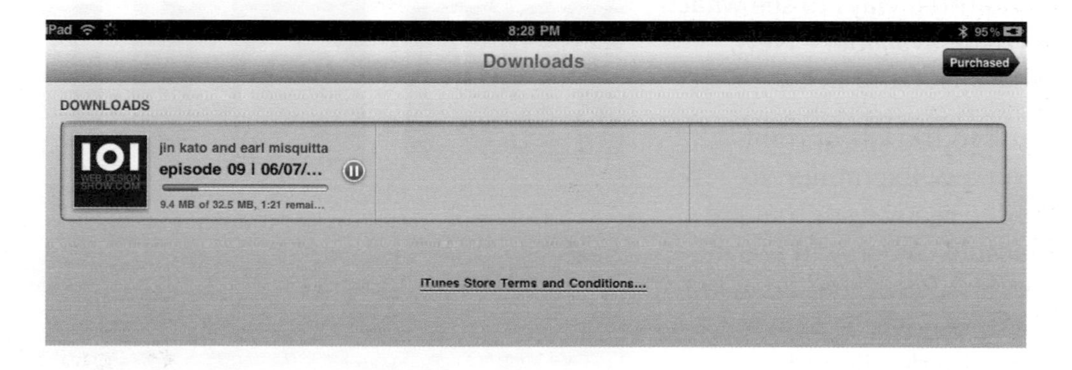

Overview of the App store

The App store is similar to the iTunes store, except it is used for purchasing and downloading apps, not media. There are hundreds of apps to choose from and more are introduced as fast as developers can make them. There are many categories of apps – books, games, health, reference, sports and much more.

1. From the Home screen, tap the App Store icon to connect to the store. Internet connectivity must be on to do so.
2. The interface to the store fills the screen. Along the bottom are small icons that provide ways to find apps. The icons are Featured, Top Charts, Categories and Updates.
3. When you tap Featured, the top of the store's screen offers three ways to see what apps are available – New, What's Hot and Release Date.
4. Scroll to the left or right using a swipe motion to see the many apps that are available. When you see an app of interest, tap on it and the screen will update to show the details and price.

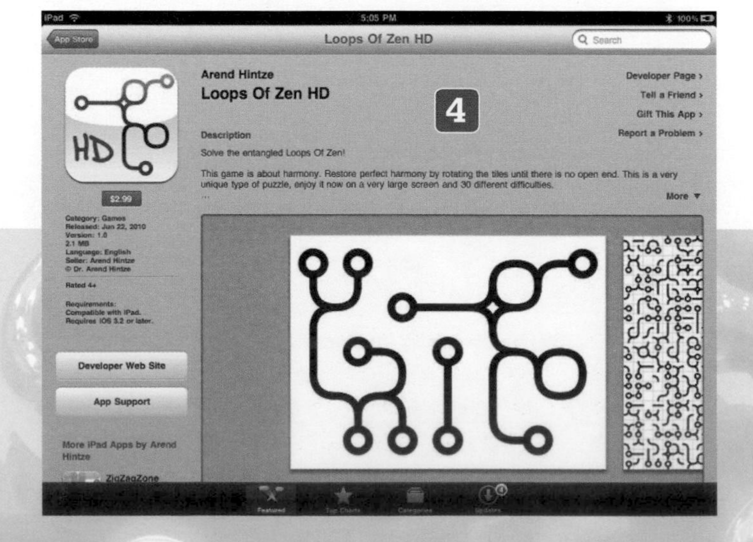

5 Using Categories at the bottom of the screen is a great way to browse through apps. Tap the Categories icon and the screen updates to the assortment of categories.

6 Tap a category of choice and the screen will show available apps in that category. Here is a listing of apps that are of the Productivity category.

DID YOU KNOW?

Some apps are free while you pay to purchase others. Even among those that cost, quite a number are reasonably priced. Also, as you use apps, you will probably find that a free app may charge a price to use extended features.

Search the App store

When you know what you want, or to see whether a certain type of app is available for purchase or free download, the search feature is just what you need.

1. In the upper right of the store screen is a search box. Enter the name of a subject or other relevant search term. Suggestions will be presented as you type into the search box.

2. Tap the desired item in the search results. The store will filter and present items related to the selected search listing. Then tap on one of the listings for details about the app.

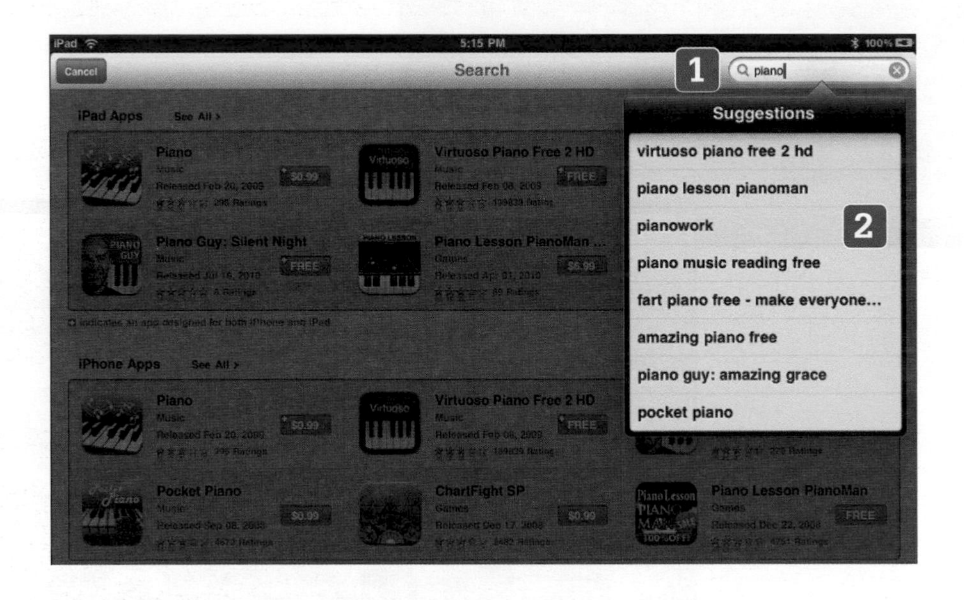

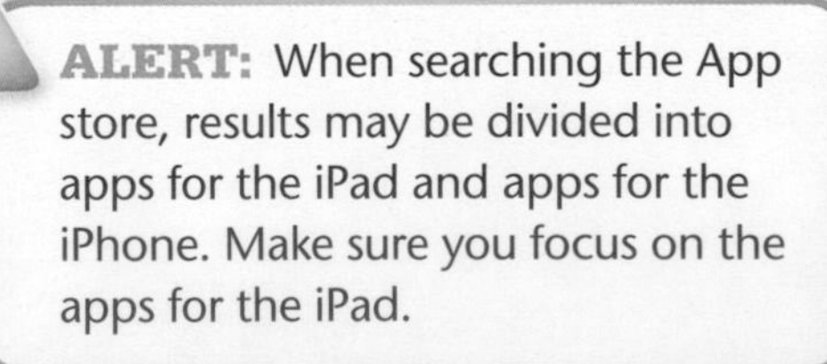

ALERT: When searching the App store, results may be divided into apps for the iPad and apps for the iPhone. Make sure you focus on the apps for the iPad.

Find out more about an app

The enormous number of apps to choose from is overwhelming. It would be helpful to use some method to weed out the mundane ones from those that are really useful. A great way to weigh the value of an app before purchasing/downloading is to read the reviews. Luckily, the apps are rated by people who have used them. There is a star system (1–5 stars) and you can also read detailed reviews.

1. In whatever manner the apps are listed, you see the star rating system. The number of stars is an average of all the individual ratings and you can also see how many ratings there are. To read reviews, tap on an app's listing to get to the details.
2. Use your finger to scroll down the screen to where the reviews are listed. Reading them often reveals quite a bit of knowledge about the app.

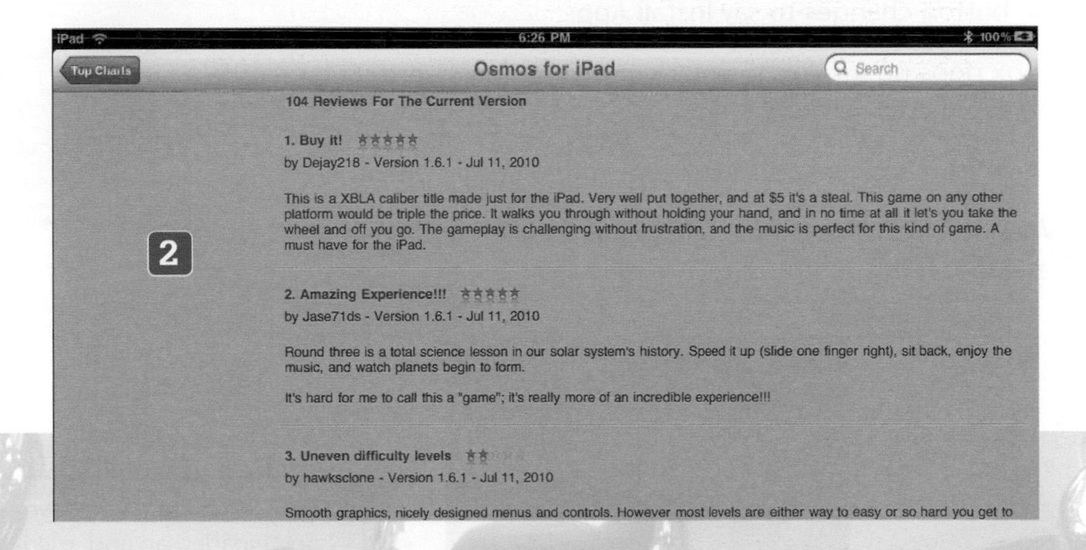

Purchase and download an app

A free app downloads without cost and an app with a cost downloads after it has been paid for. For apps that have a cost, the payment method associated with your iTunes account is used.

1. For the desired app, tap the button that says Free or that has a price on it.

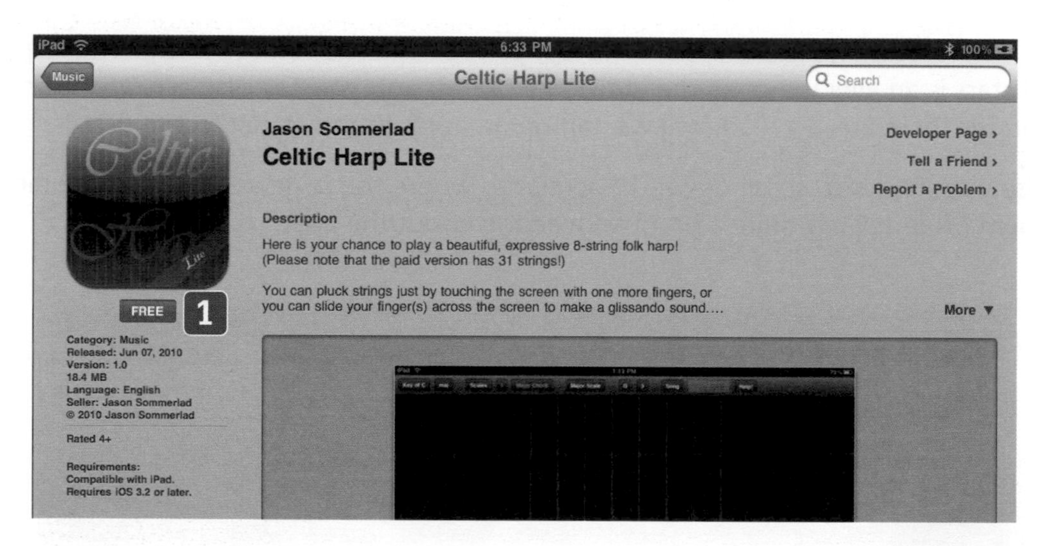

2. The button changes to say Install App.
3. A box pops up for you to enter your iTunes password. Enter it and tap the OK button.
4. A new icon appears on the screen, with a progress bar.
5. When the download is complete, tap the icon and enjoy the new app.

SEE ALSO: If you have downloaded an app, tried it out and don't like it, you can delete it. See how to do this later in the chapter.

Use an app

This is easy! Just ...

1. Tap on the app's icon.
2. If you are inclined to do so, you can go back into the App store and leave a review. Find the app by browsing or searching. Tap it in a listing if necessary to get to the details page. Scroll down and tap the link to rate it and leave a review. Tap Submit when you've finished.

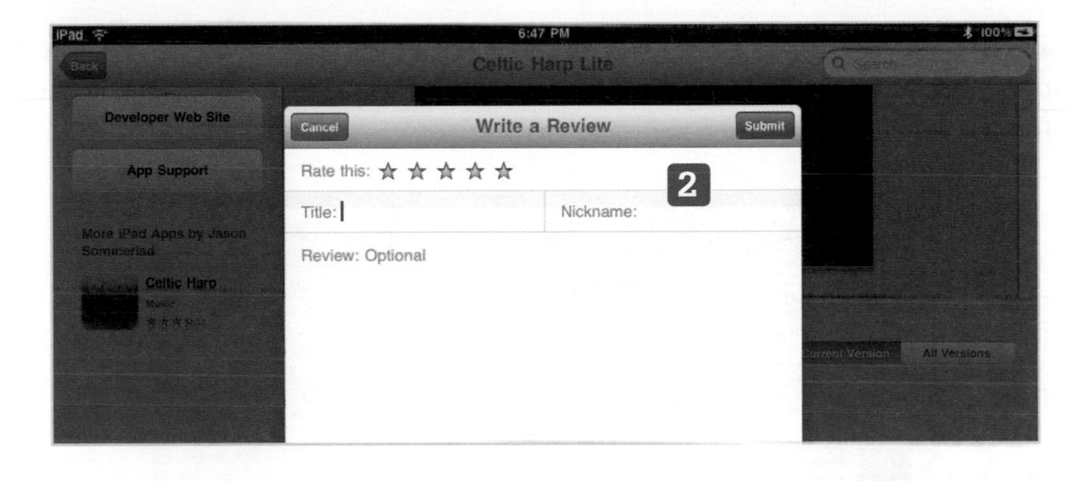

HOT TIP: Apps are all different. Some will work with a set of given features and offer more features for a fee. Some will provide a link to the developer's website. Some you will find useful or entertaining, others will seem as though they were not worth getting.

Update an app

Apps are often updated by their developer. The App Store icon on the main screen may have a number next to it. This indicates the number of installed apps that have updates.

1. Tap on the App Store icon.
2. In the bottom right of the store is an update button that will also show the number of waiting updates.

3. Tap the Updates button and a list is presented of which apps have updates. On the upper right is an Update All button. Tapping this is the easiest way to get all the updates.

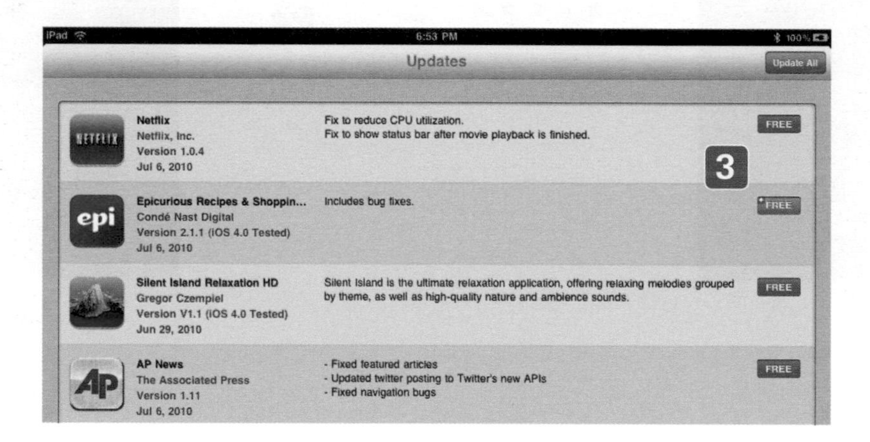

4. One by one the icons show the status of the updates. The process will attend to all the updates without any need for your intervention. While one app is updating, the others will say Waiting. All you have to do is wait for an app to finish its update before you use it.

Delete an app

To delete an app, do this:

1. Tap and hold your finger on any icon. All icons will start to shake.
2. Apps that can be deleted will have a small x on the left.
3. Tap the x to delete the app.
4. Press the Home button to stop the icons from shaking (thus returning them to their normal state).

4 Web surfing with Safari

Introduction

The iPad is a great device for surfing the Web. Safari, Apple's default web browser, is built in – and is all you need. Some of its methods are different to the typical way a browser works on a computer. For example, there are no tabs, rather you can have a succession of browser windows.

Start up Safari

Web browsing is just a tap away. Safari has a dedicated icon at the bottom of the Home screen.

1. Tap the Safari icon at the lower left of the Home screen.

ALERT: You cannot set up a default home page. Instead you set up icon shortcuts to your chosen websites, explained later in this chapter. The default behaviour when tapping the Safari icon is to open the last viewed website.

Visit a website

When Safari is tapped it opens to the last viewed site. Here is how you navigate to another site.

1. The browser has an address box at the top of the screen. Initially it is filled with the web address of the current site on the screen. Here, Safari displays the Amazon web site and the address is the one for Amazon.
2. Tap once in the address box. The virtual keyboard appears.
3. Start typing in a new web address. As you do so, suggestions are presented. The more of an address you type, the more filtered the presented list becomes. A list of suggestions may or may not appear, or may start then disappear as your typing filters the suggestions to the point at which there is none left to show. The suggestions are derived from sites which you have visited previously.
4. You can type in the full web address and then tap the Go key on the keyboard, or at any time tap the desired suggestion if it is present in the list.

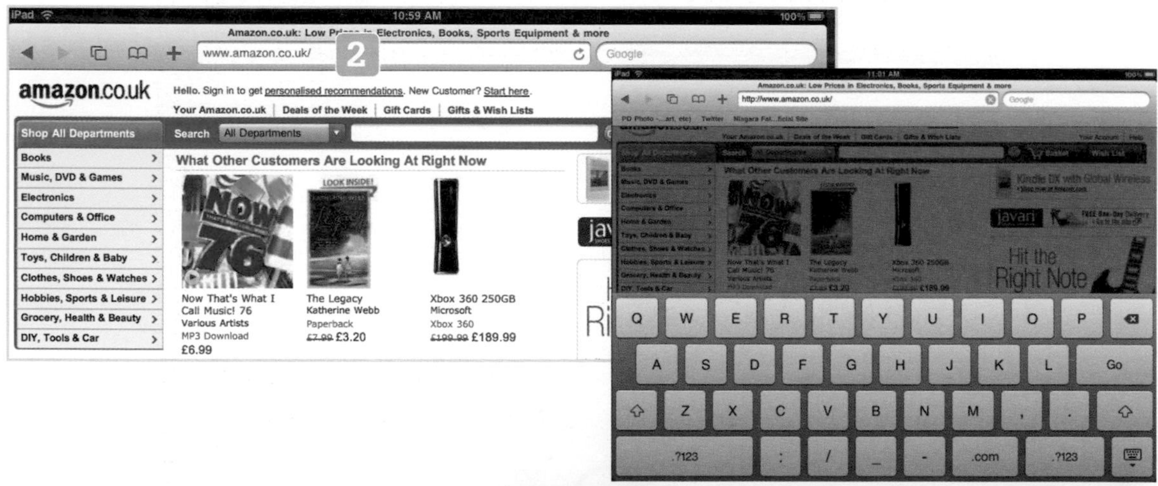

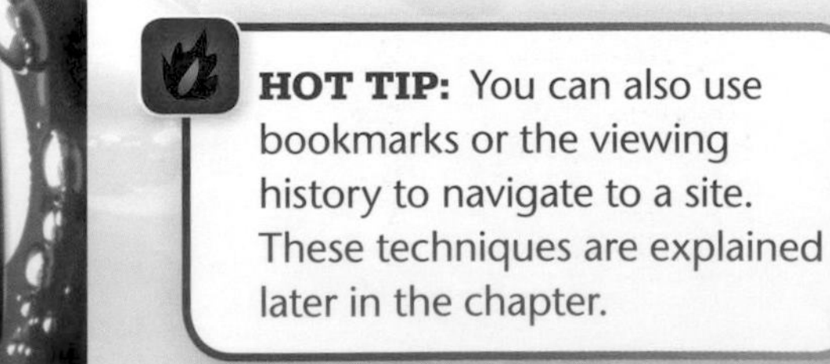

HOT TIP: You can also use bookmarks or the viewing history to navigate to a site. These techniques are explained later in the chapter.

Search the Web

To the right of the address box is the search box. You enter a word or phrase and search results are returned to the screen. Here's how.

1. Tap the search box. The virtual keyboard appears. You may also notice that the search box has expanded.
2. Start to type a search term. Suggestions will appear as you do so and the list will filter itself as you enter more of the search term. If you see the desired search term in the suggestion list, tap it and the search will be performed.
3. Alternatively, you can type in the complete search term and tap the Search key on the keyboard. Here, a search for 'fireflies' has been completed, with the search results showing up in Google.

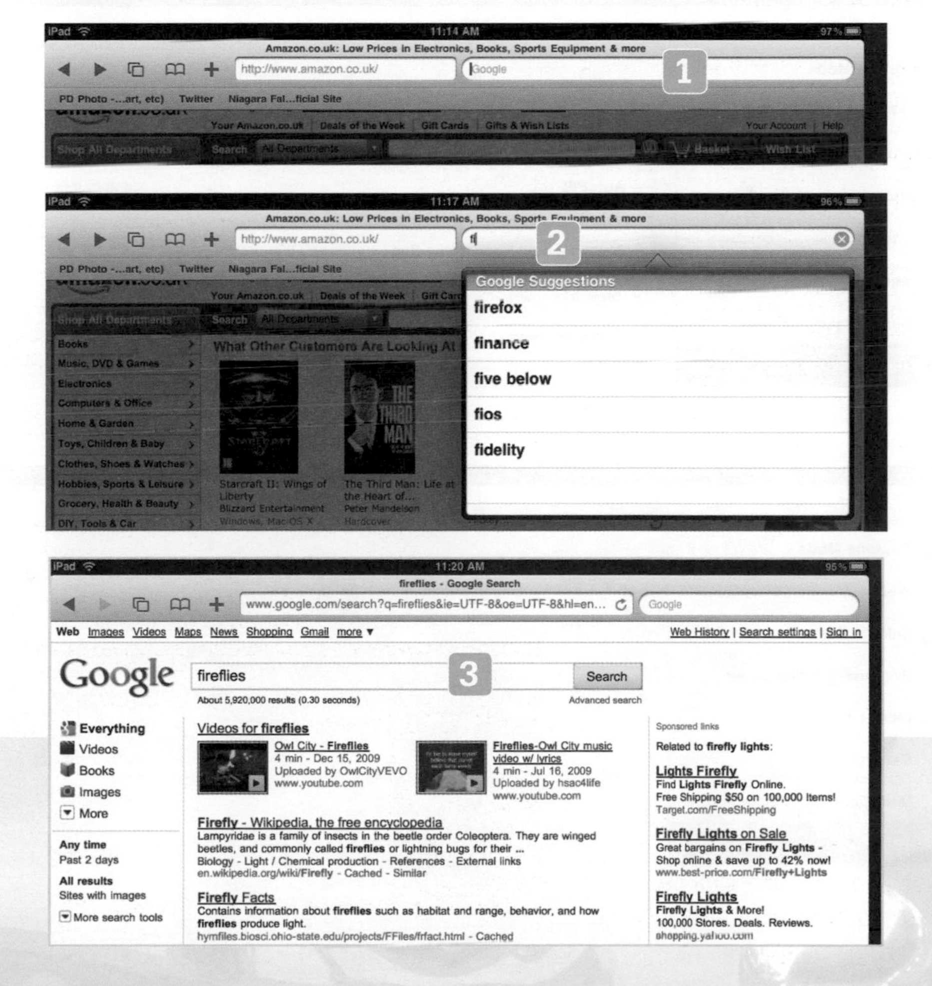

Set a default search engine

You can select which search engine to use. The choices are presented in a list in Settings.

1. From the Home screen, tap the Settings icon.
2. Tap Safari on the left side of the screen.
3. On the right side of the screen, at the top, tap Search Engine. This updates the screen to present the list of possible search engines.
4. Tap the search engine you would like to use as a default. Press the Home button to exit Settings.

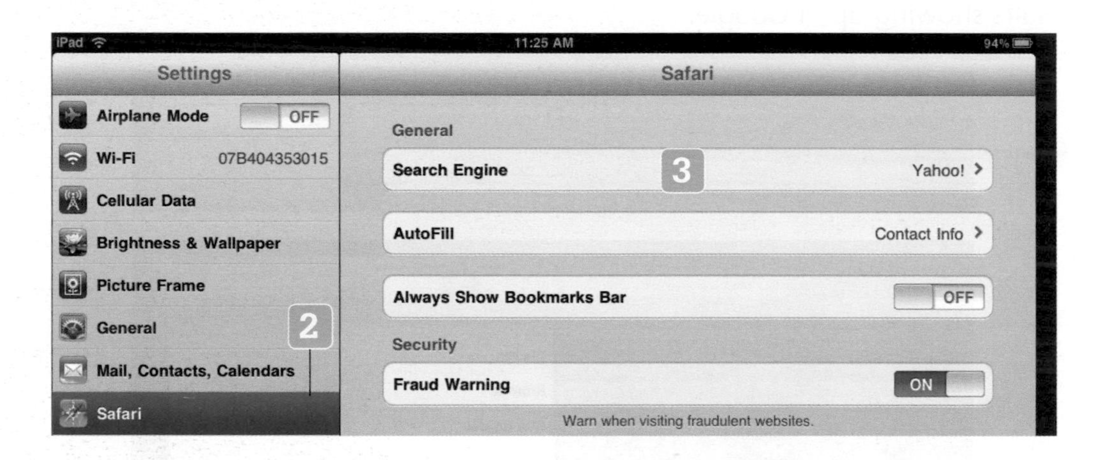

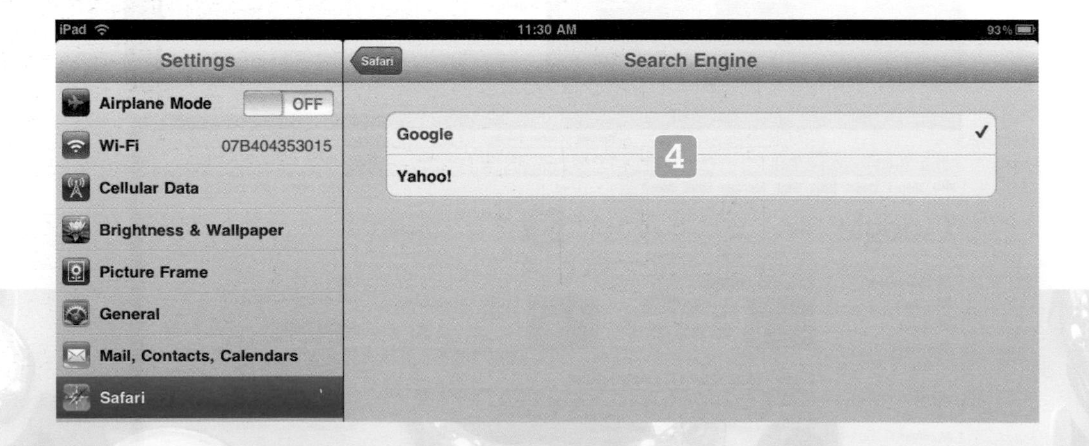

Create a screen icon to navigate directly to a website

Although you can start Safari from the Safari icon, when you do so you see the previously visited site. Then to go to another site you need to enter its URL (the web address). That is a longer process than necessary. The technique shown here is a great way to get directly to a site.

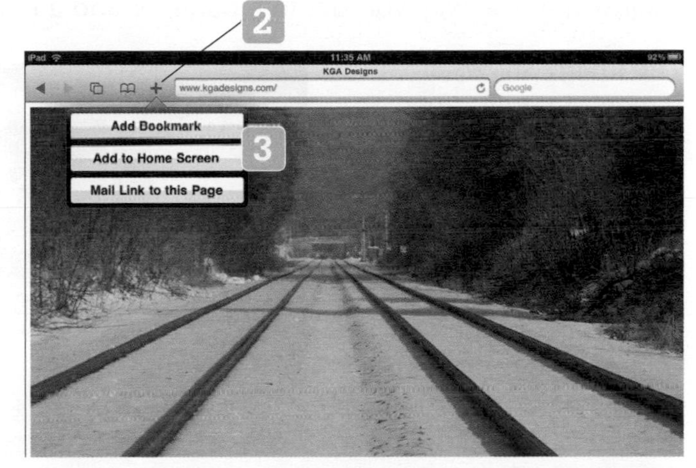

1. In Safari, navigate to your chosen web site.
2. Tap the Add Bookmark button. It looks like a plus (+) sign.
3. Tap Add to Home Screen.
4. The virtual keyboard appears, as well as a box in which you can give a title to the icon that is about to be created. Change the title if you wish.
5. Tap the small Add button in the Add to Home box. The browser closes and the Home screen is shown with the newly created icon.
6. Tapping the new icon opens Safari to the selected website.

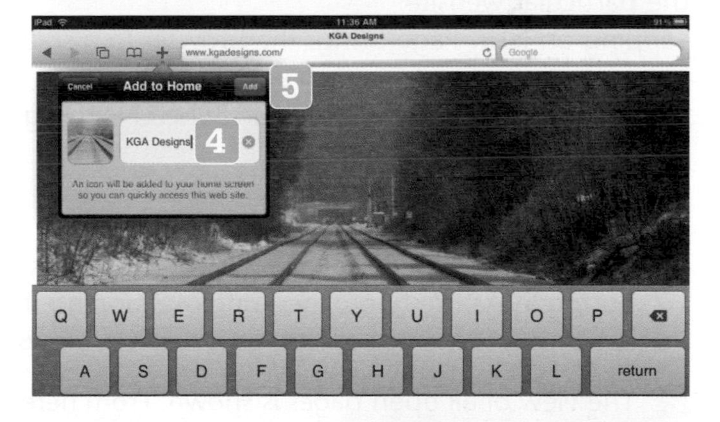

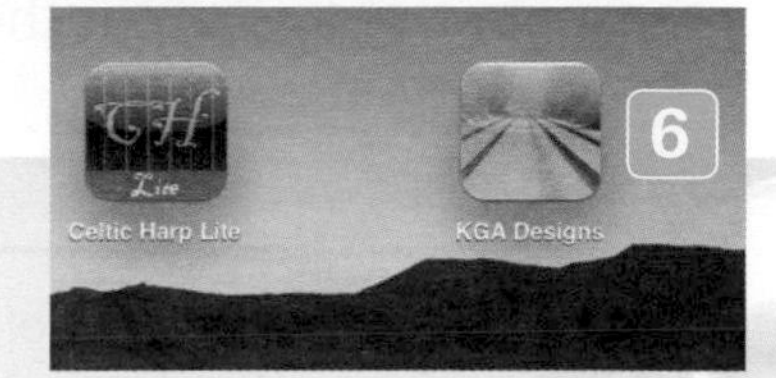

DID YOU KNOW?

You can set up many of these website shortcut icons. In a way this can be considered as giving yourself a multiple number of home pages. In Safari you cannot set a home page, so this is the best method to achieve the same effect.

Add a new page

Popular web browsers running on computers all seem to feature the ability to use tabs. That is, with a single instance of the browser running, it contains a number of tabs – each set to a different website. One tab is always the active one, on top of the others.

The version of Safari in the iPad does not support tabs, but instead has a similar way of having multiple sites available by using pages. In a sense a page is the same as a tab – it's just that the way you get to a page, or add a new one, is different.

The image shows a screen of pages 'open' in Safari and each shows a different website. On the right, second row, is a blank page. Underneath it is the caption 'New Page'. Tapping on one of the existing pages brings the browser to its normal view and displays the particular website.

Tapping on New Page brings the browser to a state in which you can enter a web address or a search term. The virtual keyboard appears when New Page is tapped.

1. When the browser is in its normal state, displaying a website, tap the Page button. This button looks like two pages, one overlapping the other. It is found in the upper left section of the browser.

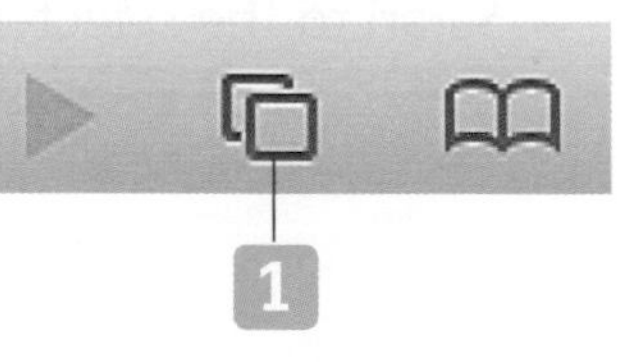

2. The view of all open pages is shown. From here you can tap a page to make it the current displayed website.

HOT TIP: In the view of pages, each page has a small x on the left. Tapping the x will close the page.

ALERT: If you visit websites that open multiple browser windows, you will find on the iPad that Safari opens new pages instead.

Create a bookmark

Bookmarking a website for easy retrieval is a boon to using Safari. The concept is similar to creating a screen icon of a web page described earlier in the chapter – the point is having an easy way to return to a website.

1. When you are on a website that you wish to bookmark, tap the + button.
2. Tap Add Bookmark. The virtual keyboard appears, as well as a box in which to give the bookmark a title.
3. Note that in the Add Bookmark box you have a choice of simply adding the bookmark or adding it to the Bookmarks Bar. Tap the bottom button in the Add Bookmark box and you will be presented with the choice of how to create the bookmark.
4. Tap the choice of Bookmarks or Bookmarks Bar. The screen reverts to the previous one, showing the Add Bookmark box. Tap the small Save button to complete creating the bookmark.

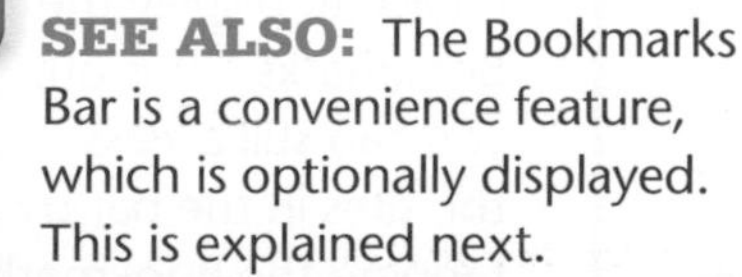

SEE ALSO: The Bookmarks Bar is a convenience feature, which is optionally displayed. This is explained next.

View the Bookmarks Bar

The Bookmarks Bar gives you a way to reach your favourite sites with a single tap. The Bookmarks Bar can be displayed or hidden, based on a selection in Settings.

1. Enter Settings, then tap Safari on the left.
2. On the right is a setting for Always Show Bookmarks Bar. Tapping the On/Off button determines its visibility in the browser.

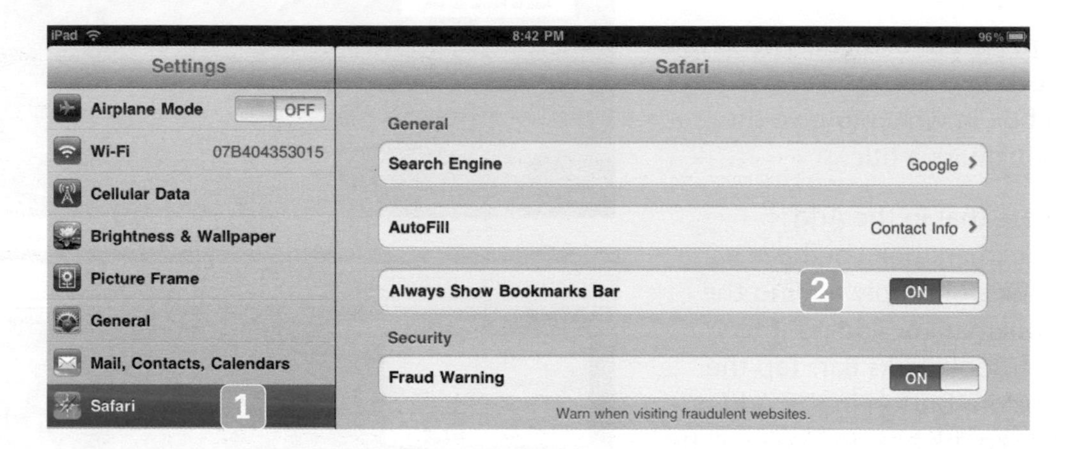

3. In Safari, the Bookmarks Bar appears just above the website window. It contains the names of sites that have been added to appear in the bar.
4. Tap a site name on the Bookmarks Bar and the browser navigates to that website.

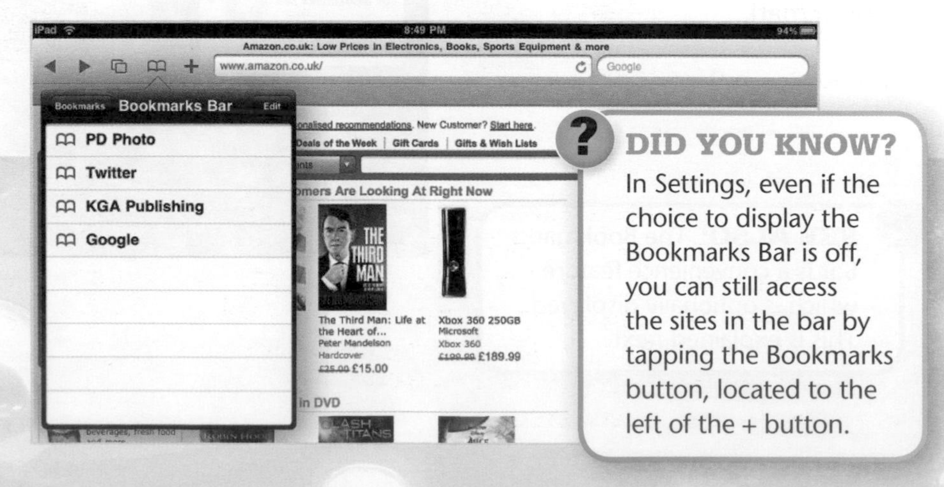

DID YOU KNOW?

In Settings, even if the choice to display the Bookmarks Bar is off, you can still access the sites in the bar by tapping the Bookmarks button, located to the left of the + button.

Edit bookmarks

Bookmarks in the Bookmarks Bar can be edited or deleted. Regular bookmarks can just be deleted.

1. Tap the Bookmarks button. The list of bookmarks appears. In the box that contains the list is a small Edit button. Tap the Edit button.
2. Each bookmark now has a red circle to the left. Each red circle has a horizontal white line.

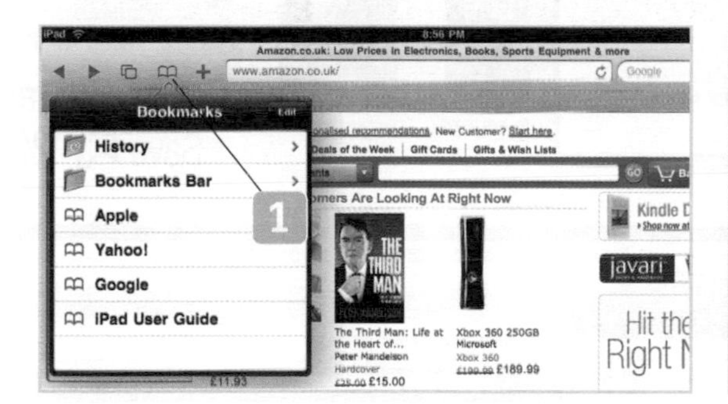

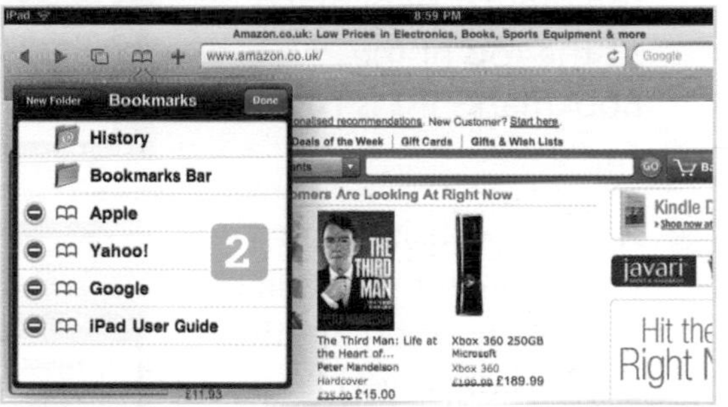

3. Tapping a red circle orients the white line to be vertical. To the right of the bookmark is a Delete button. Tap the Delete button to delete the bookmark.
4. When you have finished deleting, tap the small Done button on the right of the Bookmarks box.

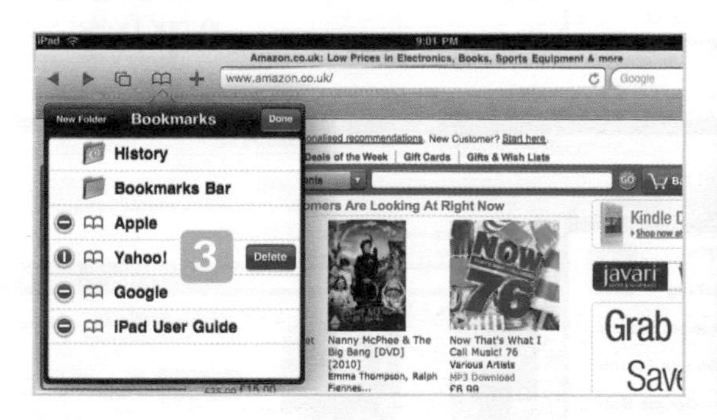

DID YOU KNOW?

When you tap the Bookmarks button, the list may open to show either History and bookmarks or the Bookmarks Bar. You can get from one view to the other. If regular bookmarks are displayed, tap Bookmarks Bar in the listing. If the Bookmarks Bar is displayed initially, the box has a small Bookmarks button in the upper left corner. Tap it to get the regular bookmarks list.

HOT TIP: If the Bookmarks Bar listing is displayed, after you tap Edit you can tap the bookmark to edit its name and/or web address.

Use the Browsing History

The Browsing History provides a way to find and navigate to a website you have visited but did not bookmark.

1. Tap the Bookmarks button. If the Bookmarks Bar is displayed, tap the small Bookmarks button on the left to display the regular bookmarks. At the top of the Bookmarks list is History. Tap it.

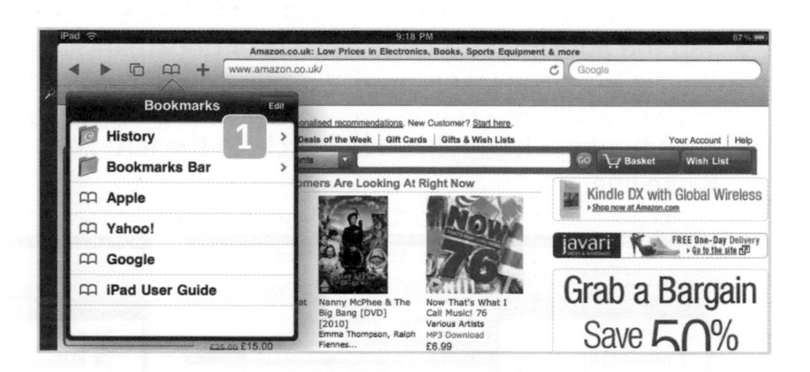

2. A list of websites you visited recently – earlier in the day or on another day – is displayed. You can tap on one of the bookmarks to navigate to the site.

3. Alternatively, you can tap one of the choices that leads to a further list of previously visited websites. For example, this image shows sites visited on July 19.

4. From this list, tap on a website name to navigate to the site.

Clear Browsing History

A common feature of browsers is to clear the history. Perhaps you have visited a site that you don't want others to know about. Or more likely you realise over time that the history fills up with numerous sites and clearing out the list is efficient.

1. Tap the Bookmarks button. Then tap the History list. It is possible that the History list appeared first anyway. To the right in the History box is a small Clear History button.
2. Tap the Clear History button. A confirmation appears.
3. Tap Clear History.
4. The listings are removed.

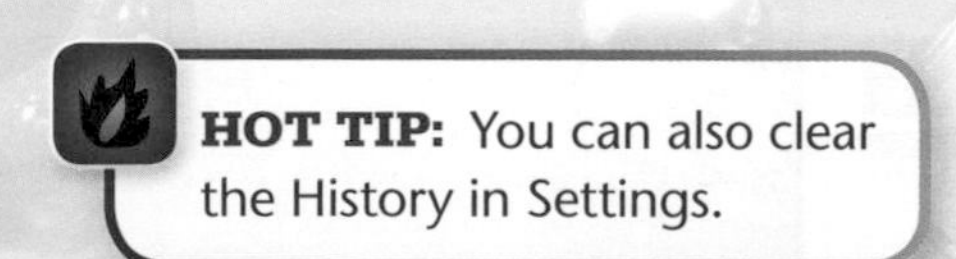

HOT TIP: You can also clear the History in Settings.

Set and use AutoFill

AutoFill is a feature that provides a unique function. When visiting a website and the page you are on is a form in which you enter your name and address, AutoFill can be used to fill in the form with a single tap. In other words, you avoid having to type in all your contact information.

1. Enter Settings, then tap Safari on the left.
2. On the right is a setting for AutoFill. Tap it and a new screen appears to set up AutoFill.

3. First, if Use Contact Info is off, turn it on by tapping the On/Off button.
4. AutoFill uses the information that you set up in Contacts (see Chapter 11). The assumption is that you set up a contact record about yourself. In the screen is the My Info setting. This setting is used to select a contact to use to fill out web forms. If your name is not the one showing (or perhaps you have multiple contact records for yourself), tap My Info. This presents a list of your contacts from which you select which contact record to use.

5. If you already have the correct contact record in place with AutoFill, just tap outside of this list to close it. Or select a different contact record (although it would not make sense to use someone else's contact info).
6. When you come across a web form, tap into one of the boxes, such as where you enter your first name. The virtual keyboard appears. In the bar just above the keys is a small AutoFill button.
7. Tap the AutoFill button.
8. The web form fills in with your contact information.

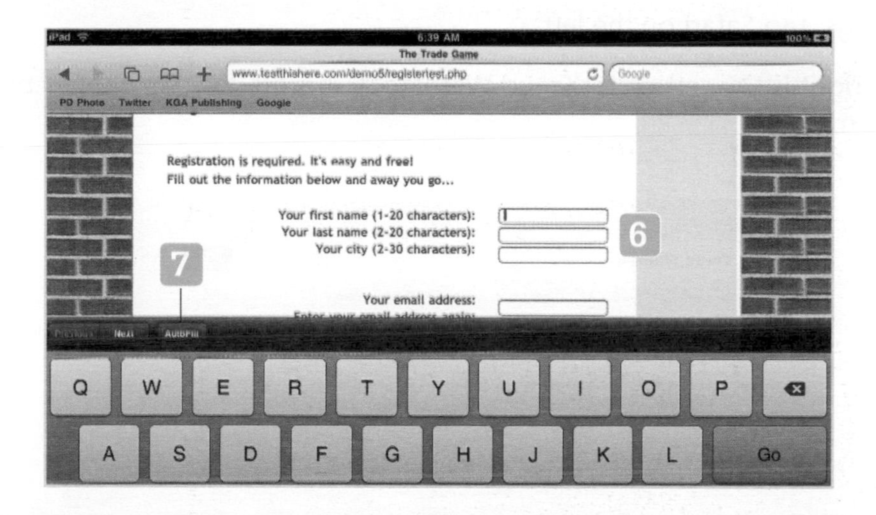

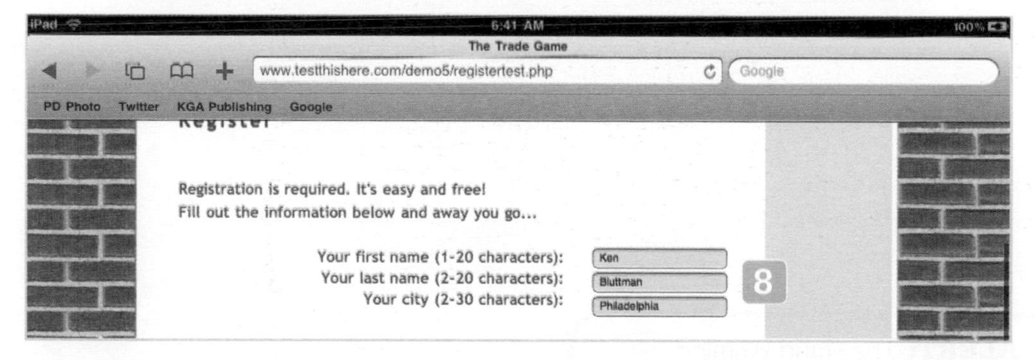

Turn on Fraud Warning

The internet, with all its variety of content and attractions, can also be a dangerous place. Unscrupulous people or groups seek to find out personal information, such as credit card numbers, or launch computer viruses and so on. Phishing is a technique meant to trick you into giving away your personal and confidential information. Often this is achieved by entering data at a website that appears to belong to a known establishment but is really just a good looking copy. You may not notice the difference and enter information. Using Fraud Warning steers you clear of making that mistake.

1. In Settings, tap Safari on the left.
2. On the right is the setting for Fraud Warning. If it is off, tap the On/Off button to turn it on.

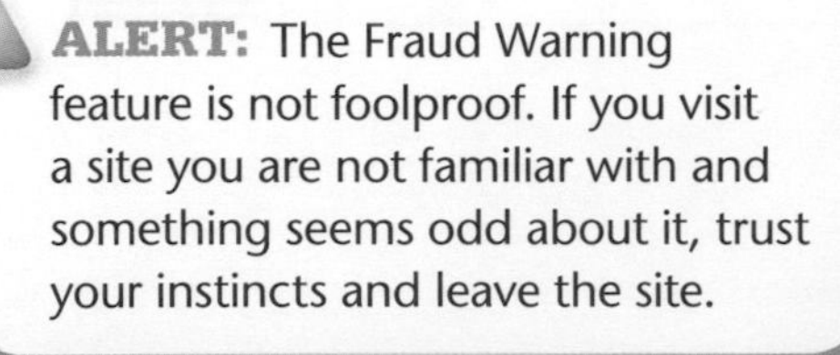

ALERT: The Fraud Warning feature is not foolproof. If you visit a site you are not familiar with and something seems odd about it, trust your instincts and leave the site.

Turn on JavaScript

JavaScript is a programming language that performs sophisticated activities in the web browser. All browsers (not just Safari in the iPad) allow you to turn off JavaScript. However, doing so will make many websites not work as they should as they have JavaScript code built into the web pages and thus the code will not do anything. Therefore, it is best to have JavaScript turned on.

1. In Settings, tap Safari on the left.
2. On the right is the setting for JavaScript. If it is off, tap the On/Off button to turn it on.

Block or allow pop-ups

Pop-ups are boxes that open on top of the website you are viewing. Some can even open underneath the website and appear only when you navigate away from the site. Pop-ups are most often used as an advertising medium. Although some good offers or information can be found in a pop-up, most people find them annoying and set their browsers to block them from appearing.

1. In Settings, tap Safari on the left.
2. On the right is the setting to Block Pop-ups. Tap the On/Off button to set the blocking feature on or off.

Set how to accept cookies

Cookies are small files that are downloaded from websites into your iPad. You will not be aware this happens, as it is programming code that does the work. Cookies serve many useful purposes, such as retaining information as you navigate from page to page or remembering your name over the span of days or weeks, which is useful with websites that are personalised.

Although the idea of letting a website insert a file into the iPad sounds like it might be a bad idea, cookies are fairly standard and cannot do anything active (they simply store information). If a website leaves a cookie in the iPad, the next time you visit that website it will test for the presence of its cookie and make use of the information stored in it.

Not all websites use cookies, but most people allow cookies to be used. The iPad gives you a choice of how cookies are implemented – Never, From visited sites only or Always.

1. In Settings, tap Safari on the left. On the right is the setting named Accept Cookies.
2. Tap it to bring up the cookie options.
3. Tap the Safari button at the top to return to Settings.

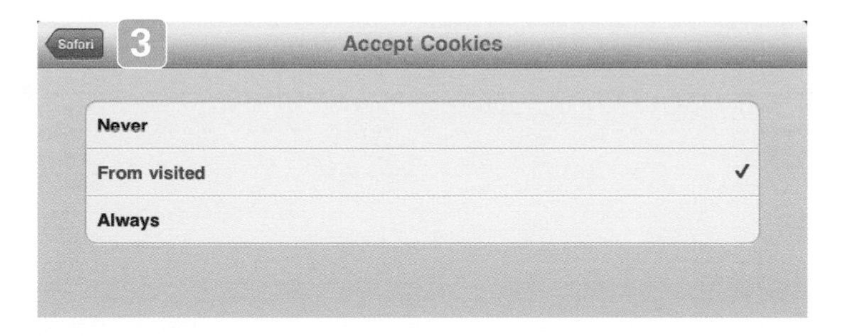

ALERT: The From visited and Always cookie options sound as if they are the same thing. They are not. When you visit a site, the site may place a cookie. If the page contains third-party advertising, then those entities may attempt to place cookies through their ads. That will happen if the cookie option is set to Always. It is recommended that you leave the cookie option on the default – From visited. This setting will let the website proper leave a cookie but not the advertisements that are on the web page.

Clear cookies

Although cookies are quite useful in your web browsing endeavours, you may want to clear them all out if you notice Safari is running slow or exhibits some other unwanted behaviour – especially if it is happening with a certain website (which probably left a cookie that has become out of date).

1. In Settings, tap Safari on the left.
2. On the right is the button to Clear Cookies. Tap the Clear Cookies button. You are presented with a confirmation box. Tap Clear and all cookies are removed from your iPad.

Clear Cookies

DID YOU KNOW?

Even after clearing cookies, as soon as you start browsing the web new cookies will be placed in the iPad.

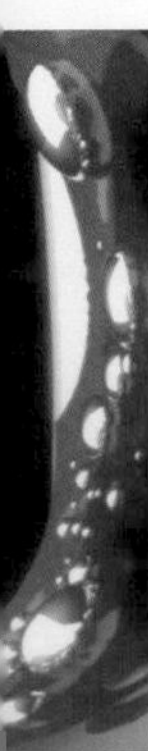

Clear the cache

The cache is a memory storage location in the iPad. Its purpose is to store images and other parts of websites that generally stay the same when you visit the sites. This speeds up the loading of web pages as some or all of the page is already in the iPad. Sometimes such pages are outdated because of using what is stored in the cache, so it's a good idea to occasionally clear it.

1. In Settings, tap Safari on the left.
2. On the right is the button to Clear Cache. Tap the Clear Cache button. You are presented with a confirmation box. Tap Clear and the cache is emptied.

Clear Cache

5 Staying in touch with Mail

Introduction

Of course, the iPad does email. The functions are straightforward as most email programs offer the same or similar features. On the iPad the email program is simply called Mail. It has a dedicated icon at the bottom of the Home screen. Chapter 2 explains how to create email accounts. This chapter explains how to use the Mail program, as well as covering some important settings.

Push and Fetch

Before diving into the particulars of creating and sending email messages, let's look at how messages are brought into the iPad. When someone sends you an email, there is an email server involved. The message is delivered to you from the email server.

The pertinent thing here is whether the iPad waits for messages to be sent to it or goes and seeks new messages on a periodic basis. The first method is Push, the latter method is Fetch. In detail, an email server will push a new message to the iPad when it receives one, whenever that might be. When Fetch is set, the iPad initiates contacting the server to see whether there are any waiting messages.

Push and Fetch are configured in Settings.

1. Enter Settings and tap Mail, Contacts, Calendars on the left. On the right, one of the buttons is Fetch New Data.
2. Tap Fetch New Data. A new screen opens with options about Push and Fetch.

3. Push, when set to On, will send messages to the iPad even when the Mail program is closed. It's a subjective choice whether to leave this feature on or off. You can toggle on and off by tapping the On/Off button. One thing is certain – leaving it on uses up more battery power than if you leave it off.
4. Fetch can be set to a frequency of 15 minutes, 30 minutes, hourly or manually. Fetch also uses up battery power, so if that is a concern (for example, you are on a long trip), you should set it to Manually. With the Mail program open, new messages will download to the iPad only when you tap to check for mail (shown later in the chapter) when Fetch is set to Manually. When Fetch is set to one of the periodic choices, the Mail program will use the timing to check for new messages.

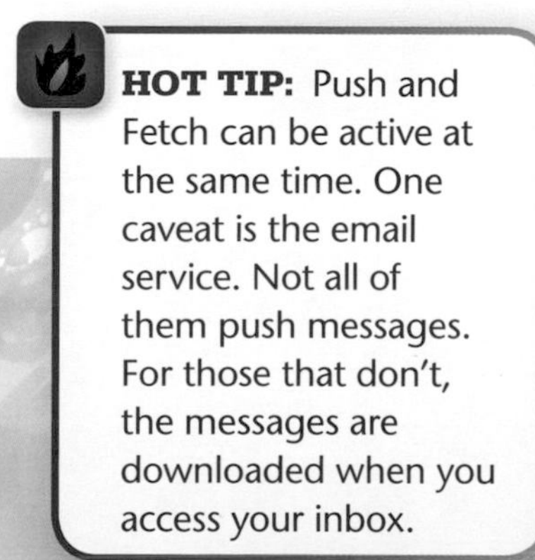

HOT TIP: Push and Fetch can be active at the same time. One caveat is the email service. Not all of them push messages. For those that don't, the messages are downloaded when you access your inbox.

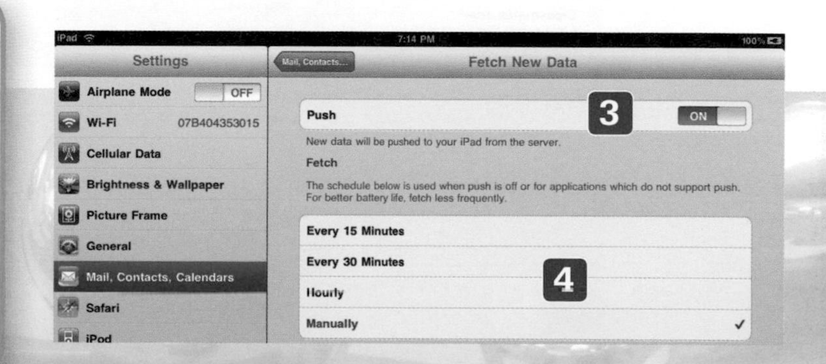

Start up Mail and read messages

The Mail icon sits at the bottom of the Home screen. A number may be present next to it. This tells you how many messages are in Mail that have not been opened and read.

1. Tap the Mail icon to open Mail. Mail will check for new messages to download. You can see a quick message about this at the bottom of the inbox.
2. The messages that have not been opened have a blue circle next to them. Tapping on a message displays it in the panel to the right. The blue circle has now gone.

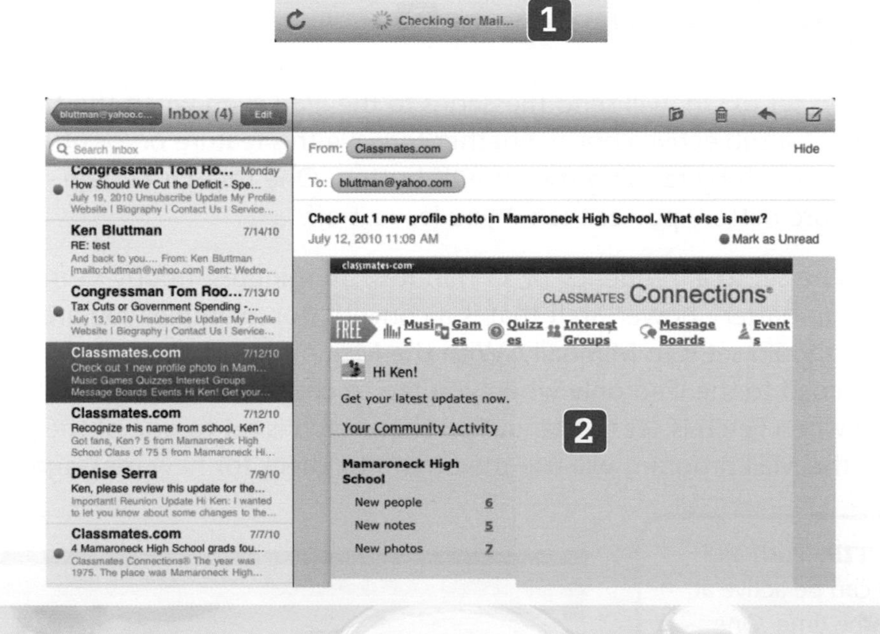

Check for new messages

You can instruct Mail to check for new messages at any time by tapping the Refresh button found at the bottom of the inbox. The Refresh button looks like a curved arrow.

HOT TIP: If you have configured Fetch to work on a periodic basis, new messages will be checked for on that schedule (for example, every 15 minutes).

Add a sender to Contacts

As you receive email from someone, you will probably like to add them to your contact list. You can do this directly from an email message.

1. Open the email message by tapping it in the inbox.
2. Tap on the sender's name. A box opens with a choice to Create New Contact.
3. Tap Create New Contact. A full contact info box opens.
4. Fill in any extra info if you wish. Tap the small Done button at the top right of the box when you've finished.

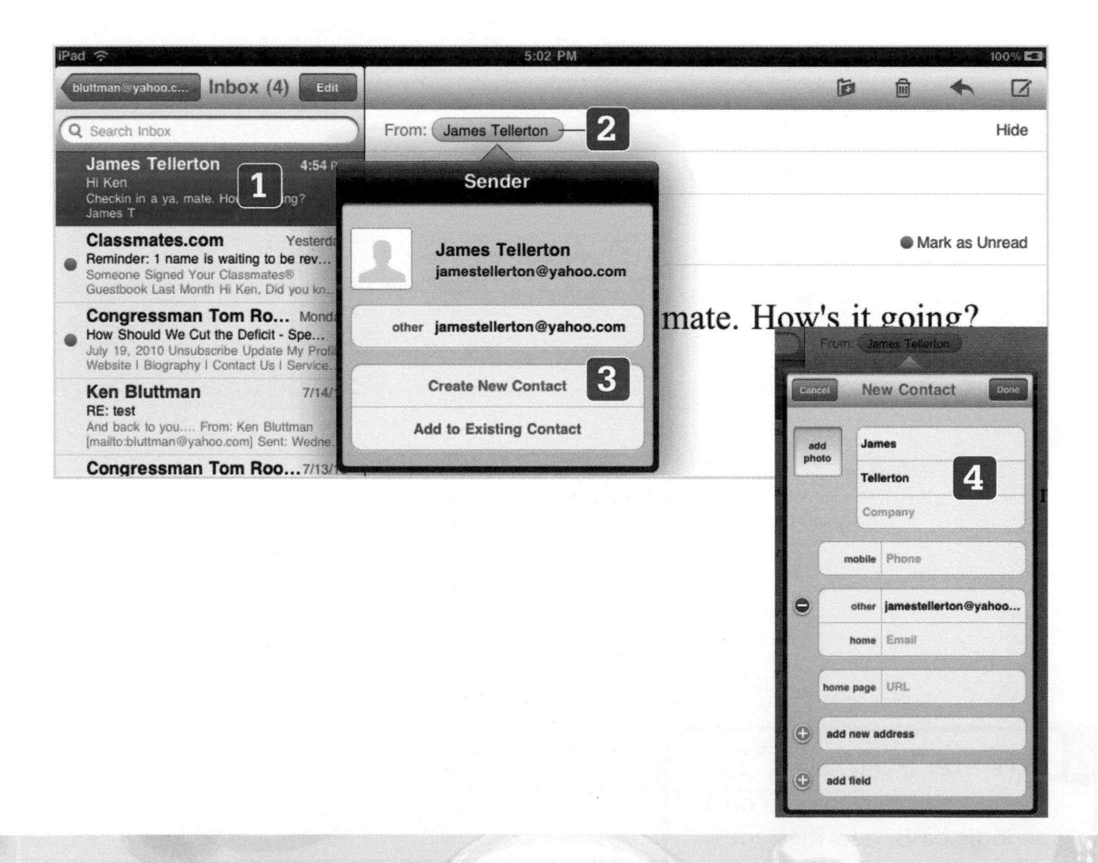

DID YOU KNOW?

When you tap Done, another box opens that provides a choice to Share the Contact. Tapping that creates a new email message with the contact's information added to the email message. You can then send the email to yet another person.

Compose an email message

A new email message is initiated by tapping the New Email button.

1. In the upper right corner of Mail are four small buttons. The one used for new mail is the furthest to the right. Tap the button and a blank new email opens up.
2. To the right of the To field is a plus (+) sign. Tapping this displays your contacts.
3. Tap on a contact's name. The To field will fill in.
4. Write your email. When you've finished, tap the small Send button at the top of the message.

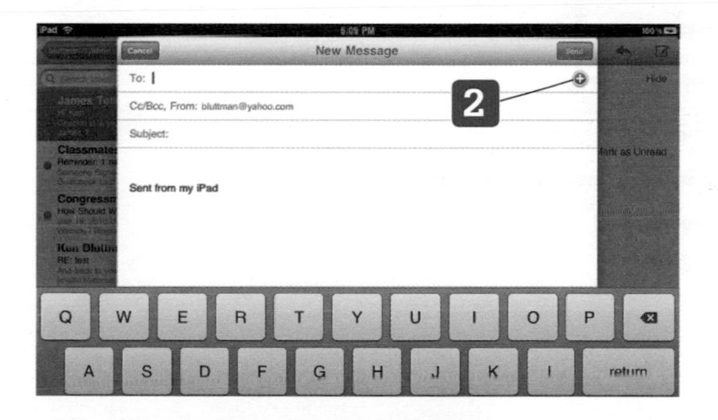

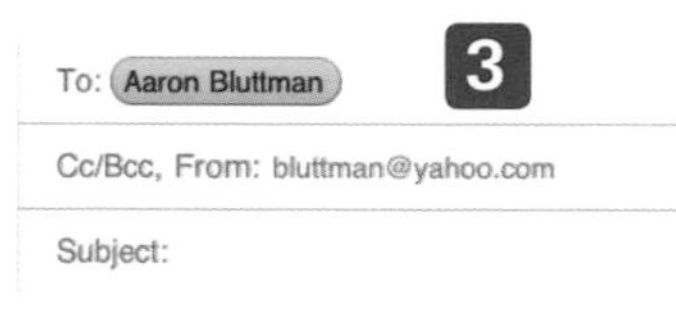

DID YOU KNOW?
You can use your finger to scroll the list of contacts.

HOT TIP: If the recipient for this email is not in your contact list, dismiss the contact list by tapping in the To box and then just type in the email address.

Save a draft of a message

There are times when you begin a new email message but don't complete it straight away. In this case you should save it as a draft. Then you can finish it at another time.

1. Tap the small Cancel button on the left. A choice appears to save or discard the message.
2. Saving the message puts it in the Drafts mailbox.

SEE ALSO: See later in the chapter for how to change mailboxes.

Reply to a message

Email is about communication, of course. Receiving messages is just half the activity – replying is the other half. Sometimes you reply to one sender, other times to multiple people – when they are in the To, Cc or Bcc fields.

1. Of the four buttons in the upper right, the third one (looks like a curved arrow) is used to reply. Tap the button.
2. Tap Reply or Reply All. Reply will create an email to send back to just the person in the To field. Reply All includes everyone on the email address fields.
3. An email ready to be sent back to the sender is created. It includes the content of their original message.
4. Type in whatever you wish to send back to the sender. Tap the small Send button when you've finished.

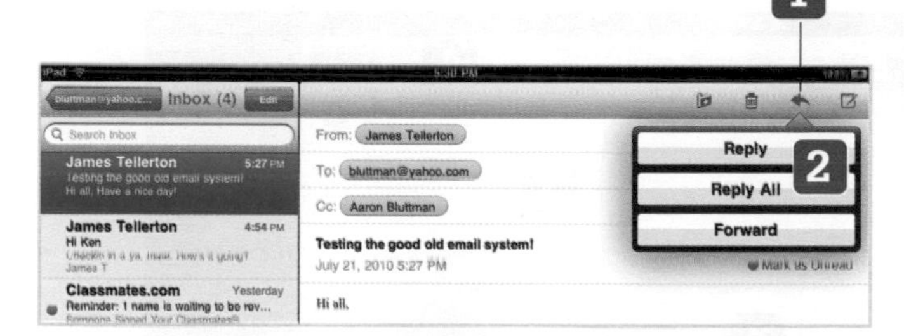

HOT TIP: Reply All shows up here because there was more than one recipient on the incoming email.

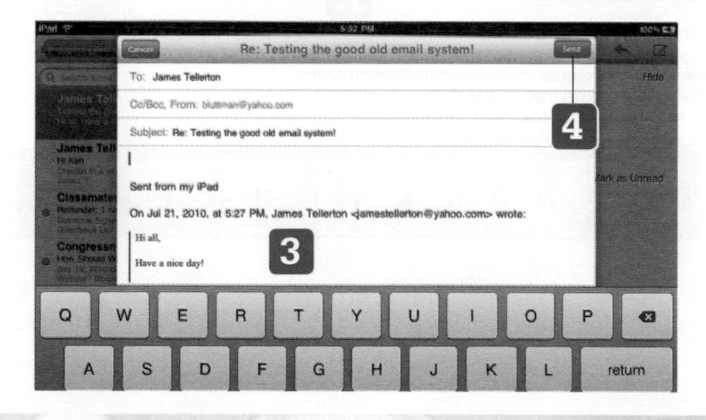

Forward an email message

Forwarding an email message lets you send a message you have received to a new recipient. It is not sent to the original sender.

1. Tap the third small button at the top right of Mail (the same button that is used to Reply). Tap Forward.
2. A new email opens and contains the content of the original message. However, the To field is blank.
3. Type in an email address or tap the plus (+) sign to the right to access your contact list.
4. When you've finished entering new information into the body of the message, tap the small Send button on the upper right.

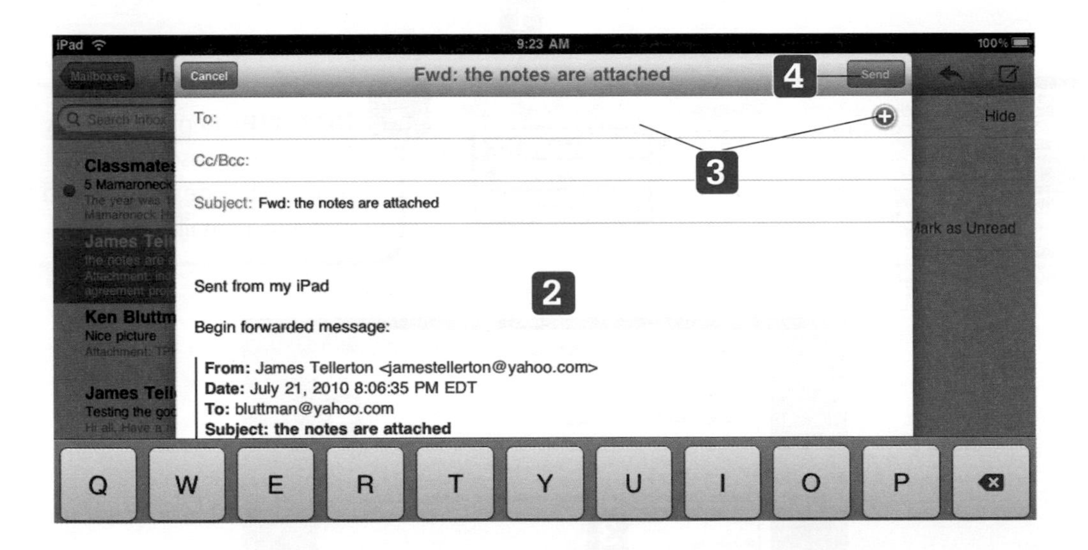

View the different mailboxes

The inbox is obviously the most viewed mailbox as this is where new messages end up. However, there are also mailboxes for drafts, sent messages, trash and bulk mail.

1. At the top left of Mail is a button that lists the particular email account in use. By default, the inbox is shown.
2. Tap directly on the account name. The inbox is replaced by a list of all the mailboxes.
3. Tap the mailbox you wish to view.

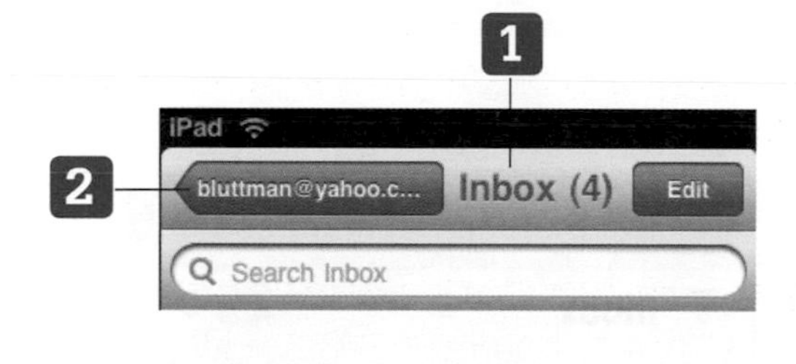

DID YOU KNOW?

You can open any message in the Drafts folder and continue working on it.

View your accounts

If you have more than one email account set up, when a list of folders of an account is in view, the button in the upper left corner says Accounts. Tapping this leads to a list of your accounts.

1. If you are in a mailbox (inbox, for example), tap on the account name to show the boxes of the current account.
2. Tap on the Accounts button in the upper left. A list of accounts appears.
3. Tap an account to enter it. You will next see the boxes belonging to that account.

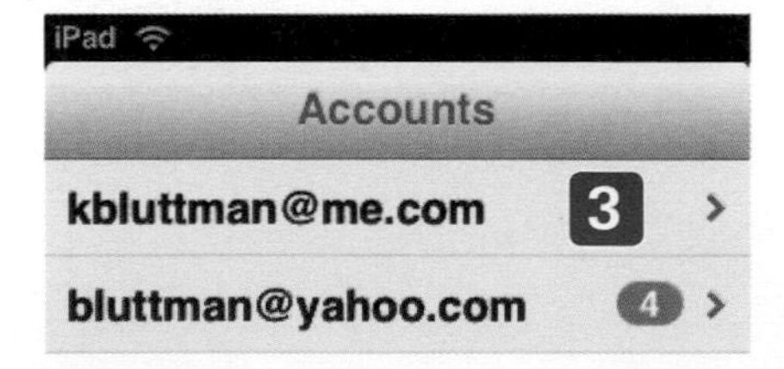

View and save an attachment

At times we all tend to receive email messages with attachments of one type or another. Here is how you can view an attachment that arrives with an email.

1. Depending on the type of attachment, it will either be visible in the body of the incoming email (a photo, for example) or the body may contain an icon referencing the attachment.

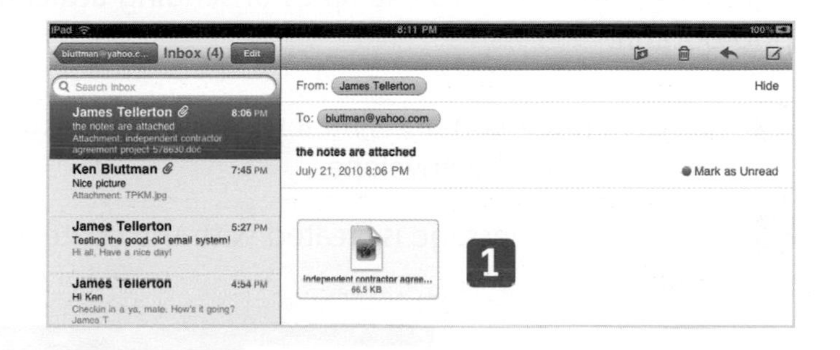

2. Tapping the attachment icon will open it in an appropriate program in the iPad.
3. To view the contents of the attachment, tap and hold down your finger until a list of options appears.

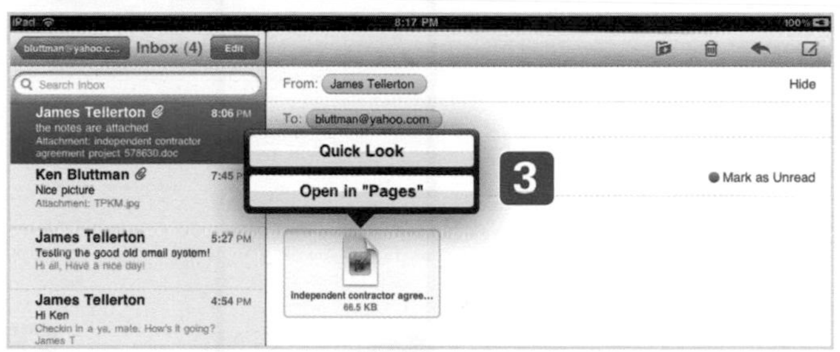

4. In the case of a photo, it will be visible in the body of the message. Tap and hold down your finger until options appear. Tapping Save Image places the photo in the Saved Photos library (see Chapter 6).

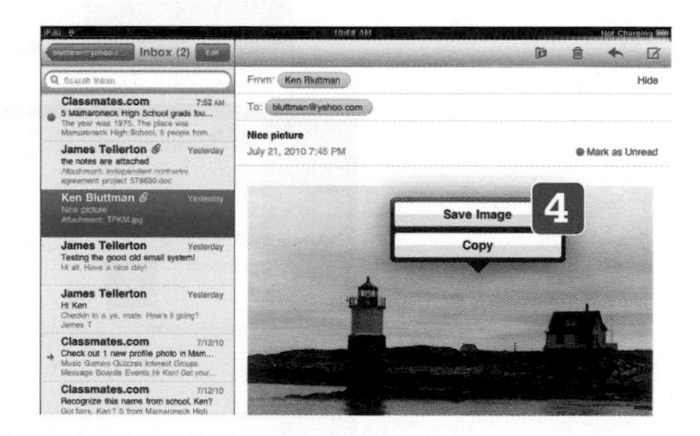

HOT TIP: Attachments that are pictures appear as is in the body of the email.

HOT TIP: The way the attachment in this example is saved is by opening it in Pages (Apple's word-processing application). The opening process actually imports the attachment into Pages' repository of saved documents.

Send an attachment

A typical way to send attachments in computer-based email programs is to add the attachment to the email message while composing it. With the iPad it works a bit differently. Here are two examples of sending attachments. One is a note, the other is a photograph.

1. Tap the Notes icon and find a note. At the bottom is a button that looks like an envelope. Tap the envelope.
2. A new email message is created with the contents of the note in the body of the email.

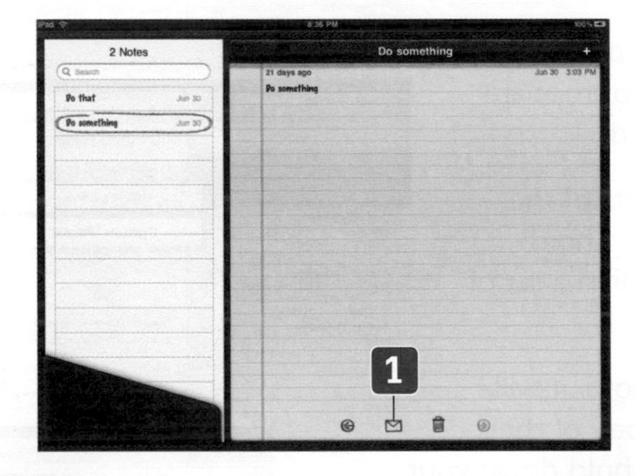

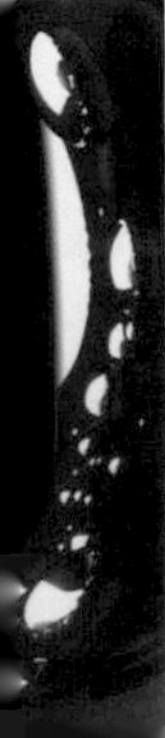

Photos are attached using these steps.

3. Tap Photos and find a photo you wish to send. Tap and hold down your finger on the photo until Copy appears.
4. Tap Copy.
5. Press the Home button and tap Mail. Tap the button for creating a new email message.
6. With the new message still being composed, tap and hold your finger in the body of the message until a choice to Paste appears. Tap Paste.
7. The photo is now in the body of the email.

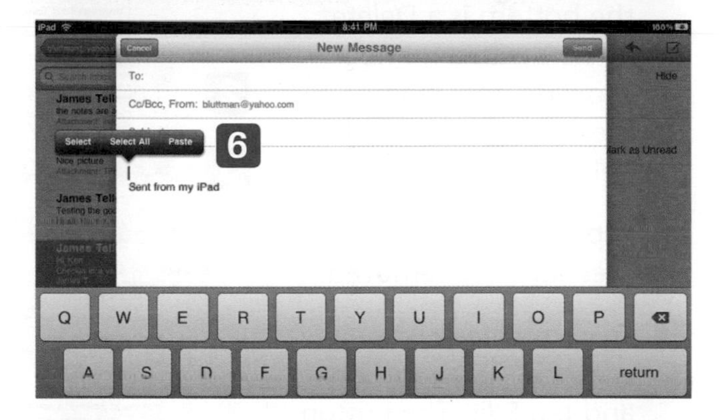

Delete email

Eventually you will want or need to clean out your inbox. Here's how to delete email.

1. At the top of the inbox (or one of the other mailboxes), tap the Edit button.
2. A circle appears to the left of each email. Tap the circle of each message you wish to delete. A tick appears in the ones you have tapped. At the bottom is a Delete button with a number showing how many messages are marked for deletion.

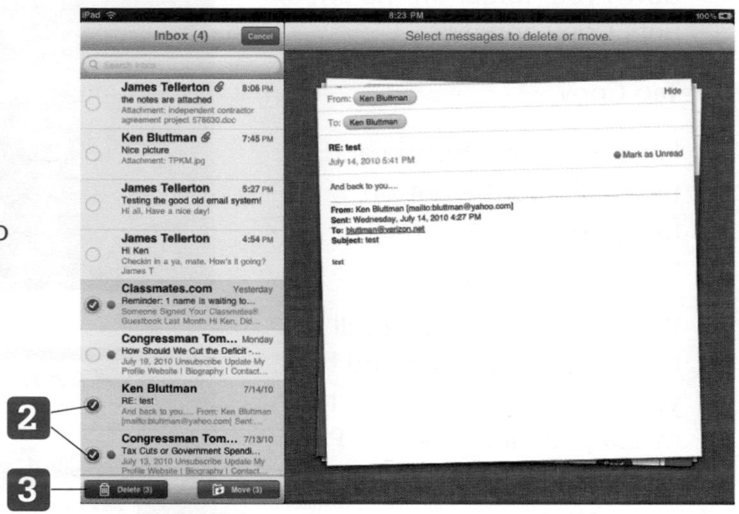

3. Tap the Delete button. The messages are removed.
4. To complete deletion, enter the Trash mailbox and tap Edit. The button for deleting now says 'Delete All'. Tapping it will permanently remove the messages.

HOT TIP: Messages from the Inbox, Drafts, Sent and Bulk mailboxes are not fully deleted – they are moved to the Trash box.

HOT TIP: A quick way to delete the current message (the one in view) is to tap the second small button in the upper right of Mail – the one that looks like a trash can. This sends the current message directly into the Trash mailbox.

Search email

A search feature that looks through email messages is a mighty tool indeed – especially as you can end up with so many email messages and can't remember which one had that certain information you need.

1. Near the top of each mailbox is a search box. Tap the box and the virtual keyboard appears.
2. Type in a word or phrase for the search. Note, however, that just under where the search term goes is a choice of how to search through the messages – From, To, Subject or All. Select the one that makes sense for your search. If you're not sure, select to search All.
3. Search results are displayed as you type. Tap on an item in the list to display the particular email.
4. To return to the inbox (or another mailbox), tap the small Cancel button next to the search box.

Move a message

Over time you will end up with an increasing amount of email. Organising the messages is helpful. This works out well when you have new folders in place to hold messages. On the iPad itself you cannot create new folders, but if you have synced with your computer's email program (this is done in iTunes), then folders from the computer will be in the iPad.

To move a message to a folder:

1. Make the message visible by tapping it in the inbox (or other mailbox).
2. Tap the first of the four small buttons at the top of Mail. The message remains visible and the list of mailboxes and folders shows on the left.
3. Tap the mailbox or folder you wish the message to be moved to.

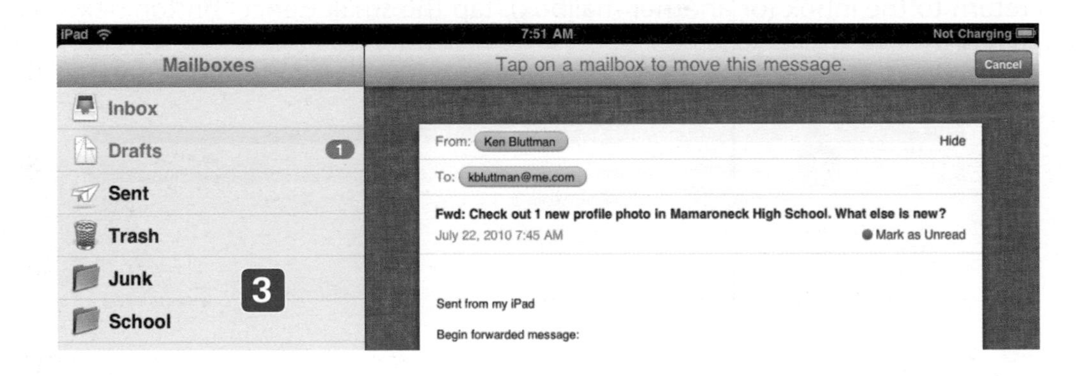

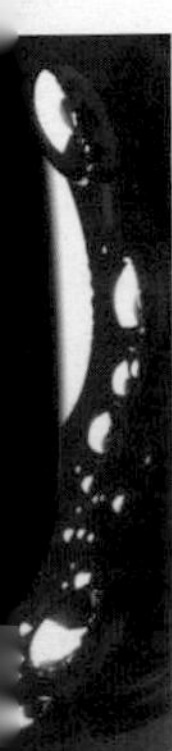

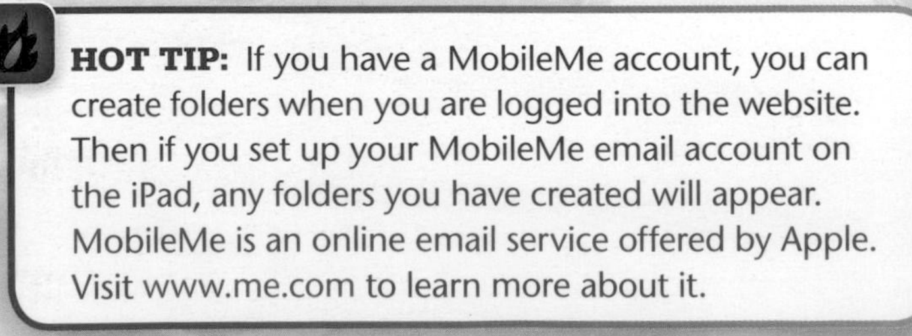

HOT TIP: If you have a MobileMe account, you can create folders when you are logged into the website. Then if you set up your MobileMe email account on the iPad, any folders you have created will appear. MobileMe is an online email service offered by Apple. Visit www.me.com to learn more about it.

6 Photos on the iPad

Introduction

The iPad provides many ways to work with photos – viewing them, emailing them, organising them, and more. Photos are kept in albums. There is a default album named Saved Photos and you can create additional albums.

If you are thus inclined you can find apps in the App store that are used for image manipulation, enhancement and viewing options. Photos are brought into the iPad either by syncing with your computer or using the camera kit accessory. All this is explained in this chapter.

One item to note is how to make a screenshot. Press the On/Off, Sleep/Wake button and the Home button at the same time. The iPad takes a snapshot of the screen and stores the image in the Saved Photos album.

View photos

There is a dedicated Photos icon located at the bottom of the Home screen. Tapping it leads to a collection of photo albums. To start you may just have the single default Saved Photos album.

1. Tap the Photos icon.
2. A view of available albums is shown. Tap one to open it.
3. Tap on a photo to make it fill the screen.
4. You can move from photo to photo by swiping the screen with your finger.

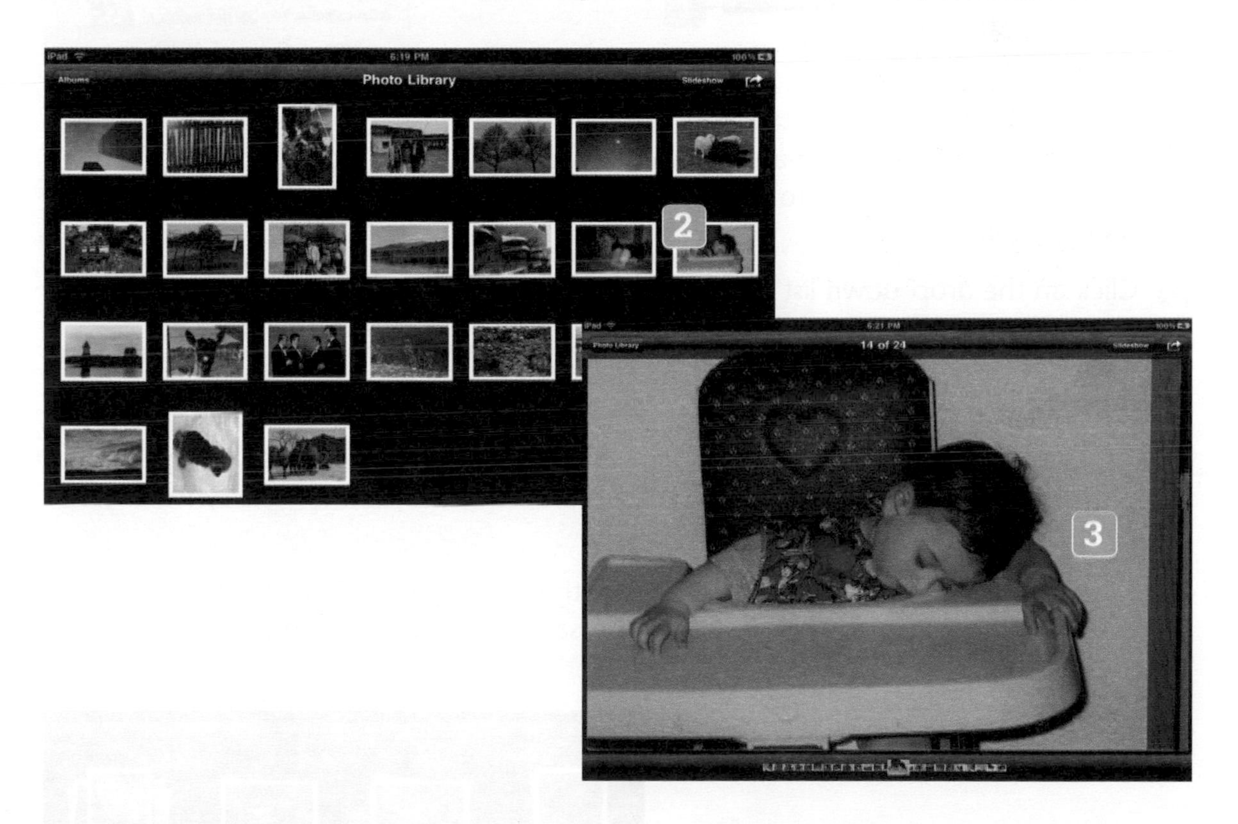

HOT TIP: Along the bottom of the screen is a small navigation bar with which you can scroll through the pictures in the album by moving your finger along the bar. If you don't see the bar, tap once on the picture and it will appear.

HOT TIP: To return to the view of available albums, tap the small Photo Library button in the upper left of the screen. If you do not see the button, tap once on the photo first.

Create a photo album

The iPad contains the default Saved Photos album. However, you can add albums when synced up with your computer. You sync folders that contain photographs. This places the folders as new albums on the iPad.

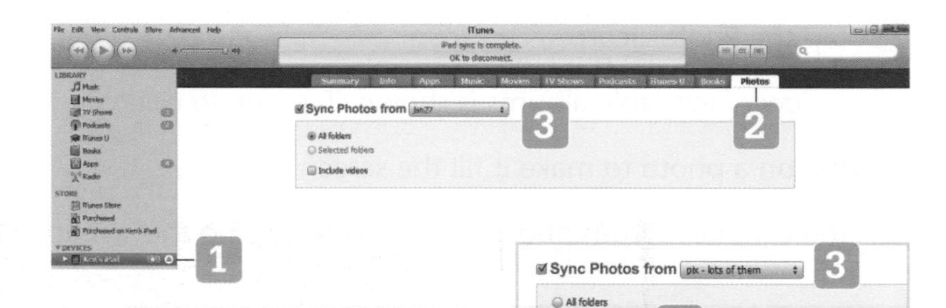

1. Connect the iPad to your computer and start iTunes on the computer (iTunes may auto start). In iTunes on the computer, click on your iPad under Devices on the left.
2. Near the top of the screen are tabs that relate to different types of media. To the right is Photos. Click on the Photos tab.
3. Click on the drop-down list to the right of the Sync Photos from tick box. In the drop-down list is a choice to select a folder. Navigate to a folder in the drop-down list and select it.
4. Then click the Selected folders option. A list of subfolders appears (assuming your photos are organised this way). Select from the list which subfolders to sync – these become photo albums on the iPad.
5. Click the Apply button in the lower right of the iTunes screen. The iPad displays a message that a sync is in progress. This message may come and go quickly if there are just a few photos being synced.
6. In the iPad is now an album for each folder you selected to sync.

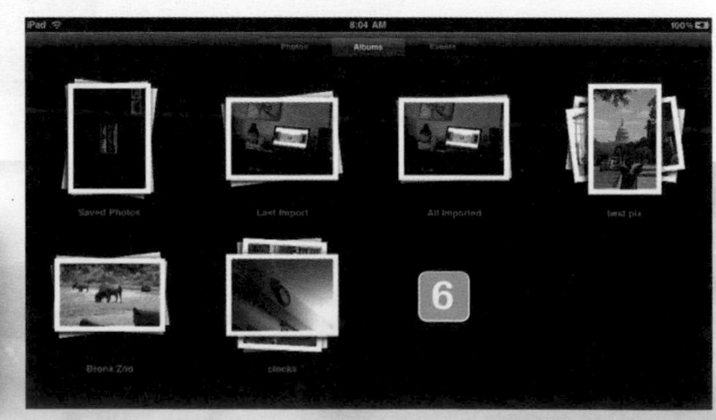

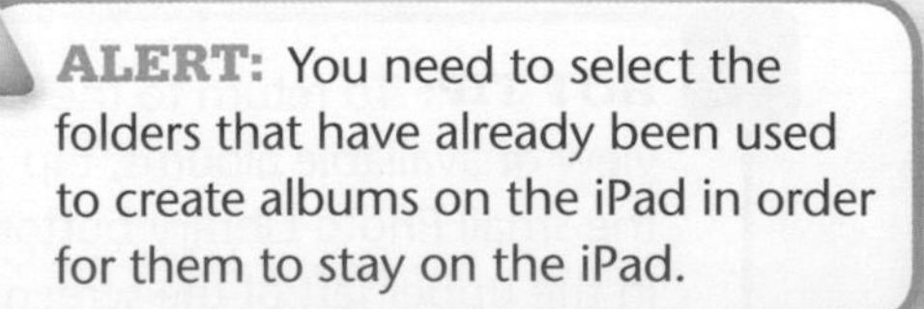

ALERT: You need to select the folders that have already been used to create albums on the iPad in order for them to stay on the iPad.

Shrink or enlarge a photo

This is easy. Let your fingers do the work!

1. Open a photo.
2. Press the screen with two fingers and move the fingers away from each other. The photo will stretch out (be enlarged).
3. Use two fingers again. This time move the fingers towards each other. The photo will shrink.

HOT TIP: You can enlarge a photo directly from the thumbnail images in the album.

Run a slide show from an album

You can view your photos as a slide show. This means the screen will show picture after picture without needing to touch the screen.

1. From the view of an album, tap the Slideshow button in the upper right of the screen. A list of options appears.
2. Select whether to play music during the slide show. If you have this option set to on, tap Music to select from the music already in the iPad. Select a transition – this is the animation effect of how slides change from one to the next.
3. Press the Start Slideshow button.
4. At any time while the slide show is running, simply tap the screen to stop it.

Run a slide show from the Picture Frame

When the iPad is showing the lock screen (the screen with the 'slide to unlock' slider switch), there also appears an icon for the Picture Frame. Tapping this starts a slide show.

1. In Settings, tap Picture Frame on the left and select desired settings on the right. These control how the slide show will work, as well as which album or albums to use as the source of pictures.

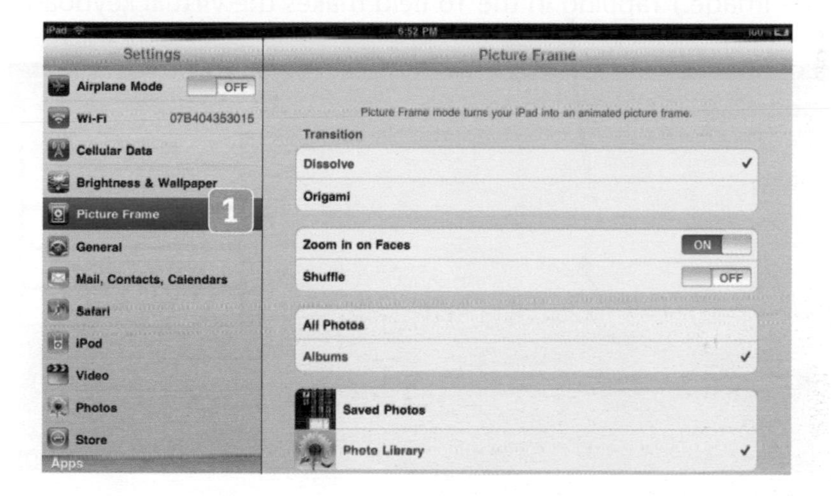

2. When the lock screen is present, tap the Picture Frame icon (looks like a flower in a box). The slide show begins.
3. At any time, tap the screen to display the slide to unlock switch. Slide the switch. The slide show ends and the Home screen is displayed.

Email a photo

It's likely that you will want to share your photos with family and friends. Here's how.

1. With a photo displayed, tap the Options button in the upper right of the screen. The button looks like an arrow inside a square. A list of options appears.
2. Tap Email Photo.
3. A new email appears with the photo embedded in the body of the message. The virtual keyboard appears. (In this example the keyboard was closed to avoid blocking the image.) Tapping in the To field makes the virtual keyboard appear.

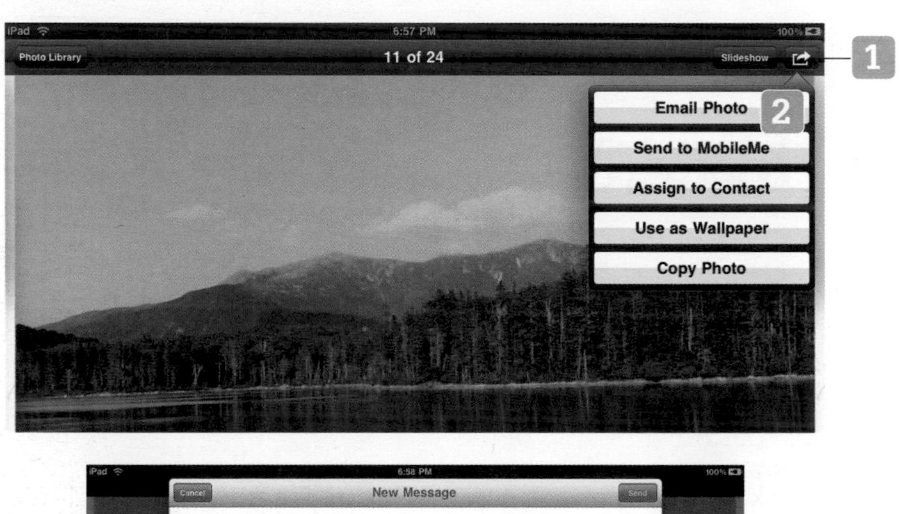

Assign a photo to a contact

The list of contacts is essential for holding names, addresses, phone numbers and such. An optional but handy feature is to assign a picture to a contact. The image will probably be of the person, although there's nothing stopping you from assigning the picture of a cow to one of your relatives (only if they have a sense of humour!).

1. Display the photo you wish to use. Tap the Options button in the upper right of the screen. The button looks like an arrow inside a square. A list of options appears.
2. One of the options is Assign to Contact. Tap it.
3. The list of options is replaced by your list of contacts. Tap on the name of the contact.
4. A Preview window opens in which, using stretch or squeeze gestures with your fingers, you can essentially crop the picture. When you've finished, tap the small Use button at the top of the Preview window.
5. To confirm, press the Home button and tap the Contacts icon. Tap on the name of the contact and see that the picture is next to the contact's information.

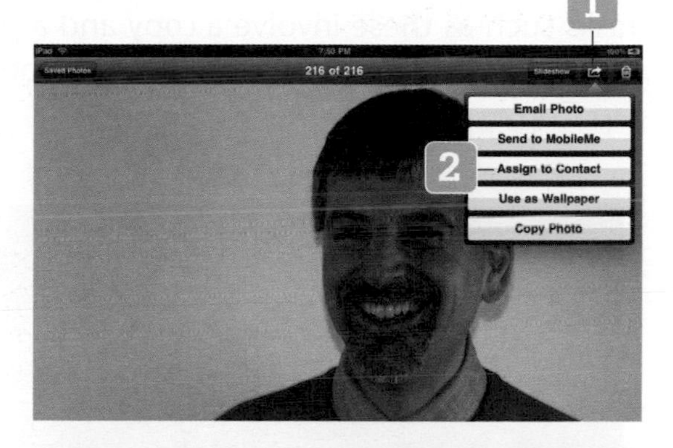

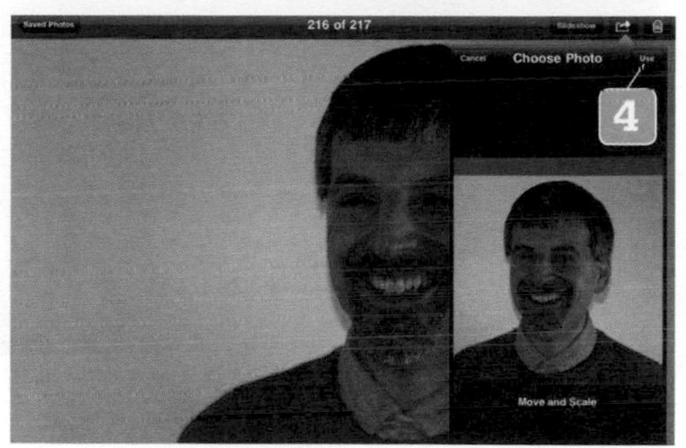

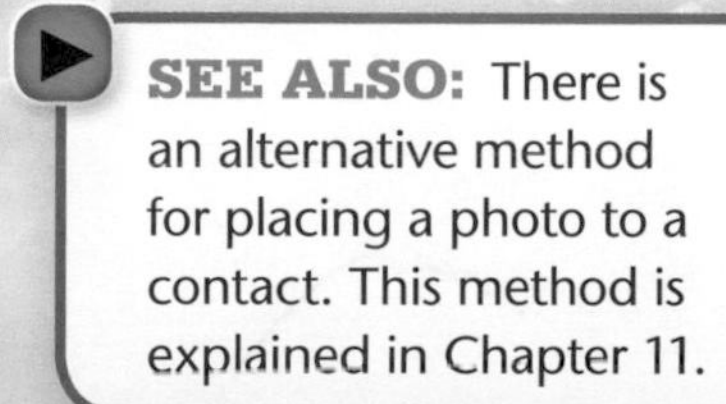

SEE ALSO: There is an alternative method for placing a photo to a contact. This method is explained in Chapter 11.

Copy a photo

The obvious reason for copying a photo is to place the copy somewhere. In terms of the iPad this would be to place the photo as an email attachment or to place the photo in a contact's record. The instructions for these two tasks are explained in Chapters 5 and 11 respectively.

Tasks such as these involve a copy and a paste. Here we'll look at how to get the copy of the photo. It's easy. Just hold down your finger on a photo until Copy appears, then tap Copy.

Delete a photo

When you tire of a photo or accidently get a bad shot into a photo album (for example, saving a shot from an email that you didn't mean to save), it's time to delete.

One caveat here: you can delete only from the default Saved Photos album. Any other album is in the iPad as part of a sync operation with the computer. Deleting a photo from such an album is done by removing the photo from the folder it is in on the computer and then the next time the iPad and computer sync, the photo will be gone (but make sure you selected to include the folder in the sync).

Otherwise, to delete from the Saved Photos folder:

1. Display the photo.
2. In the upper right of the screen is a trash can button. Tap it. A confirmation to delete the photo appears.
3. Tap the Delete photo button. The photo is deleted.

Import photos using the camera connection kit

The camera connection kit is an accessory. It does not come with the iPad and needs to be purchased separately. Its function is to allow you to copy pictures directly from your camera into the iPad.

The kit comes with two connectors. One is for SD camera memory cards and the other is a USB connection. Here is how to copy pictures using the USB connection. (Of course, this assumes that your camera has a USB connection.)

1. Connect the USB adaptor to the iPad dock. One side of the connector fits in the dock, the other accepts a USB cable.
2. Connect a USB cable to the camera and into the connector. Turn the camera on.

3. The iPad should sense there are photos from the 'new source' – the camera. The iPad screen will show the photos as thumbnails and there is a small Import All button in the upper right of the screen. Tap the button.
4. After the import is complete you may see a message asking whether you wish to delete or keep the photos from the camera.

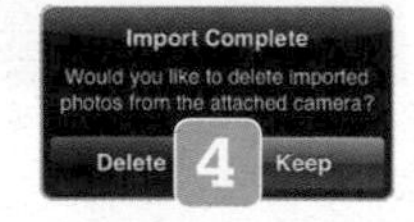

ALERT: There are many camera manufacturers and there are not necessarily any standards when it comes to using a USB connection to copy photos. The iPad may or may not recognise there are photos that can be copied from the camera – primarily due to how the particular camera makes use of the USB port on the camera. Check the camera's manual to see whether you need to apply certain settings to use the USB port on the camera.

7 Watching videos and YouTube movies on your iPad

Introduction

The ultimate media experience, of course, is video. Photographs are nice. Music is great to listen to. But video trumps all since it has both audio and moving visual action.

The iPad plays movies, television shows, visual podcasts and music videos. A movie could be a professional one you bought or rented through the iTunes store; it could be one you created with your digital camera or camcorder. Television shows, podcasts and music videos are all available through the iTunes store.

The Videos icon leads to all the video types.

Within the Videos area are categories that segregate the types of videos.

Watch a video

Playing a video is just two taps away from your viewing enjoyment. Full featured movies provide an extra option to go direct to a section (a chapter) of the movie before play begins.

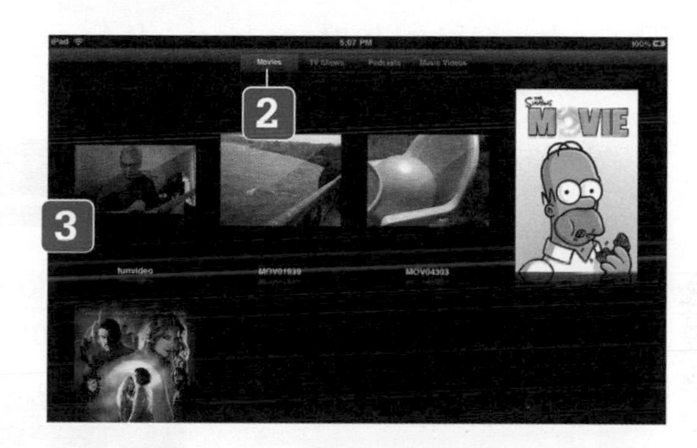

1. On the Home Screen, tap the Videos icon.
2. Tap the Movies heading, which appears if there are movies stored in the iPad.
3. Tap a movie to get started.
4. If the movie is home-made, an information window opens with a Start button (an arrow) to start the movie.

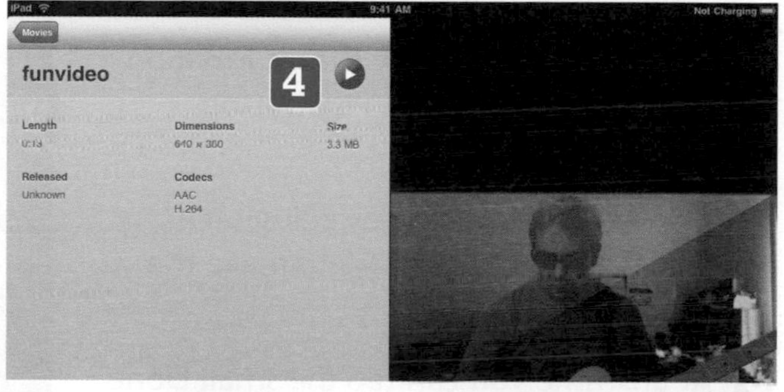

5. Professional movies provide an information window with an option to list the chapters within a movie. These are useful for starting at a certain point in the movie. Tapping a chapter starts the play at that point.
6. You also play TV shows, podcasts and music videos as described.

ALERT: The iPad plays only certain video file types: .mov, .m4v and .mp4. If your home-made videos are of another video type, they have to be converted to work on the iPad. A search on the internet will provide links to many conversion utilities. Any video downloaded from the iTunes store is already optimised to play on the iPad.

Control video playback

Videos have both an indicator of elapsed time and a set of controls to start, pause, rewind or fast forward (sometimes referred to as VCR controls), along with a volume control. When a video ends, the screen reverts to the video's information window.

The video control buttons from left to right are fast backward, pause (double lines) and fast forward. Underneath these is a slider switch to control the volume.

Tapping the Pause button changes it to look like the Play button (an arrow). The video is paused; tapping the Play button resumes play of the video.

1. Tap a movie to display the information window, then tap the Play button (looks like an arrow).
2. The movie starts to play, full screen. Tap it once while it plays to make the controls appear.
3. At any time you can tap the small Done button in the upper left to stop the video and make the screen revert to the information window.

DID YOU KNOW?
You can use the volume control on the side of the iPad as an alternative to the slider control underneath the VCR controls.

HOT TIP: From the information window, you can tap the small Movies button in the upper left to return to the full set of movies. If you were watching a different video type, a podcast for example, then the button is captioned with Podcasts.

HOT TIP: At the top is a slider control with which you can quickly move through the movie.

Download and watch a video from the iTunes store

The iTunes store is the place to find the latest and greatest videos. Or you can search through the many bargain titles, which are older but just as good.

1. On the Home screen, tap the iTunes icon.
2. Along the bottom of the store screen, tap Movies (if not already on Movies).
3. Select a movie. You may find that a movie is available for rental only. If you wish, rent the movie to watch; otherwise browse for another movie that you can buy.
4. Once the movie is downloaded into the iPad, it is available under Movies (after tapping the Videos icon). Tap the movie to get started.

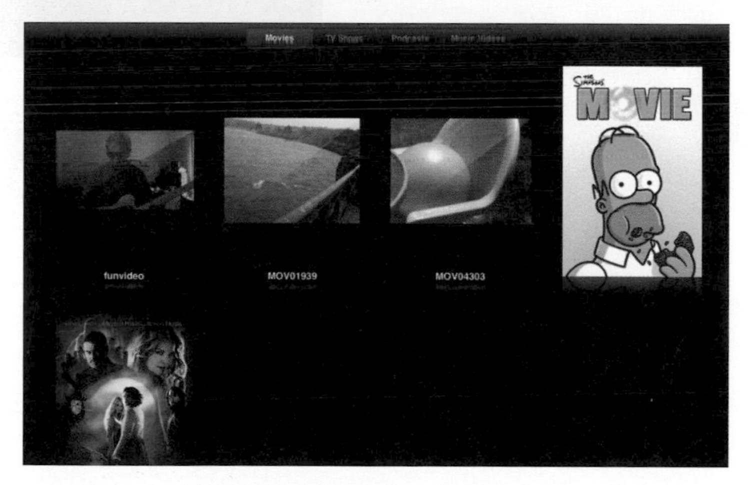

SEE ALSO: See Chapter 3 for further details about purchasing from the iTunes store.

Delete a video

At some point in time you will probably wish to clean out some of the old videos in the iPad that you no longer watch.

1 Tap and hold your finger on the video until a small x appears.

2 Tap the x to delete the video. You will be asked to confirm the deletion.

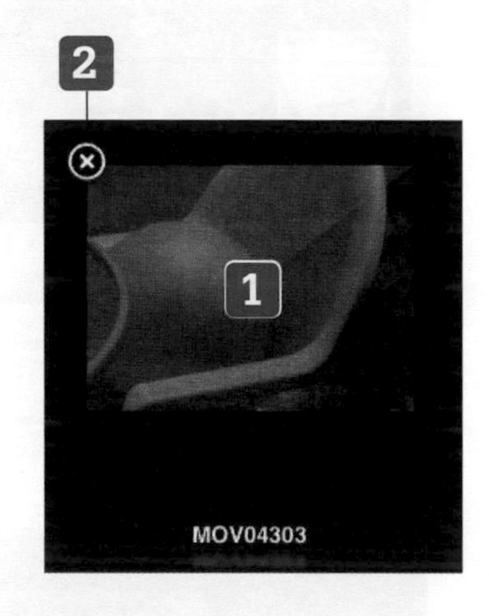

Connect your iPad to a television

With the use of the dock connector to VGA adaptor accessory, you can hook up the iPad to a television. The television must have a VGA-type connection for this to work.

1. Connect the dock connector to VGA adaptor to the iPad.
2. Connect the other end of the dock connector to VGA adaptor to the VGA connection of the television.
3. On the iPad, start a movie or other video. The media will play on the television screen.

HOT TIP: You will probably have to change the source on the television.

ALERT: The iPad makes use of a television to play videos. Other features and apps will not be sent to the television screen.

Watch a YouTube movie

YouTube movies are accessed through the YouTube icon on the Home screen. In case you are not familiar with YouTube, it is the world's biggest repository of user-supplied videos. Millions of movies exist on YouTube. These are not full-length, theatre-type movies, they are uploaded by individuals and companies. Usually you can go directly to www.youtube.com, but for technical reasons it is necessary to use the YouTube app on the iPad.

The best way to learn what YouTube offers is to dive right in and watch a movie. Movies are segregated out by Features, Top Rated and Most Viewed. You can search for movies, subscribe to a YouTube movie provider and upload your own movies. Uploading your movies has to be done through the website – and you need an account (explained below). For now, let's watch!

1. On the Home screen, tap the YouTube icon.

2. Along the bottom of the YouTube screen are Featured, Top Rated and Most Viewed. Tap any of these categorisations to see what is available to watch. Here, Top Rated has been selected and previews are shown of Top Rated movies.

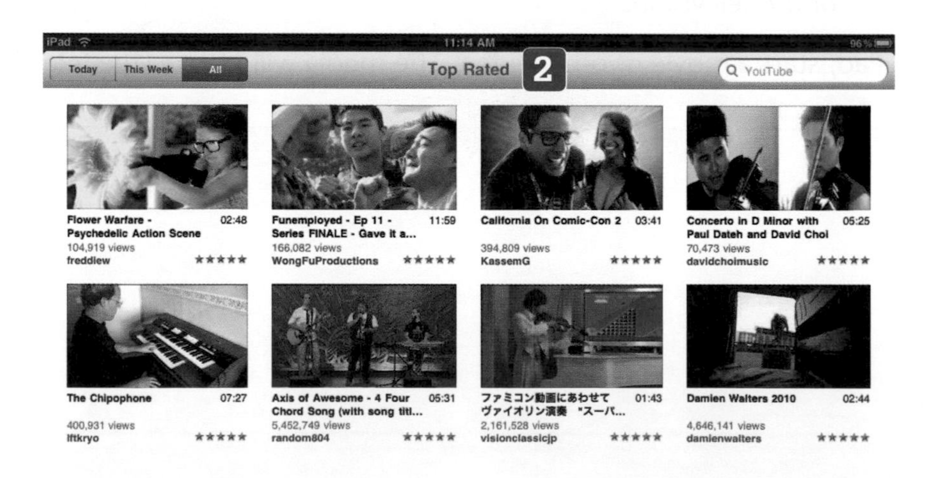

DID YOU KNOW?

A movie's rating is an average of all ratings supplied by those who have viewed the movie.

3. Tap a movie to get it started. It may take a moment or two for the movie to load. Then it will start to play.

4. Once a movie is playing, you can tap the screen to display the controls. The typical VCR controls (backward, pause/play, forward) are available for playback control. The volume slider is underneath. There are two additional controls – on the left is a button for adding the movie to your list of favourites; on the right is a button that looks like two arrows pointing at each other. This button is used to show the movie's information.

5. To exit the movie, tap the small Done button in the upper left of the screen.

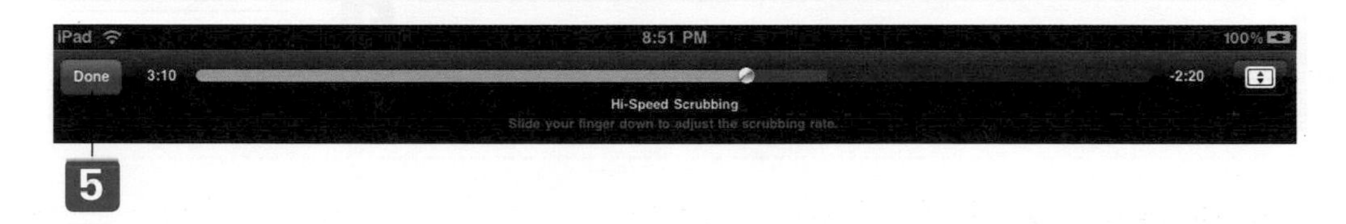

6. On the right side of the slider at the top is a small button. This toggle shows the movie in full-screen mode.

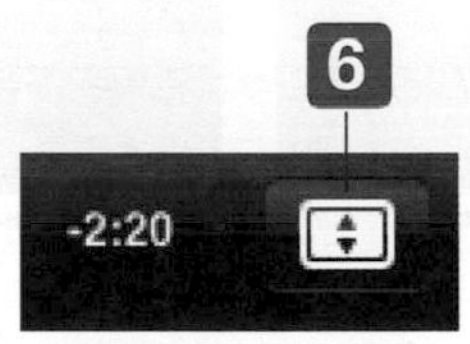

HOT TIP: At the top of the screen is a slider switch to quickly navigate through a movie. Tap and hold your finger on it, then slide your finger forward or back. You may see a message underneath that Hi-Speed Scrubbing is in effect.

Search for a YouTube movie

It's easy to be overwhelmed with the vast number of movies on YouTube. Where do you start? What should you watch? Often it is best to search for movies that are of interest to you. The search feature is perfect for this.

1. Tap into the Search box in the upper right of the screen. The virtual keyboard appears.
2. Type in a search term, then press the Search key on the virtual keyboard. You will be shown movies that are related to your search term. Here, for example, 'cooking' was used as a search term.

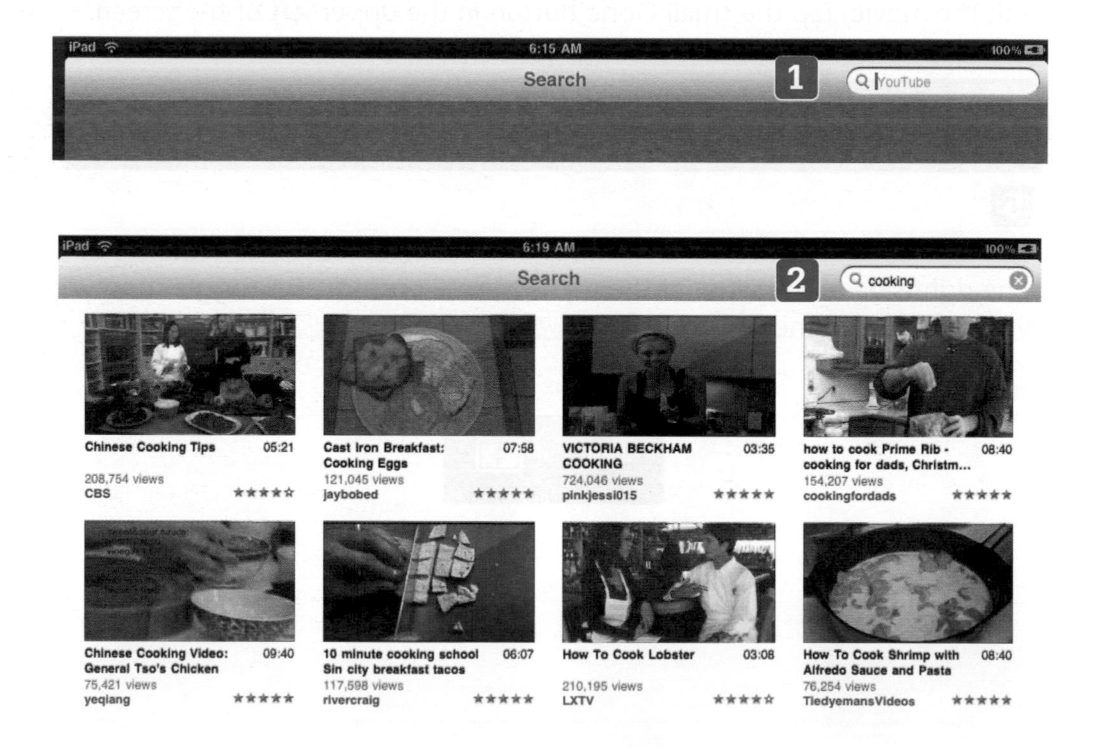

DID YOU KNOW?

It is likely that more movies will be returned from the search than you see on the screen. Scroll down to see them all.

HOT TIP: Narrow your search for better results. For example, 'cooking fish' is a more focused search than just 'cooking'.

Create a YouTube account

You need a YouTube account to upload your own movies, leave ratings and feedback, and more. An account is created on the YouTube website, not through the YouTube app on the iPad.

1. Tap the Safari icon to start the browser.
2. Go to the YouTube website (www.youtube.com). (See Chapter 4 for help with using the Safari browser.)
3. From the main page of YouTube, tap the My Account tab.
4. In the next screen you can log in or create a new account. Look for the link to sign up for a new account. Tap the link.
5. The next page that appears is where you enter information to open an account.

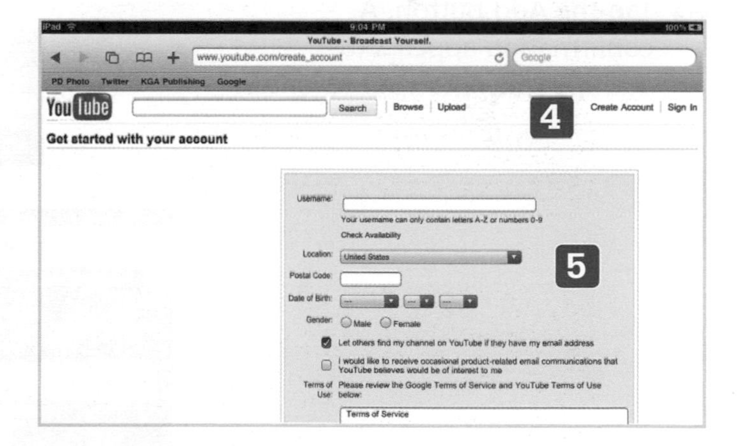

HOT TIP: You can also create an account by visiting the site using a web browser on your computer instead of using Safari on the iPad.

Add a movie to Favorites

When you have watched a movie that you enjoyed, you may want to add it to Favorites (also known as bookmarking). Then you can easily watch the movie again by accessing your Favorites list.

1. When a movie ends, whether by reaching the end or by you tapping Done, the movie information appears, with a small still visual of the movie.
2. Tap once on the movie. New buttons appear: Add, Share, Rate and Flag.
3. Tap the Add button. A confirmation appears to add the movie to your Favorites.

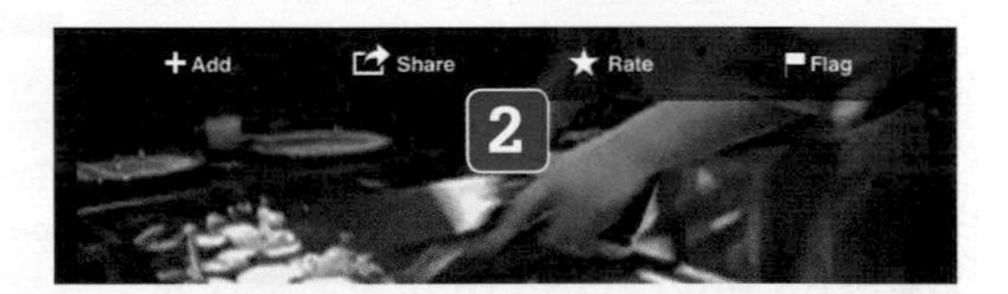

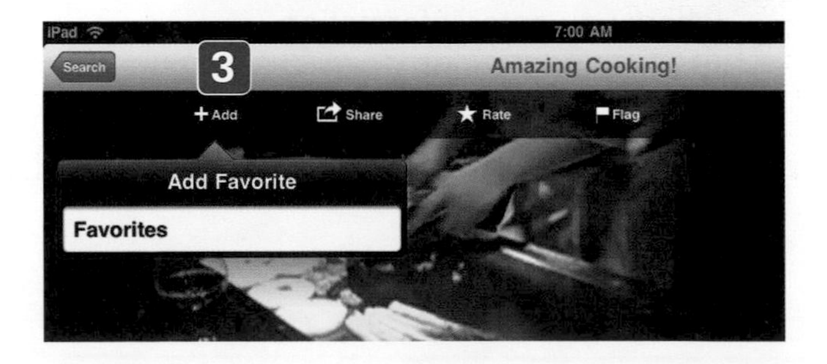

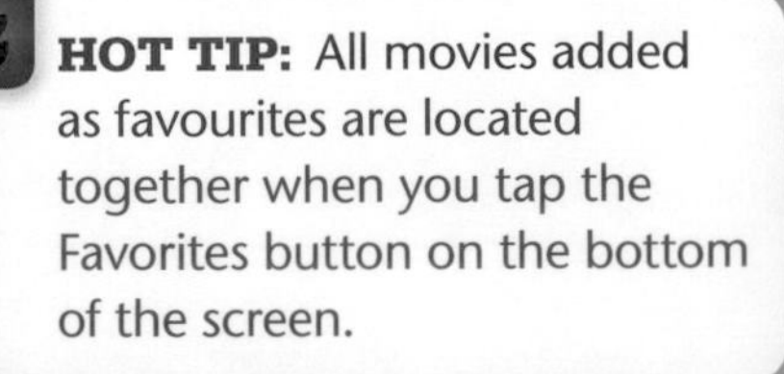

HOT TIP: All movies added as favourites are located together when you tap the Favorites button on the bottom of the screen.

Share a movie

When you wish to show someone a movie you enjoyed, you can email the link to the movie. You don't actually send the movie itself (which is a good thing because the file can be quite large). Instead, a link back to the YouTube website will be carried in the email.

1. Tap the Share button.
2. An email message appears with a link to the movie inserted into the body of the email.

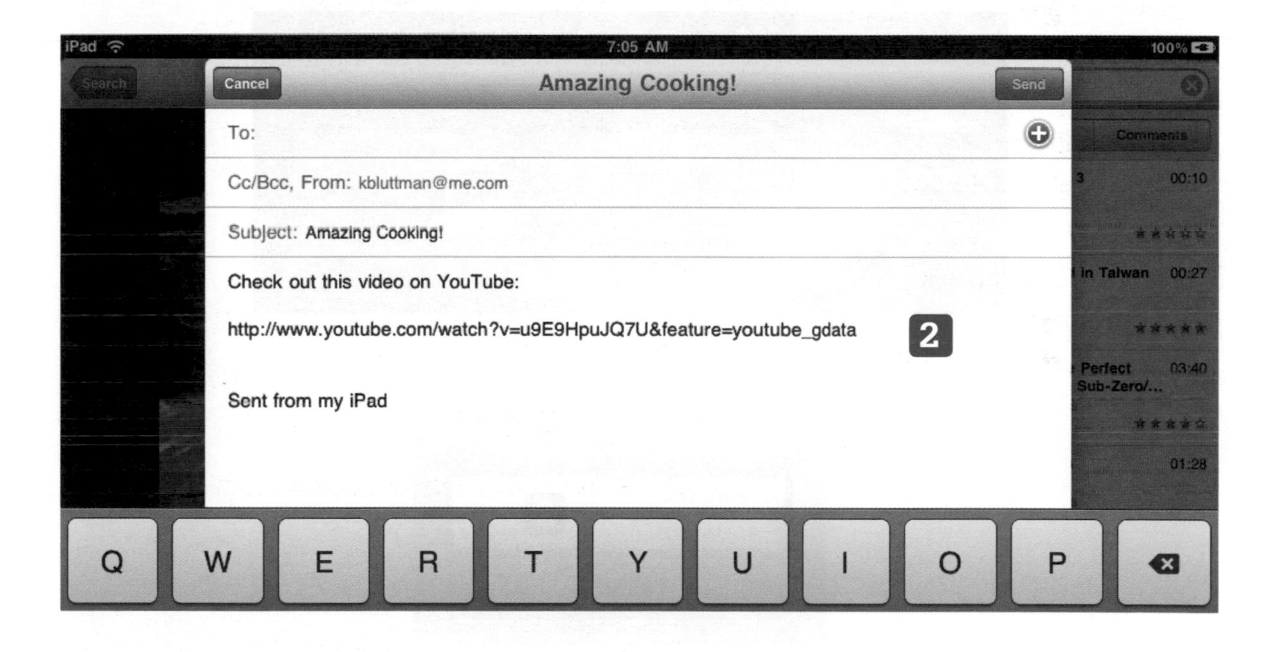

Rate a movie

If you really liked a movie (or thought it was not that good), you can rate it accordingly. You may have noticed that nearly all movies have ratings. These ratings come from viewers like you and me.

1. Tap the Rate button. A panel of five stars appears. Swipe your finger across to the number of stars you wish to rate the movie (five stars is the best rating).
2. If you are not already logged in you will be prompted to do so.

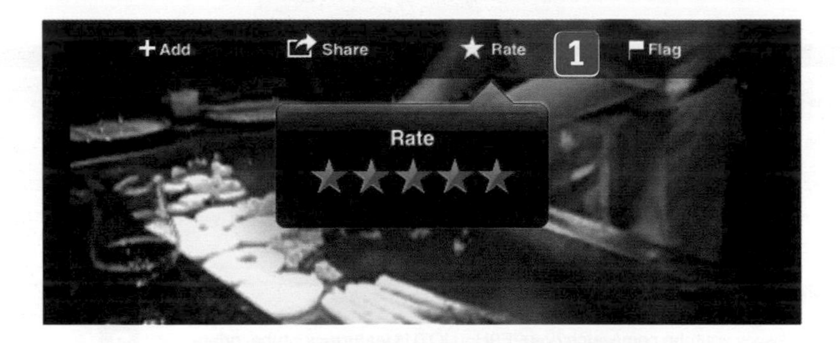

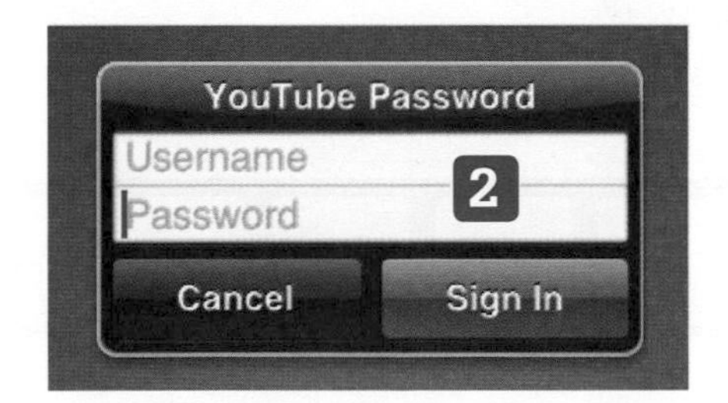

DID YOU KNOW?

It is possible to flag a movie as inappropriate. This is not a common action, as there are many classes of viewers, so what is appalling to one person is appealing to another. Most people simply rate the movie, and possibly leave a comment, as shown next.

Leave a comment

Besides rating or flagging a movie, you can leave a detailed comment. On the right are three tabs – Related, More From and Comments.

1. Tap the Comments tab. Tap into the entry box. The virtual keyboard appears and you can type in your comment.
2. Tap the Send key on the keyboard.
3. Your comment appears instantly, as mine just did here.

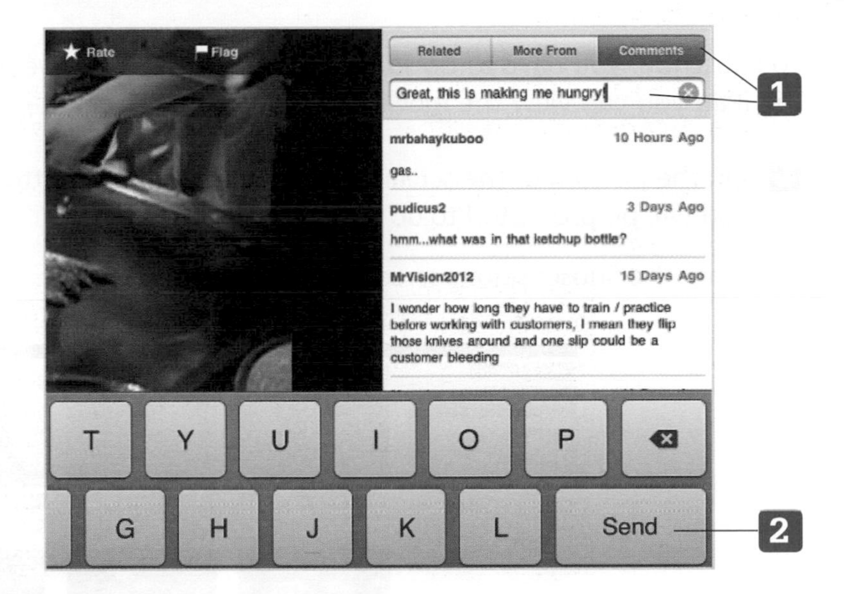

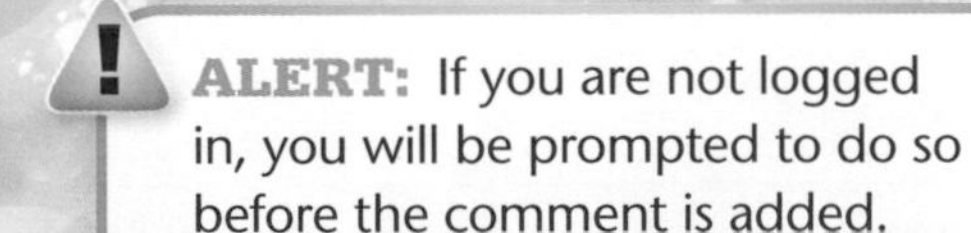

ALERT: If you are not logged in, you will be prompted to do so before the comment is added.

Subscribe to a YouTube user

Many people and organisations regularly post movies on YouTube. You can subscribe to them, which keeps you alerted to new activity and makes it easy to find their existing movies.

To subscribe, you have to do so directly on the YouTube website, when logged in. On the iPad you can view the movies from your subscriptions.

1. On the bottom of the screen, tap the Subscriptions button. If you are not logged in, you will be prompted to do so.
2. From the Subscriptions screen, tap a movie to watch it.

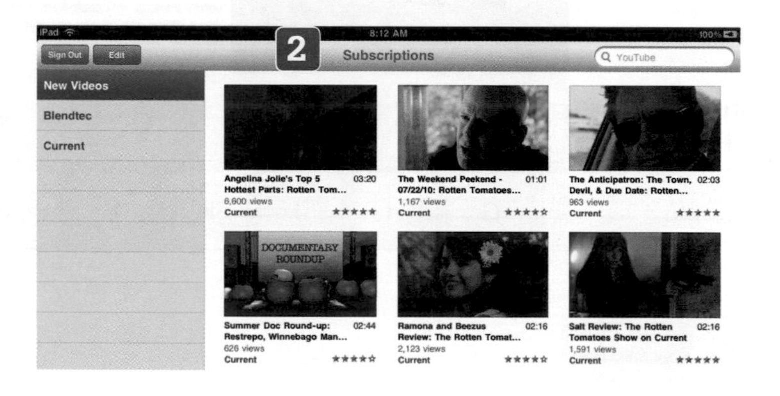

Configure video settings

In Settings are a few selections you can make that affect how you watch videos. There is not much to select, but it is still useful for your needs.

1. Tap Settings, then tap Video.
2. Keep or change the settings.

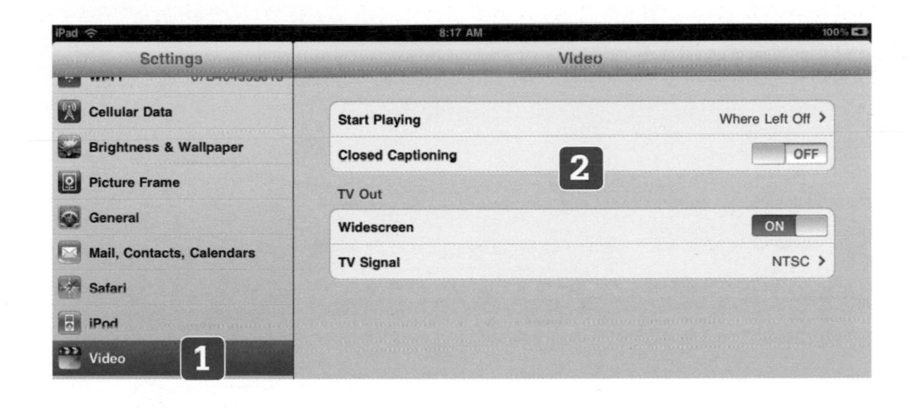

8 Sound advice – using the iPod app

Introduction

The iPod is an Apple product that has been a long-time market success. Sensibly, then, it comes as a core part of the iPad. The iPod is an audio player, but a full-feature one. You can listen to songs, podcasts and audio books. You can create your own playlists and access music videos.

Browse your music library

First things first. If you have not purchased or downloaded any music, podcasts or audiobooks, visit the iTunes store to find some audio. See Chapter 3 for more information on finding audio in the iTunes store.

Assuming you have some music or audio in the iPad, here is what you do.

1. On the Home screen, tap the iPod icon. It is located along the bottom of the screen.
2. The iPod opens. There are several ways of viewing the content. The initial view you have may be different than what is shown here, which happens to be Albums.
3. Note that on the left are different ways to view the library. Music shows all music. Podcasts shows all podcasts and so on. There are even items to select such as Recently Played. Tap on any of the listings to see what media appears.
4. Along the bottom are categories – Songs, Artists, Albums, Genres and Composers.
5. By selecting different views and different categories, you can see the available audio in an organised way. For example, here is a picture of the Top Rated songs (which qualifies as a playlist).

HOT TIP: A view such as Music shows all available music, but a view such as Classical Music filters to show just music that matches the selection. This is the basis of a playlist – an assortment of music put together based on a subjective theme.

Listen to a song

From any organised presentation of the available audio, just tap a song to play it.

1. Find a song to play using the Library selections on the left and/or the categories on the bottom. Tap the song title to start the music.
2. The screen will change to show what is currently playing. On the lower left is 'Now Playing'.
3. At the top left is a volume slider control. In the centre top are the standard play/pause, forward and back buttons and underneath is a timeline showing the point in the song which is currently playing.

4. From the albums category, you tap the album to select it. Here an album has been tapped. A box opens showing the songs on the album.
5. Tap any song to start the music. You can tap any song in the album list and the play will start with that song. When playing an album, the music will continue to the end of the album – all the songs will be played.

DID YOU KNOW?
You can slide your finger along the timeline to change the play to any point in the song.

HOT TIP: To stop the music, tap the Pause button at the top centre (looks like two vertical lines on a button).

Control song playback

Being able to fast forward, pause, start over, repeat a song and other options makes the iPad's iPod a powerful media player. The controls for these various actions can appear in a different place depending on the view. What does this mean?

1. Consider this first image of the iPod while it is playing. In the lower left is a thumbnail picture of the album. Tapping it expands the picture to full screen.
2. Tapping the full-screen picture makes the playback controls and other screen elements appear. In this view, there are numerous settings and controls.
3. The standard playback controls are in the upper right of the expanded view. The back and forward buttons move the play to the beginning or the end of the song. If it is an album that is in play, you can tap these controls to navigate back and forth between songs on the album.

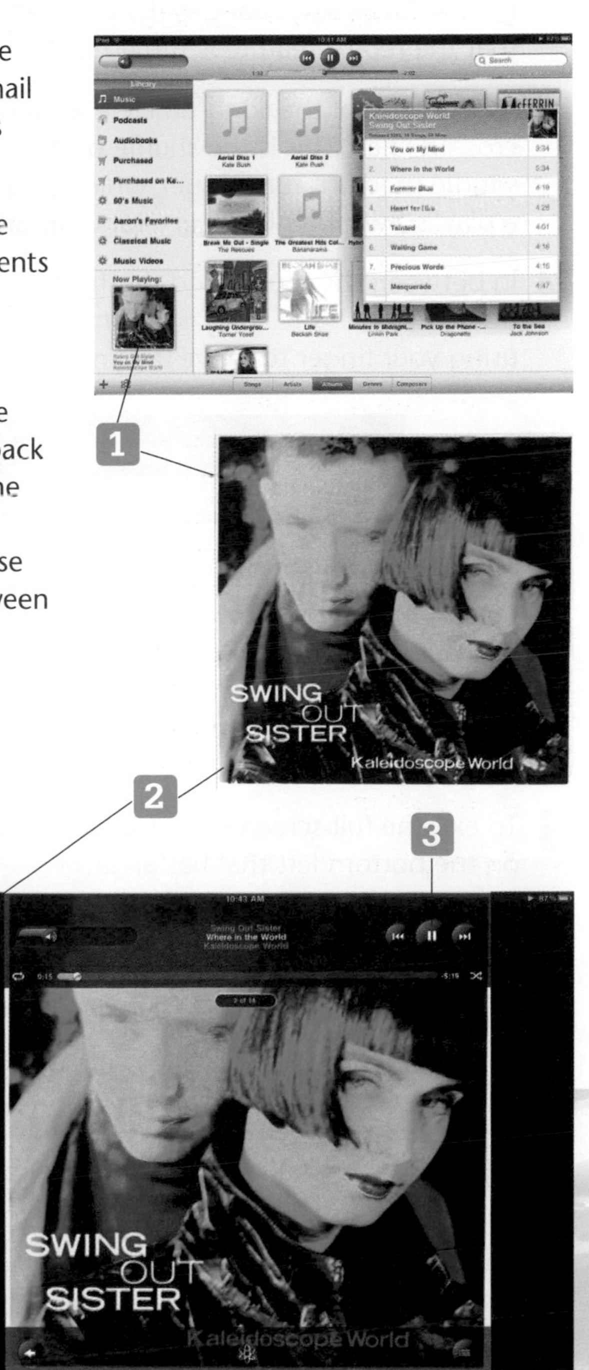

4 Tapping the pause button (looks like two vertical lines) pauses the music. As soon as it is tapped it changes to an arrow, which when tapped resumes playing the music.

5 A small button with two rounded arrows pointing at each other is the control for repeating play. Tapping it puts the iPod in repeat mode and changes the button's colour to blue to indicate that the repeat feature is turned on.

6 To the right of the song timeline is a small button that appears as crossed lines. This is the shuffle button. Tapping it puts the play into shuffle mode (it turns blue), which means the songs on an album (or a playlist) will be played in a random order. Tap it again to turn off shuffle.

7 In between the repeat and shuffle buttons is the song's play timeline. It shows the point at which the song is playing. You can skip to a different part of the song by using your finger to move the knob in the slider.

8 At the bottom right is a button that you tap to change the view to a list of the songs. When the view changes, the button is replaced with a thumbnail of the album cover. If you tap the album cover, the view changes back.

9 To exit the full-screen view, tap the button on the bottom left that has an arrow pointing left.

HOT TIP: If a song which is not from an album is playing, repeat will keep playing that song. When an album is playing, tapping the repeat once sets the iPod to repeat the album, not just the current song. To repeat the current song, tap the repeat button again and a small number 1 will appear. This indicates the current song will repeat.

Create a playlist

A playlist is a customised set of songs. Playlists are most commonly used to assemble your favourite songs for playback.

1. At the bottom left of the screen is a plus sign (+) button. Tap the plus sign. The virtual keyboard appears.

2. You will be prompted for a name for the new playlist. Enter a name and tap Save.
3. A list of all songs appears. Tap songs to add them to the playlist. Tap as many as you like, then tap the small Done button on the right.
4. The playlist now appears in the Library list on the left. The contents of the playlist are shown on the right.

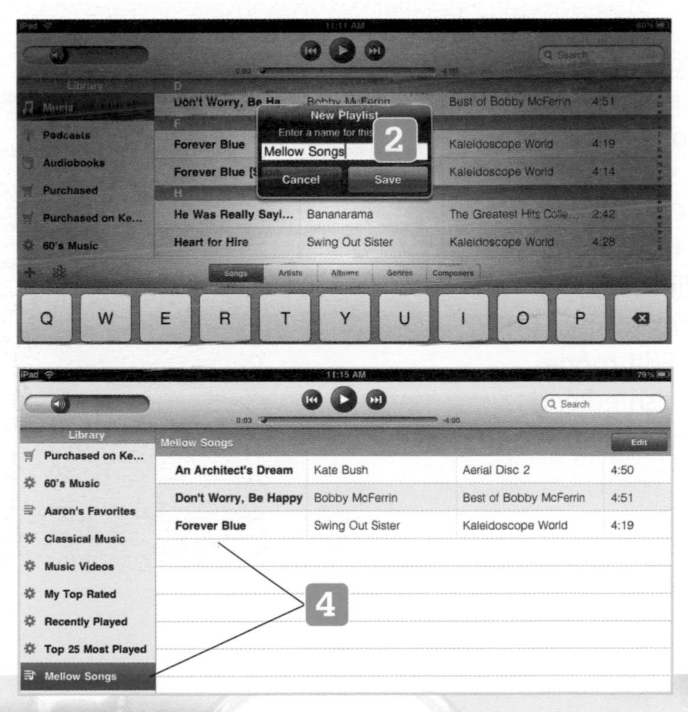

DID YOU KNOW?

A song can appear in more than one playlist.

Edit a playlist

Often we tire of one song and want to listen to another. Playlists provide a great way to hear our favourite songs, but sooner or later a playlist becomes stale. You can create a new playlist, of course, but perhaps even better is to just change an existing playlist.

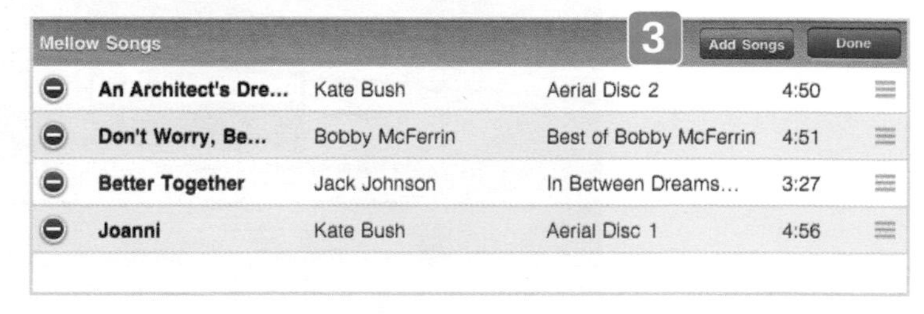

1. With a playlist in view, tap the Edit button on the right.
2. The playlist is ready for editing. To delete a song, tap the red circle to the left of the song, then tap the Delete button that appears to the right of the song.
3. Tap the Add Songs button. The view changes to the full list of available songs. Tap on songs you wish to add to the playlist. Tap the Done button when you've finished. The view returns to the playlist, still in Edit mode. Tap Done to finish editing the playlist. The playlist is updated.

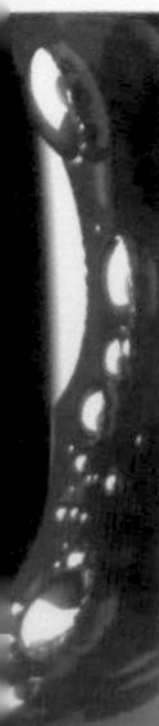

ALERT: The category choice at the bottom of the screen must be Songs in order for the Editing features to be available.

Search your music library

When you can't remember a full title or artist, or an album name, use the Search feature.

1. Tap into the search box. The virtual keyboard appears.
2. Type in a search term. A list of matching songs is displayed. Any podcasts or audiobooks that meet the search criteria are also displayed.

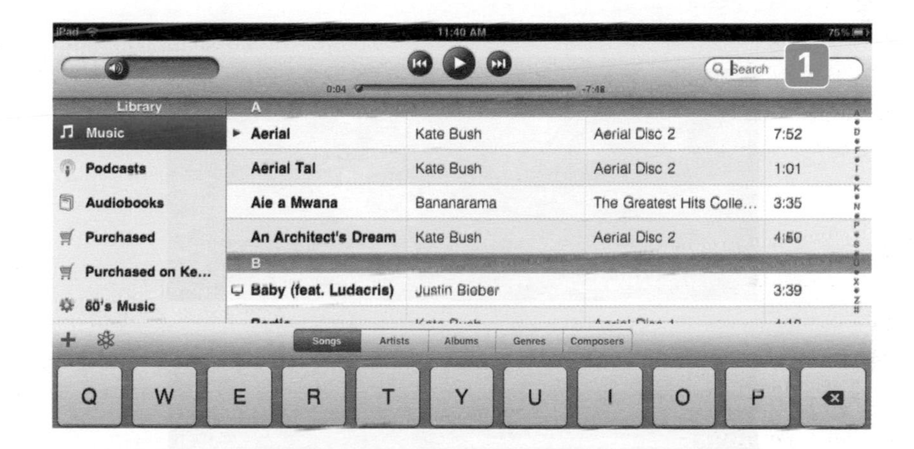

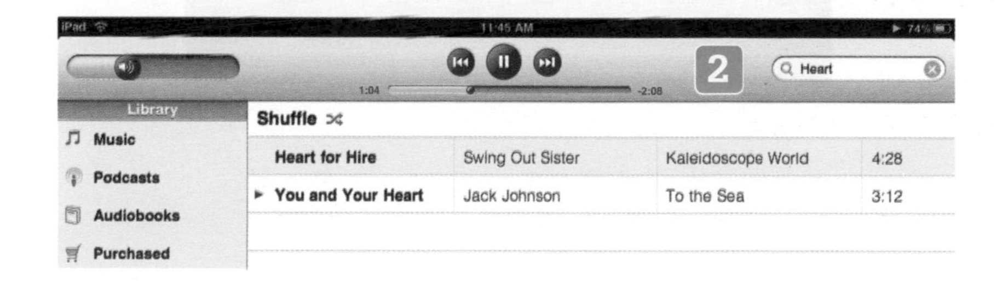

HOT TIP: You can tap on a song in the search results. The song will start to play, but the virtual keyboard continues to cover part of the iPod. Tap the lower right key on the keyboard to close it. You now have the search results visible with the rest of the iPod – for example, some of the Library column that was covered by the keyboard is accessible.

Rate a song

As you obtain new songs and albums, perhaps you may find it useful to rate the songs so that you can seek your own best rated ones to listen to.

1. Start playing a song or an album. Manipulate the view to show the song list. See the 'Control song playback' task earlier in this chapter. Note that under the song timeline are five dots.
2. Swipe your finger along the dots and they change into stars. Five stars is the top rating.

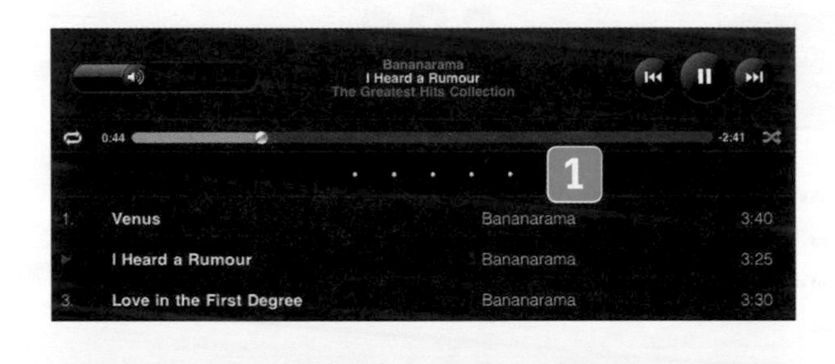

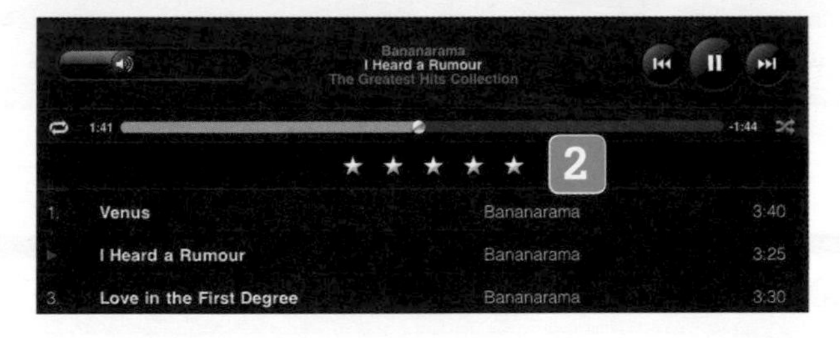

HOT TIP: Songs rated with four or five stars appear in the My Top Rated playlist in the Library.

Listen to music while using another application

Do you like to listen to music while you work or play? You're in luck! It's possible to start music playing in the iPod and then use some other feature of the iPad. The music will continue to play.

1. Start up the iPod app and play some music of your choice.
2. Press the Home button. The music will continue to play. Use the iPad for some other activity.
3. To stop the music, enter the iPod app again and stop the music by pressing the pause button.

ALERT: If you use some other feature that also involves audio, such as watching a movie, the music will stop (which is actually a helpful feature).

Configure iPod settings

There are a few iPod settings you can set.

1. Enter Settings. Tap iPod on the left.
2. Setting Sound Check to On instructs the iPod to play all songs on an album or playlist at the same volume. Subjectively, this is best left off.
3. Tap EQ. A comprehensive list of EQ selections appears.

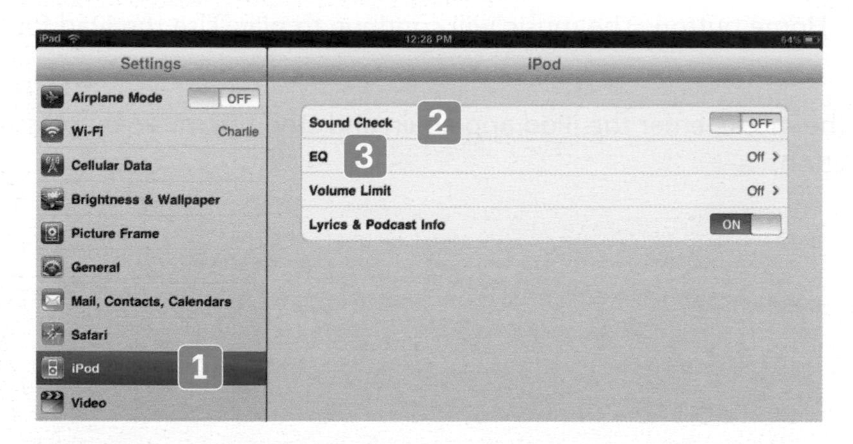

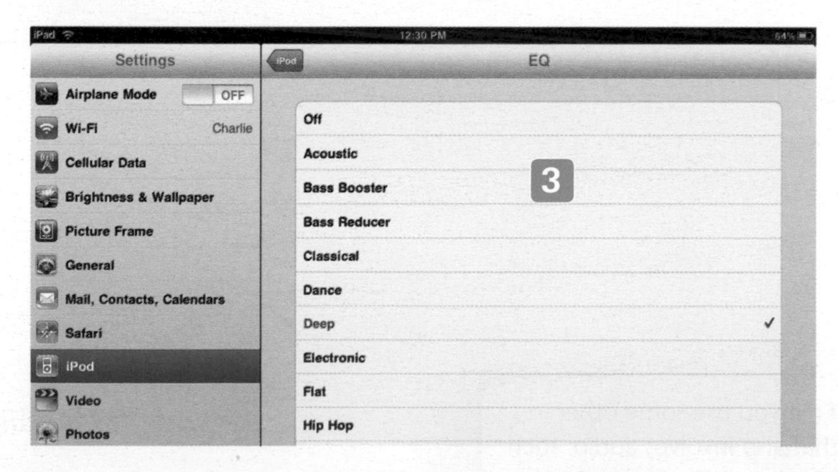

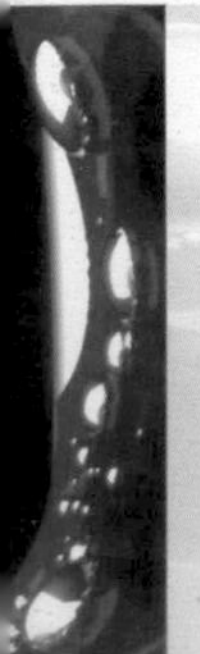

WHAT DOES THIS MEAN?

EQ: Abbreviation for equaliser. An equaliser is a musical device that shapes the tonal ranges for music playback. Each available setting alters the tonal qualities.

HOT TIP: A great way to find an EQ setting you like is to start music playing in the iPod app, then go to Settings and into the EQ selections. As you tap different EQ settings you can hear how they change the sound of the music.

9 Reading on the go – iBooks for ebooks

Introduction

Electronic book readers have been around for years but with a lukewarm reception – until recently. The success of the Amazon Kindle and other new entries into the market has brought reading on a tablet-type device to new levels of popularity.

Not to miss out on the excitement, the iPad has a great app named iBooks. iBooks is not a core app, it needs to be downloaded; however, it is free and is full featured. Reading books takes a jump forward with iBooks.

Install the iBooks app

The first action you need to take is to get iBooks. It is in the App Store. So let's start there.

1. Tap the App Store icon.
2. Use the search feature in the upper right to search for iBooks. A number of apps are returned from the search. The app of interest here is simply named iBooks.
3. Download the iBooks app. Chapter 3 explains in detail how to do this.

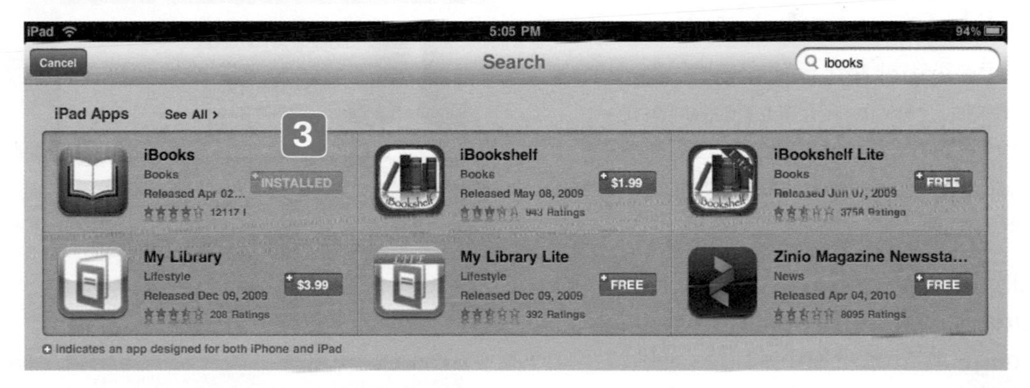

4. When installed, the iBooks icon is now on the Home screen.

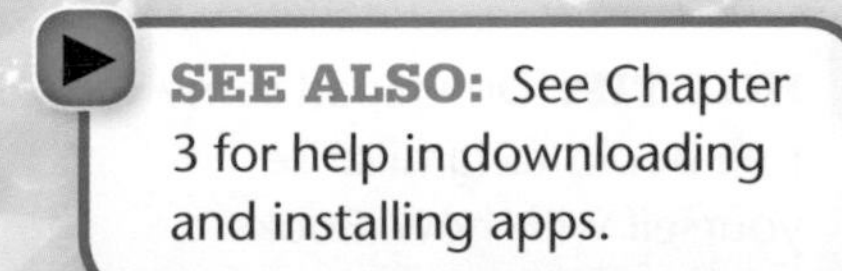

SEE ALSO: See Chapter 3 for help in downloading and installing apps.

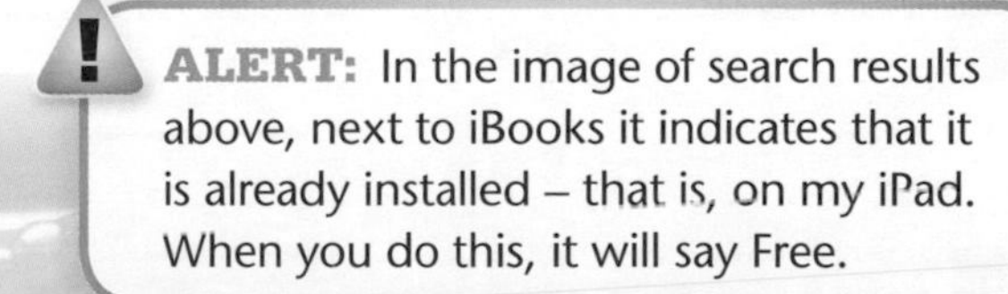

ALERT: In the image of search results above, next to iBooks it indicates that it is already installed – that is, on my iPad. When you do this, it will say Free.

Browse the iBookstore

When the iBooks app is started up, it displays your library of downloaded books, if you have any. There may not be any when you use the app for the first time, so the initial activity is to download one or more books.

1. Tap the iBooks icon.
2. In the upper right is a small button captioned Store. Tap the Store button.

3. The iBookstore opens. It is similar to the iTunes store, but features just books.

4. In the upper left is a small Categories button. Tap it. A list of categories opens. You can tap on a category if you choose to browse within a certain category.

5. Along the bottom are a few buttons. One is Featured, which is what the image in Step 3 shows (featured books). Another interesting button is Top Charts. Tap this button. On the left is the list of top-selling books that have been purchased. On the right is a list of the most popular free books.

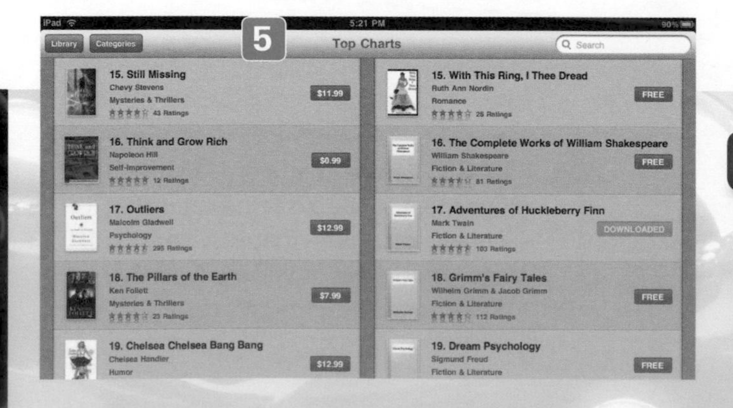

HOT TIP: Download some free books to familiarise yourself with how iBooks works.

Preview a book

A great feature is that you can get a preview of a book before downloading the entire book or purchasing it. Instead, the smaller preview is downloaded into your library.

1. From anywhere in the iBooks store, tap on a book. A new screen opens with details, rating and comments.
2. Note that along the right side of the book information are links to the author page, an alert for your convenience, tell a friend and often the ability to get a sample. Tapping Get Sample will place a preview of the book in your library.

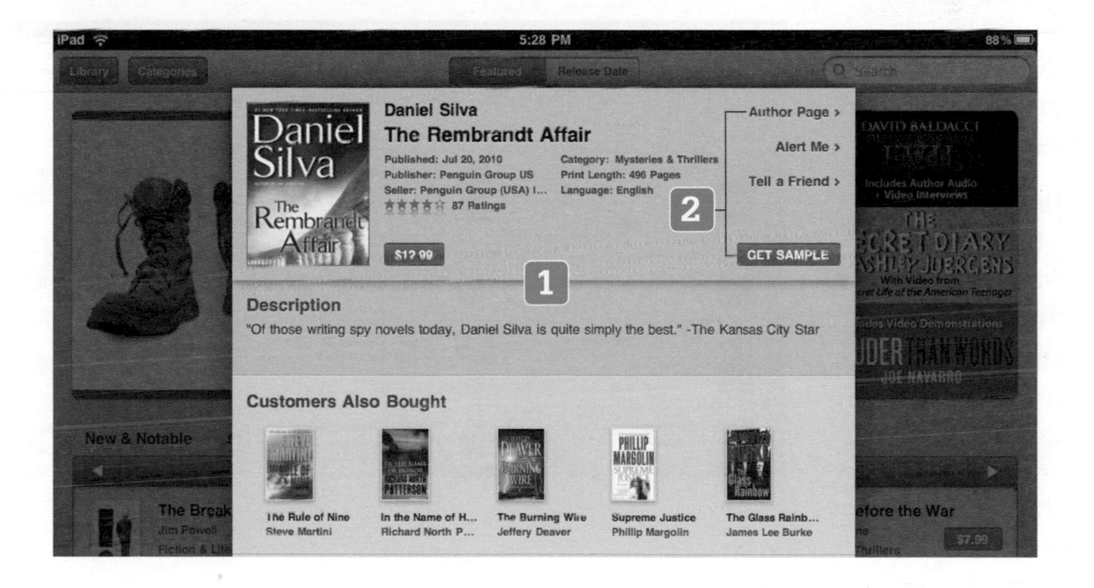

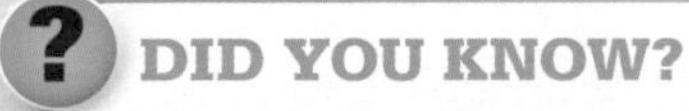

DID YOU KNOW?

The window that opens with information about the book can be scrolled downwards to find customer reviews.

Search for a book

Mysteries might be your thing, or history or romance. These are categories (perhaps referred to as genres). You don't need to search for categories as there is a list of them already in place (see earlier in this chapter). The search feature is more useful for finding a particular author or a subject that is not presented as a category.

1. On the right side of the screen, tap into the Search box. The virtual keyboard appears.
2. Enter a search term. Here a search is done for the author Robert Ludlum.
3. Tapping on a book title will present the detailed information.

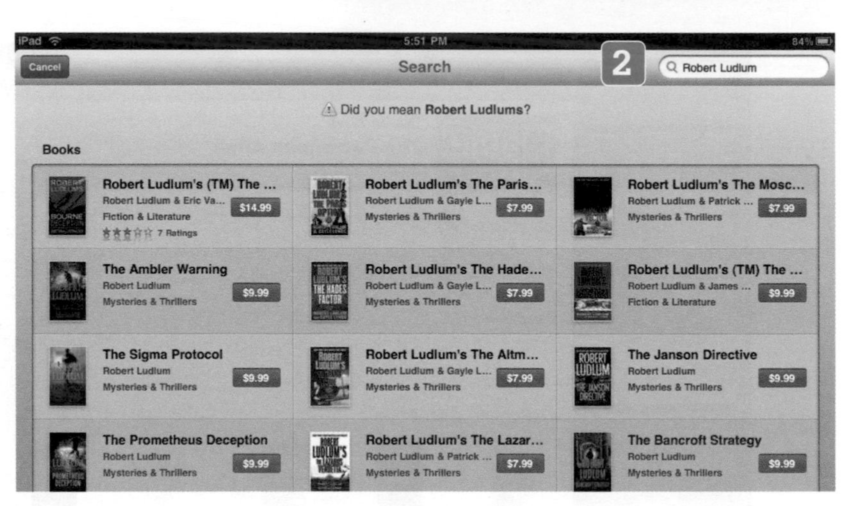

HOT TIP: Another way to find free books for download is to use the search feature and enter Free as the search term.

Download a free book

Many books are free primarily because the copyright has expired. Many free titles are just as rewarding a read as anything new. Here is how to get one of these great freebies.

1. In the iBookstore, tap the Top Charts button at the bottom of the screen. On the right is the list of the most popular free downloads.
2. When you see a book you would like to download, tap the button that says Free. The button changes to say Get Book. Here, *The Adventures of Sherlock Holmes* is about to be downloaded.
3. Tap the Get Book button. You will next be prompted for your iTunes password. Enter your password and tap OK.
4. The download is placed in your library. The screen will have changed to display your library and the store is no longer shown. If you want to return to the store, just tap the small Store button in the upper left corner.

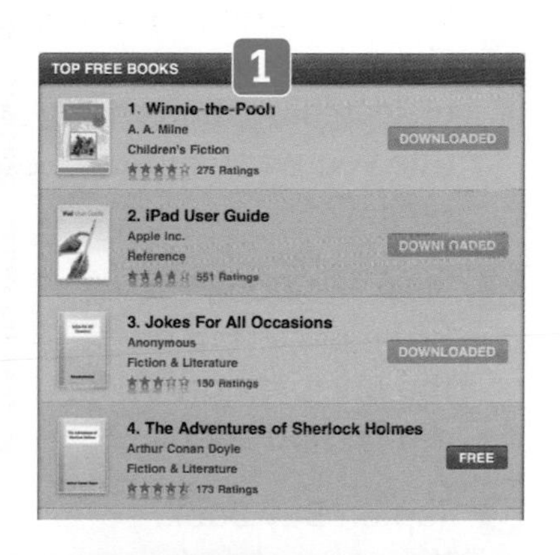

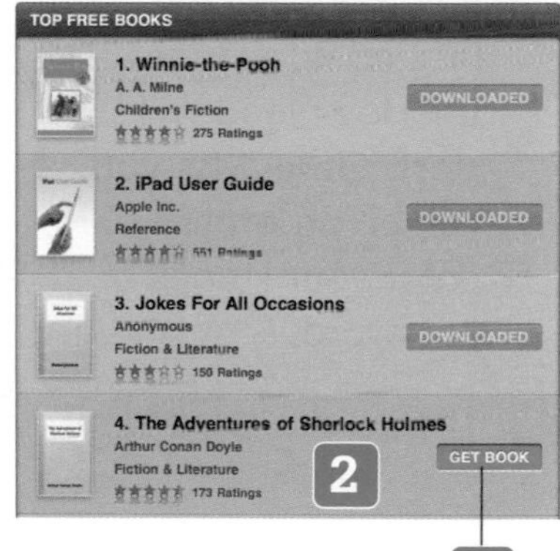

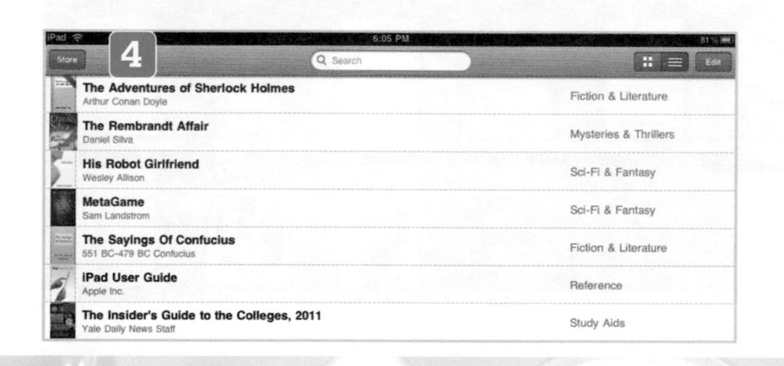

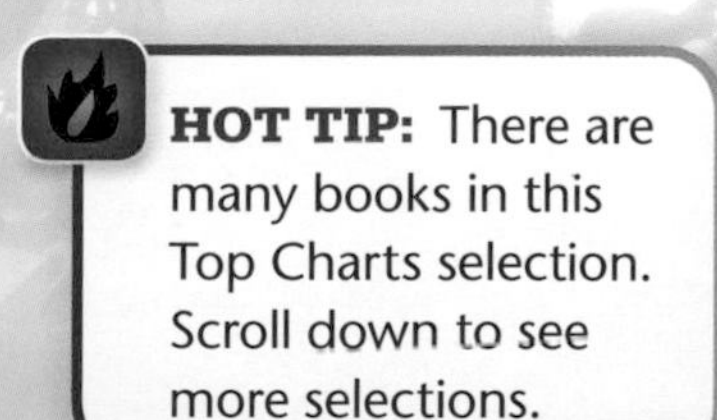

HOT TIP: There are many books in this Top Charts selection. Scroll down to see more selections.

SEE ALSO: See Chapter 3 for help on setting up an iTunes account.

Purchase a book

Even with all the free books to choose from, there are many desirable books that you have to pay for. For example, one of your favourite authors releases a new book. Time for a purchase.

1. Either by browsing or searching, find the title you want and tap on it.
2. Near the book's cover is the price. Tap on the price. It now displays Buy Book.
3. Tap on Buy Book. If you are already logged into iTunes the download will start. Otherwise you will be prompted to enter your iTunes password.
4. The book is placed in your library.

HOT TIP: You may have a gift card to redeem. The Redeem button is generally found at the bottom of any page in the store. You will have to scroll down to see it. There are some other helpful items on the bottom of a store page, including links to interesting categories such as Books into Movies or Popular Pre-Orders.

View your library

If you are in the iBookstore, tap the small Library button in the upper left of the screen. Or you may already be in the library. The library has two views – one is presented as a list, the other looks like a bookcase. To toggle the view, use the two buttons at the upper right.

Note that in the list-type display, there are buttons along the bottom that change the order of how the titles are displayed, explained next.

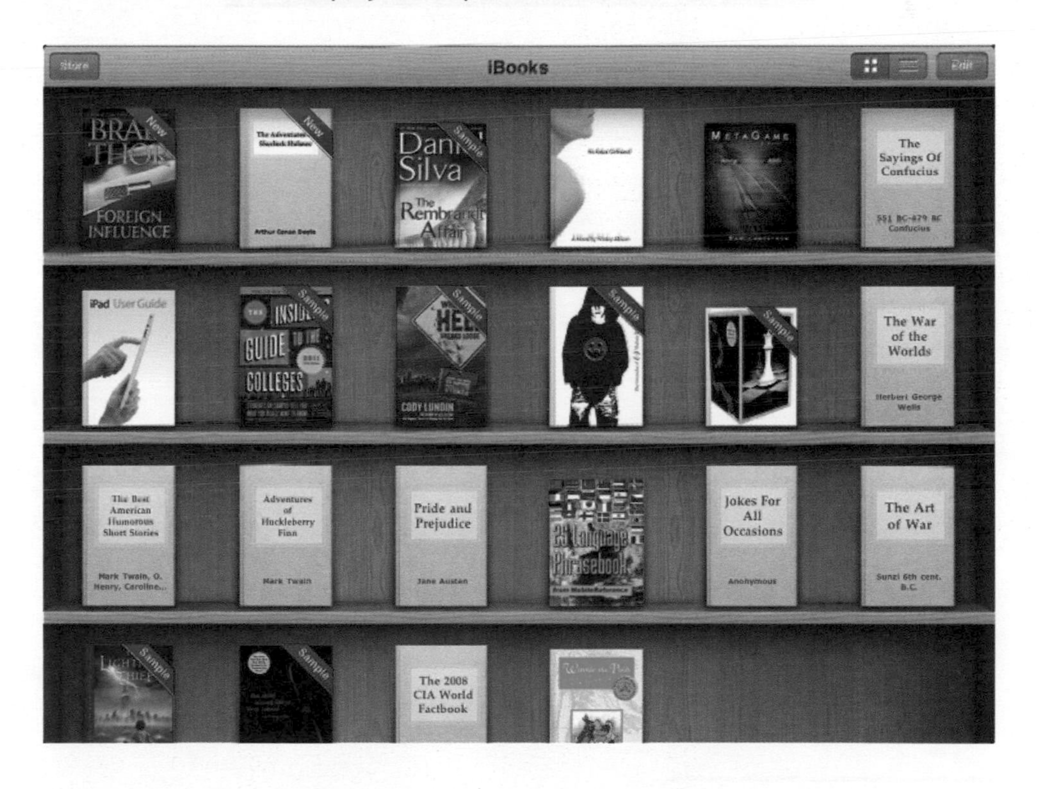

Sort the Library

There are four ways to sort the list of books in the Library:

- Bookshelf – the sort is latest to oldest download.
- Titles – the book titles are in alphabetical order.
- Authors – the books are sorted alphabetically by author.
- Categories – the listings are put into categories.

DID YOU KNOW?

When the Library view is of the bookshelf, the books are sorted by download – latest to oldest.

Open and read a book

Here is the main point of all the downloading and organising: reading! Peruse your library, settle on a title, and then …

1. Tap on the book you wish to read. The book opens – to the last place you read or to the beginning if it is being opened for the first time.

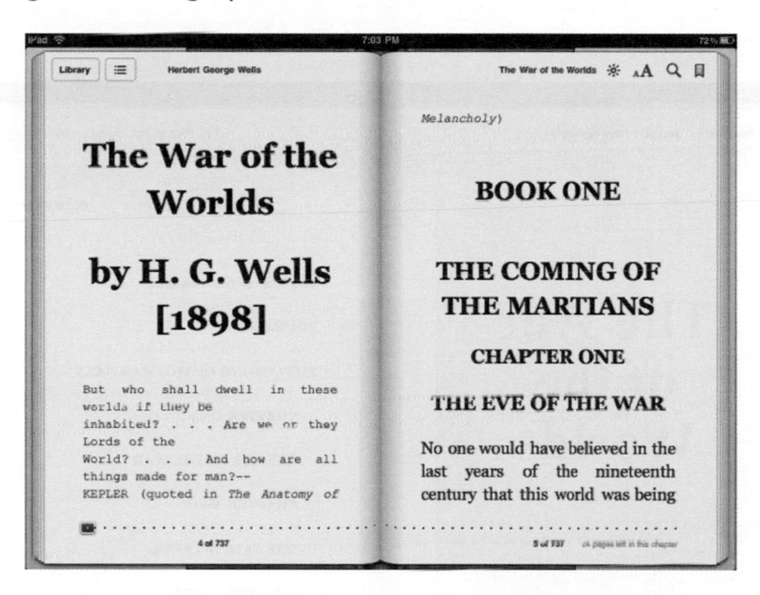

2. There are a few key things you need to know to make your way through a book.
   - Swiping with your finger moves the pages along.
   - There is a fast page finder at the bottom. Swipe your finger along it to quickly get to a page or part of the book.

- At the top left is the Library button. Tapping it brings the screen back to the Library.
- Also in the left corner is a button that looks like three dots next to three lines. Tapping it brings you back to the table of contents or the beginning of the book.

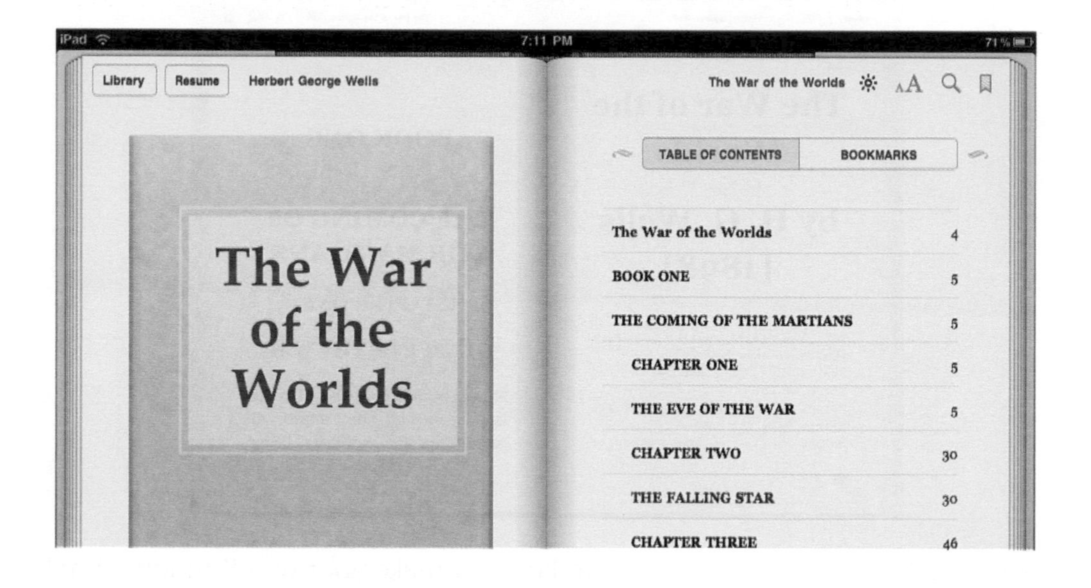

ALERT: The button that returns the book to the table of contents is present only when not on the table of contents. When at the table of contents, a Resume button appears which, if tapped, returns you to the page you last viewed.

Set the brightness

A bright book in a dark room or a toned-down book in sunlight? We all have our preferences for how bright the screen should be. It's easy to change the brightness. In the upper right of the screen are four buttons, one of which controls the brightness.

1. Tap on the first button on the upper right. It looks like a representation of the sun.
2. A slider control appears. Use your finger to drag the knob in the slider to adjust the brightness.

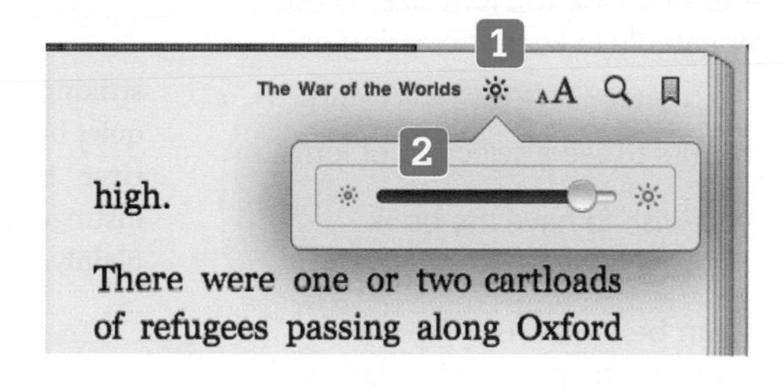

Set the font size and type

If you misplace your reading glasses, not to worry. You can set the font size of the book. In fact, you can set it quite large (or small).

1. Tap the second button in the upper right corner. It looks like the letter A.
2. A box appears in which font selections are made. On the top of the box are two As. The one on the right is larger.
3. Tap the larger letter A to increase the font size or tap the smaller A to decrease the font size. These can be tapped repeatedly to keep increasing or decreasing.
4. Tap on the word Fonts to see a selection of fonts.
5. Tap on the font you wish to have the book presented in.
6. The Sepia option can be turned on. Tap the On/Off button. It makes the pages a bit darker, sort of an old-fashioned look.

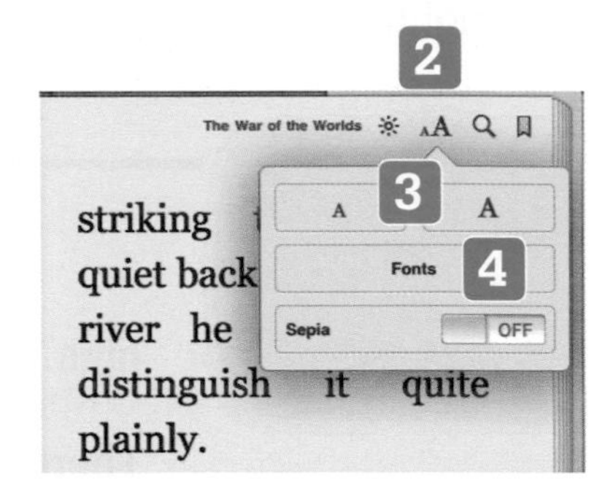

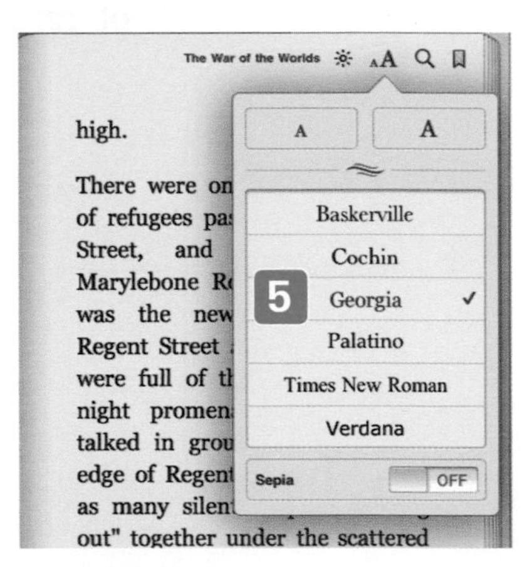

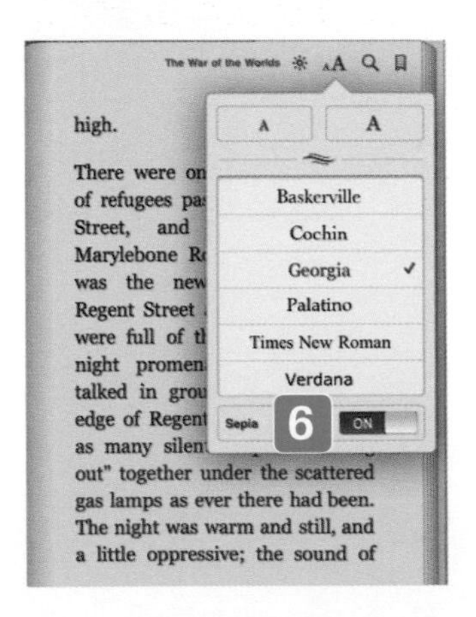

ALERT: When one of the As is tapped, it may take a few moments for the font size to change. The lag in time is dependent on the length of the book.

DID YOU KNOW?
Turning Sepia on is not quite the same as lowering the brightness. Altering the brightness affects the page and the text. Turning Sepia on affects only the page and not the text.

Search inside a book

I bet there have been times when you have read a book and tried to recall where a certain passage was. This is often a tedious and sometimes unsuccessful endeavour. Wouldn't it be peachy if you could search in the book for the part you want to reread? Well, now it's a snap to do!

1. Tap the third button in the upper right corner. This is the search feature – the button looks like a magnifying glass. A search box opens and the virtual keyboard appears.

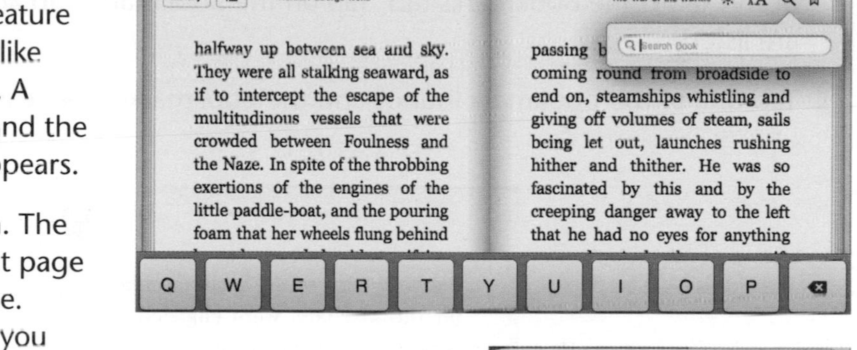

2. Enter a search term. The results tell you what page and in which phrase. Further options let you search Google and Wikipedia.

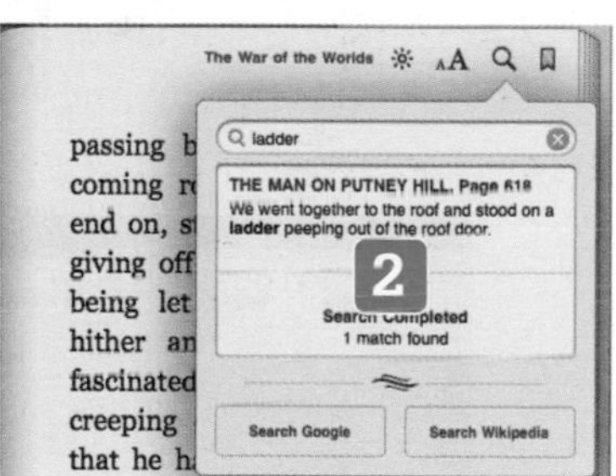

3. Tapping on a search result navigates the book to where the word or phrase was found, as in this example for the word 'ladder', which is highlighted.

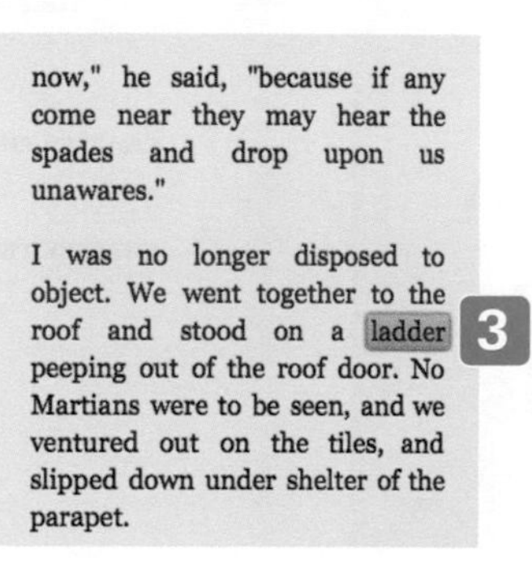
now," he said, "because if any come near they may hear the spades and drop upon us unawares."

I was no longer disposed to object. We went together to the roof and stood on a ladder peeping out of the roof door. No Martians were to be seen, and we ventured out on the tiles, and slipped down under shelter of the parapet.

Set and use a bookmark

The iBook app has a feature that lets you set a bookmark in the book. Then at some future point, you can resume reading from where the bookmark has been set.

1. Tap the fourth button in the upper right corner – it looks like a ribbon. It expands in size and changes to red. So what you end up with is a clearly visible bookmark.
2. To resume reading from a bookmark, navigate to the table of contents. To the right of this tab is the Bookmarks tab. Tap on the Bookmarks tab and all the bookmarks are listed.
3. Tap one of the bookmark listings and the bookmarked page is displayed.

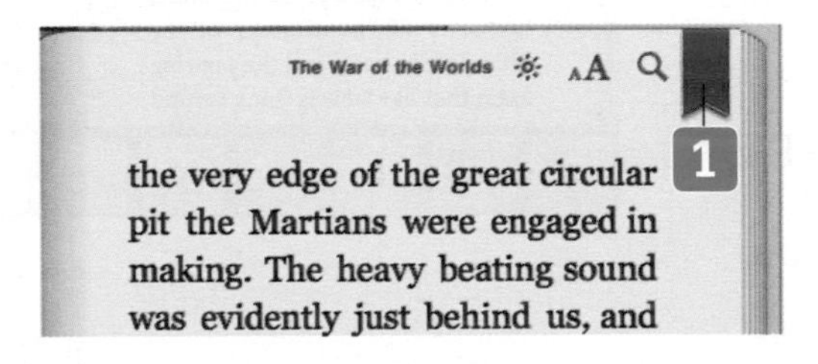

HOT TIP: You can set multiple bookmarks – each on a different page.

DID YOU KNOW?
At the beginning of the book is the Resume button. Tapping it returns you to where you left off, which does not necessarily have to be where a bookmark was set.

Use the dictionary

When you come across a word you don't know there's no need to go fumbling around looking for a dictionary. The iBooks app provides one.

1. Tap and hold your finger on a word for a moment. A list of options appears.
2. One of the options is Dictionary. Tap it and a description of the word is shown. Tap anywhere else on the screen to close the dictionary.

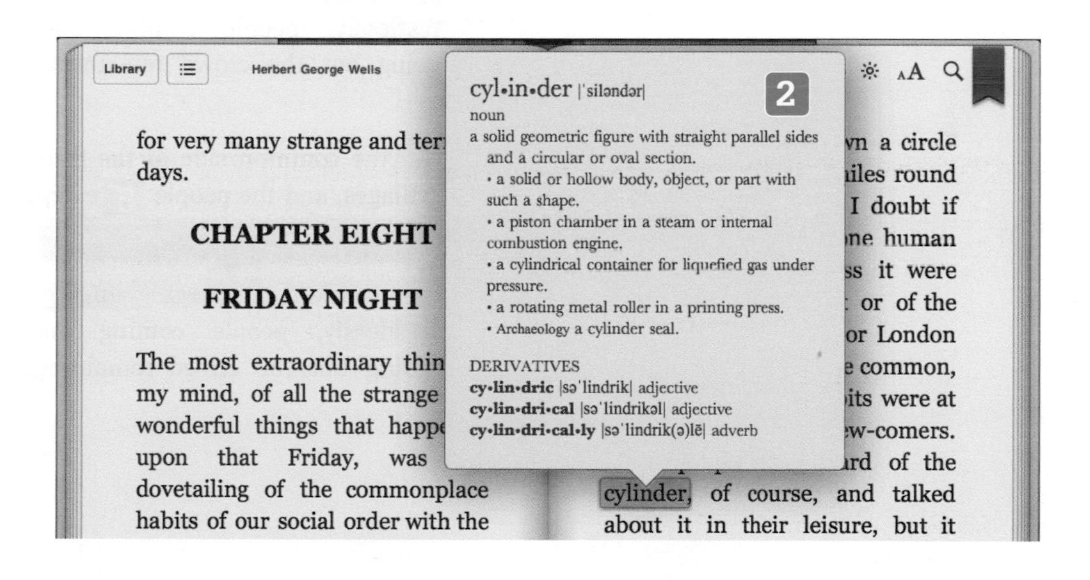

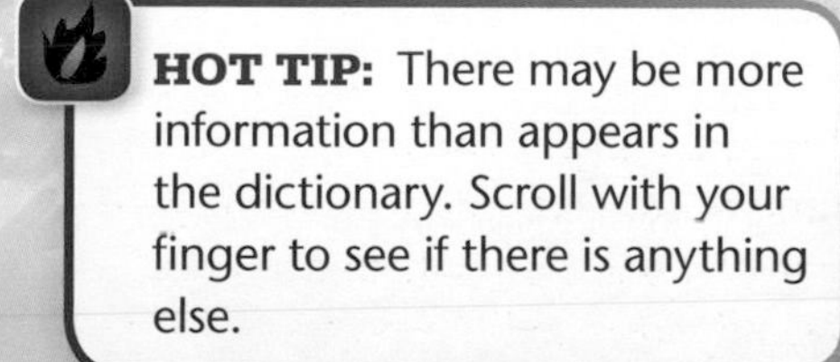

Highlight text

One of the options in iBooks is to highlight text. You can even use different colours for highlighted sections.

1. Tap and hold down your finger for a moment until the list of options appears.
2. Tap Highlight to colour the highlighted text.
3. Tap the highlighted text and new options appear. One of them is Colors.
4. Tap Colors and you are presented with a list of colours.
5. Tap on the colour you wish the text to be – assuming the current colour is not your first choice.

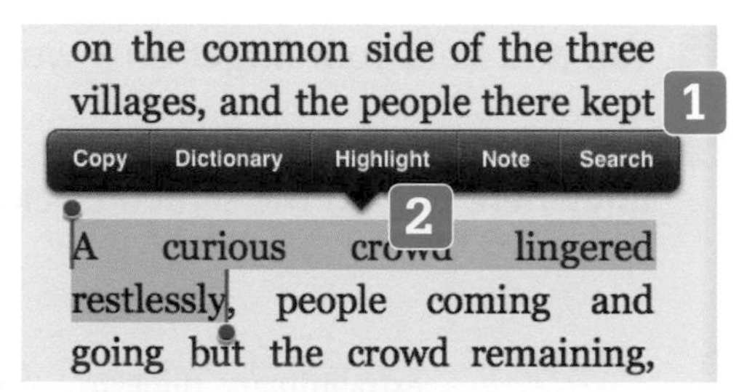

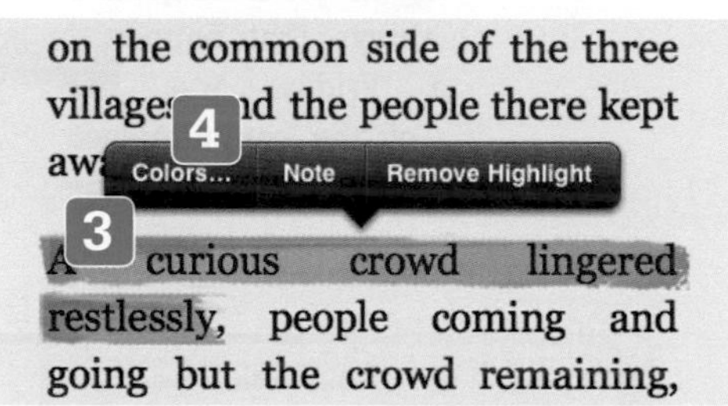

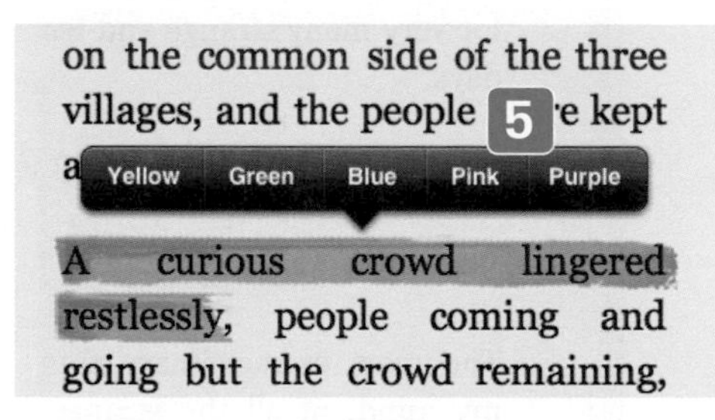

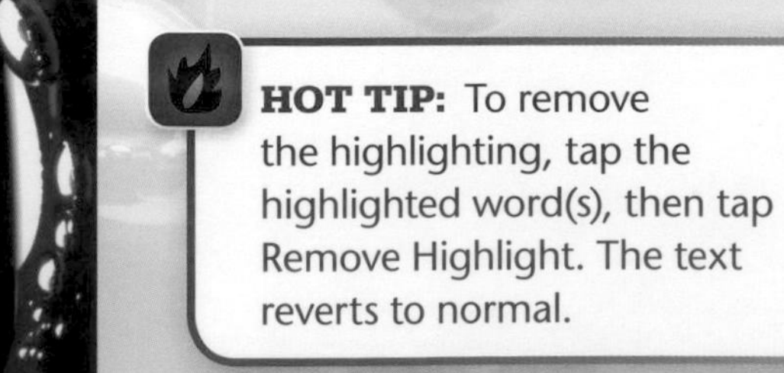

HOT TIP: To remove the highlighting, tap the highlighted word(s), then tap Remove Highlight. The text reverts to normal.

Insert a margin note

This feature is not likely to be used much, but when you need it, it will prove to be valuable. Essentially you can leave notes in the margin. It works like this:

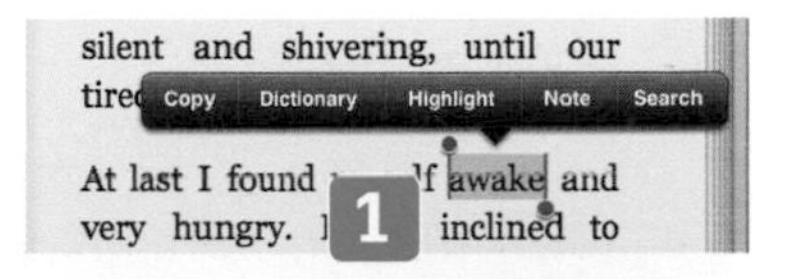

1. Tap a word and hold down your finger until the options appear.

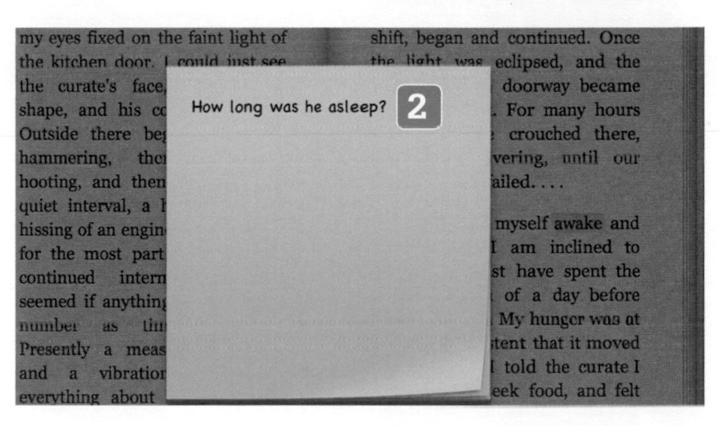

2. One of the options is Note. Tapping Note displays what appears as a pad of sticky paper. You can type a note in here and then tap on the side (not on the note) to save the note.

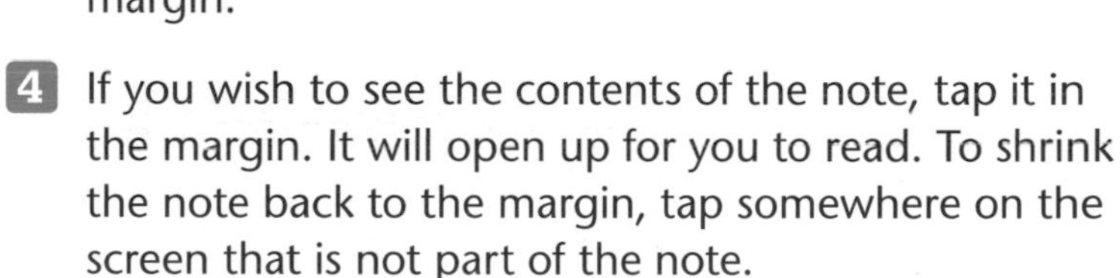

3. The note is positioned in the margin. The date on which the note was written is displayed, but not the contents of the note. This lets the note fit in the margin.

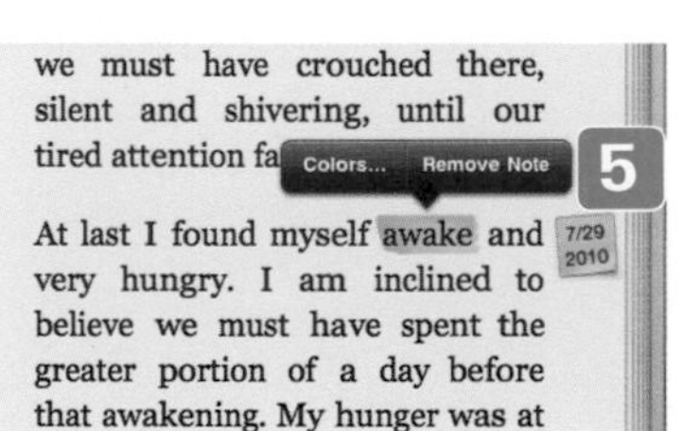

4. If you wish to see the contents of the note, tap it in the margin. It will open up for you to read. To shrink the note back to the margin, tap somewhere on the screen that is not part of the note.

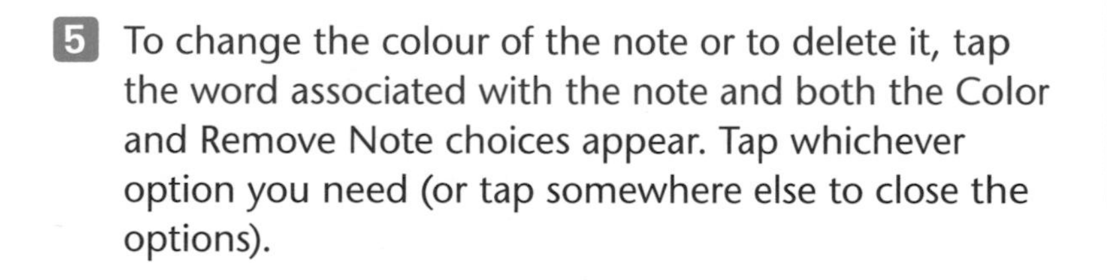

5. To change the colour of the note or to delete it, tap the word associated with the note and both the Color and Remove Note choices appear. Tap whichever option you need (or tap somewhere else to close the options).

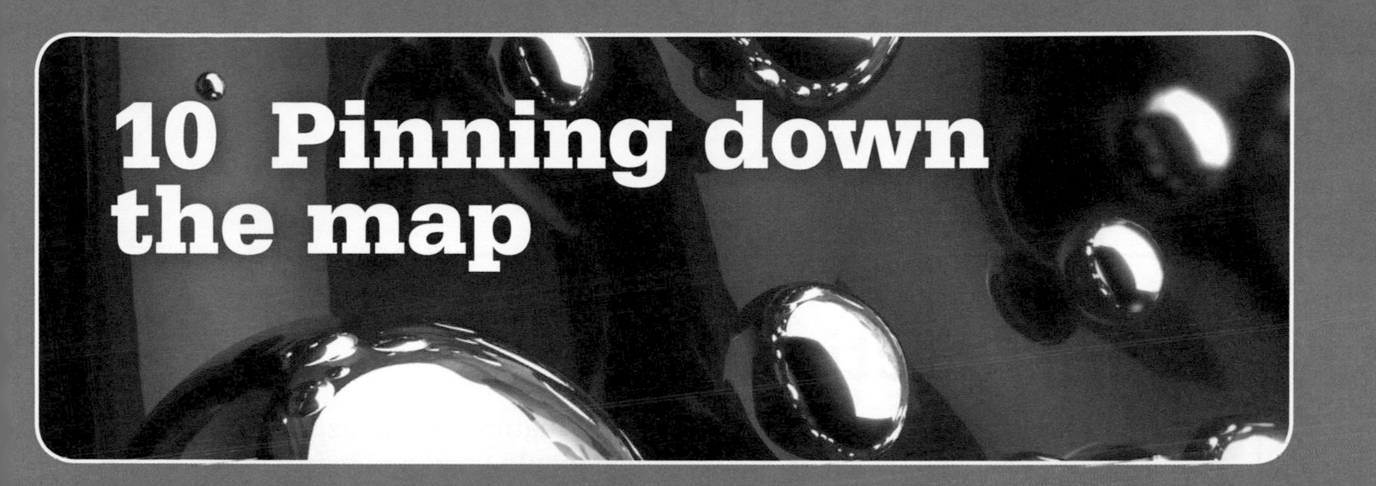

10 Pinning down the map

Introduction

Maps have become a commonly used online feature. It's amazing to think that just less than a decade ago, you would need a physical map and perhaps a pad and pen to figure out how to get from one place to another. Now all you need is internet access.

There are many map utilities available on the web – Google, Yahoo!, etc. all have them. Better yet, though, you have the iPad with its built-in Maps app. Its features rival those of the ones you find on the Internet. This chapter shows you how to access what the Maps app can do.

Start up the Maps app

The first step, of course, is to start the Maps app. The Maps app is a core part of the iPad and therefore its icon cannot be deleted, so it should be easy to find – it looks like a piece of a map.

1. Tap the Maps icon.
2. The app opens to its last viewed use.

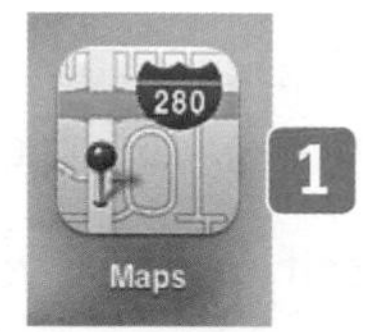

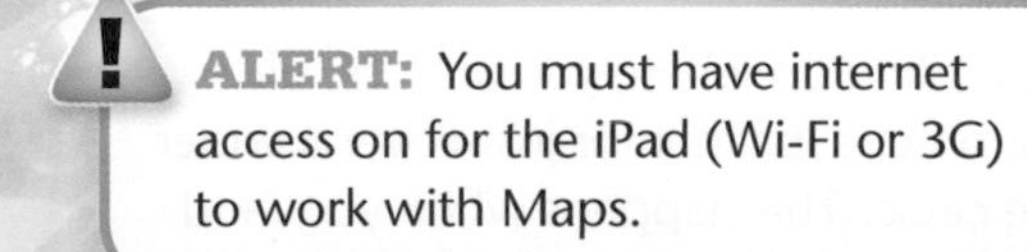

ALERT: You must have internet access on for the iPad (Wi-Fi or 3G) to work with Maps.

Find your location on the map

Thanks to the wonders of technology, the iPad can identify its physical location and display it on the map. Assuming you and the iPad are in the same vicinity, you could find your location on the map.

1. Along the top of the map are two buttons. One looks like a circle or a compass. It's called the Tracking button. Tap the Tracking button.
2. The map will scroll itself to show your location, which is indicated by a blue dot.

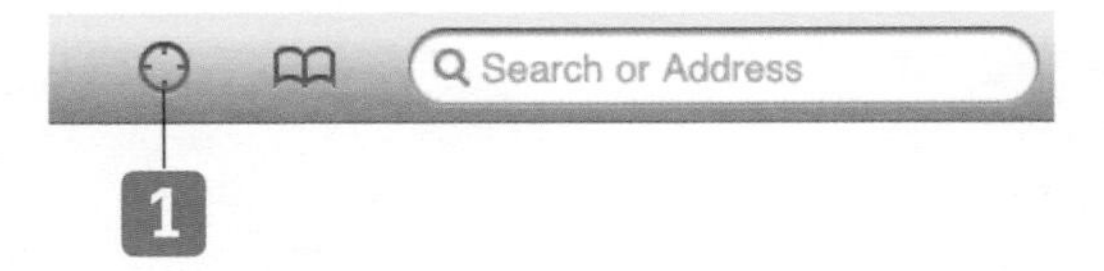

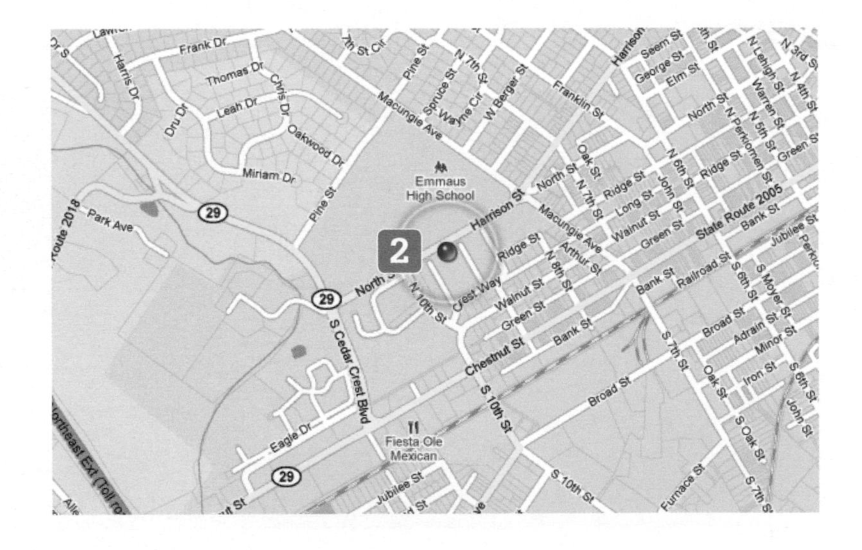

DID YOU KNOW?
Although the iPad finds its location on the map, most people think of this as finding where they are on the map.

HOT TIP: Depending on where you are, the blue dot may show a precise location or just cover a wider area with a blue circle. This happens when you (and the iPad) are not close to a mobile phone tower while using 3G as your internet connectivity. With a Wi-Fi connection, you will get a precise location on the map.

Zoom in and out

At times it helps to see a big geographical area to get an idea of distance from one place to another or to find a certain location. Other times it's necessary to zoom into the map so that you can see street names. Zooming in or out is literally just a walk with your fingers.

1. Starting with any location on the map, note the level of zoom.
2. To zoom out, put two fingers on the map and move them towards each other. The map will zoom out, seeming as though you are pulling it in from the sides. You can repeat this action as much as you need to.
3. To zoom in, put two fingers on the map and move them away from each other. The map will zoom in. You can repeat this action to achieve a precise view (such as at street level).

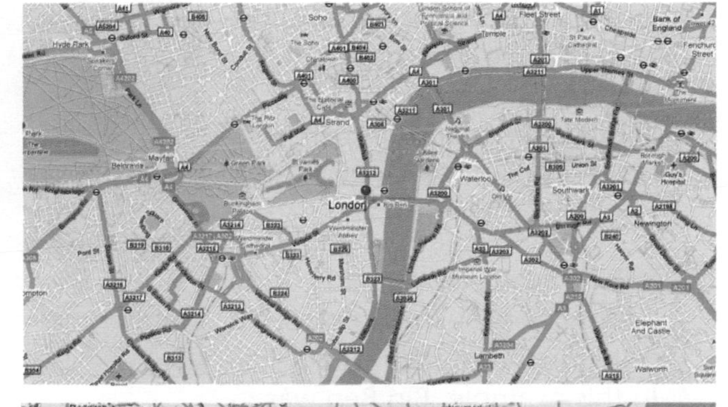

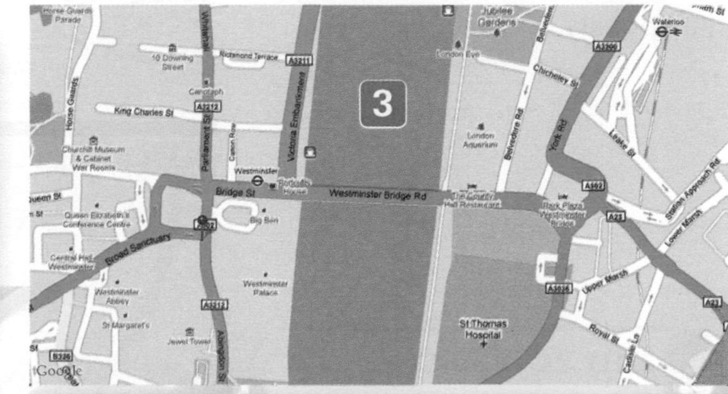

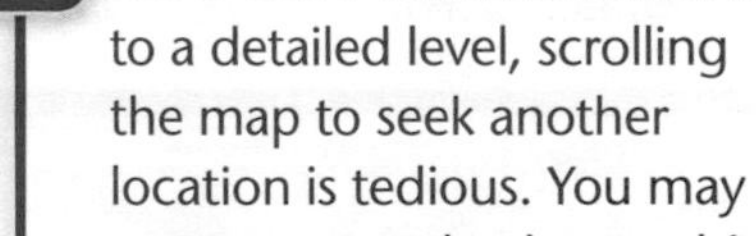

HOT TIP: When zoomed in to a detailed level, scrolling the map to seek another location is tedious. You may want to zoom back out a bit first. Scrolling is explained next.

DID YOU KNOW?

To look around at parts of the map not in view, put your finger on the screen and drag the map around.

ALERT: If you tap and don't start moving your finger around, a pin will drop to mark the location where you put your finger. Pins are explained later in the chapter (including how to remove them.)

Search for a location

At the top of the map is a search box. This is where you can enter an address you need to find. In fact, you can try entering the name of a famous landmark or a type of establishment, such as bookstores or pubs.

1. Tap into the search box. The virtual keyboard appears. You may also see a list of recent searches. If what you were about to enter in the search box is in the Recents list, just tap it in the list.
2. Enter a search term – an address, a well-known place or a type of establishment. In this example, Big Ben was entered for the search term and the map centred on it.
3. Here, Bookstores was entered as the search term. A number of pins dropped onto the map – each one is where a bookstore is located. By tapping the head of a pin, the name of the bookstore appears.

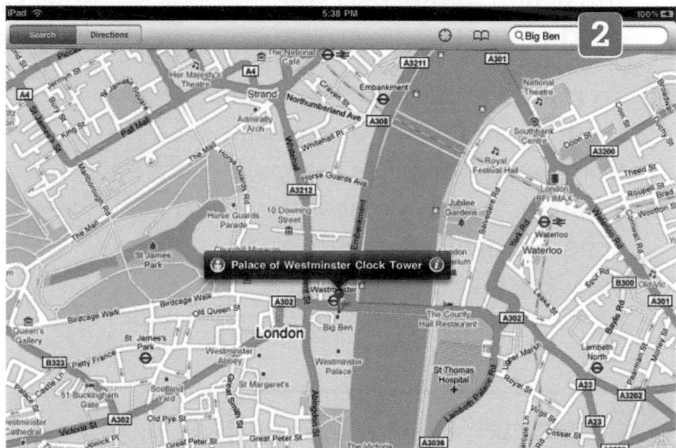

DID YOU KNOW?

You can get detailed information about the location or establishment found in a search, explained next.

Find more information about a location

When a location is identified by a pin, more information and a view of the location are available.

1. Assuming a location is marked with a pin, tap the head of the pin. The address or name is shown along with a red button on the left and a blue button on the right.
2. Tap the blue button on the right for more information. A box opens with a variety of things depending on the location. Here we see the phone, website address and street address.
3. Tap outside the information box to close it. This also removes the heading above the pin, so tap the pin head again to get it back.
4. Tap the red button on the left side of the pin heading. The screen now shows the actual location as it actually looks (like a photograph). This is called Street View.
5. In the lower right is a circle. Tap it to return to the map.

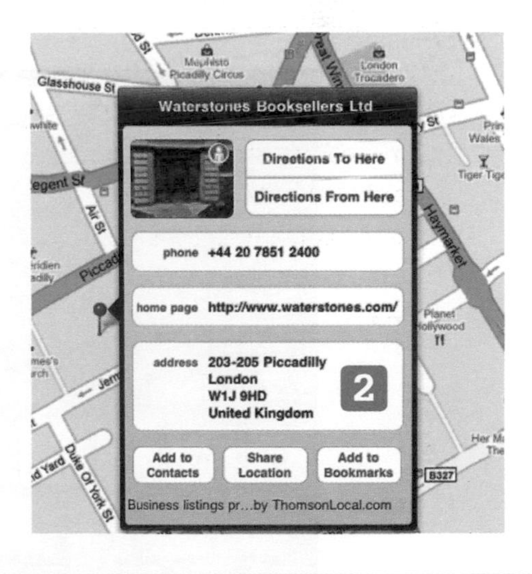

HOT TIP: When you are viewing the actual location you can use your finger to move the view around and see what else is nearby.

Directions to a location from where you are

Since the iPad can pinpoint your location, getting directions from where you are to another location means you have to enter the destination only.

1. Tap the Tracking button on the top. The map will display your location.
2. At the top left of the map, tap the Directions button. The screen changes in a few ways:
   - the virtual keyboard appears
   - the search box is replaced with a destination box
   - to the left of the destination box is the starting location box. It should say Current Location.
3. If necessary, tap the destination box so that it accepts your entry. Type in the address where you wish to go. It can be a full address, or just the name of a town or city.
4. Tap Search on the keyboard.

HOT TIP: The Recents list may have appeared. You can tap a location from the list to fill the destination box.

5. A route is shown. A blue pin is your location and a red pin is the destination.

6. Near the bottom is a bar with car, bus and pedestrian buttons on the left and a Start button on the right. After selecting the mode of transport (most likely car), tap Start button.

7. This creates a list of directions. To open the list, go to the new button with three lines on the left of the bar. Tap that button.

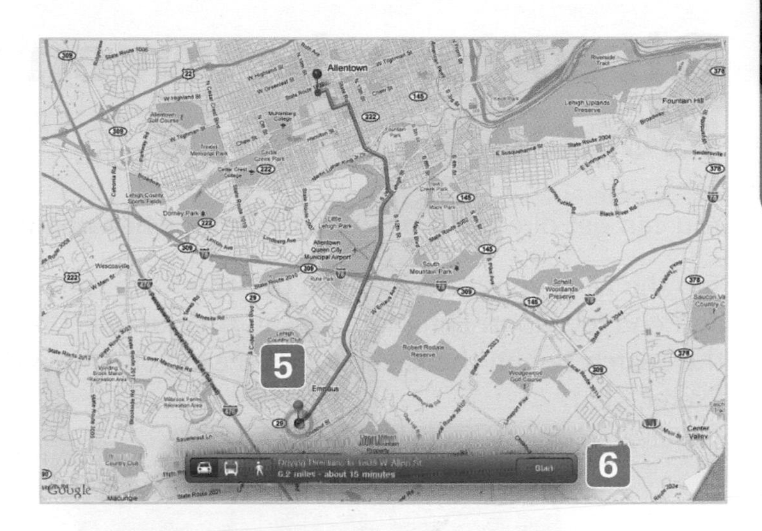

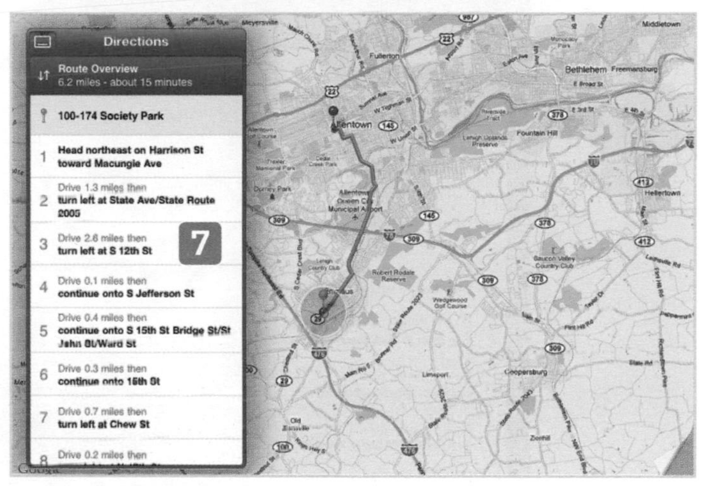

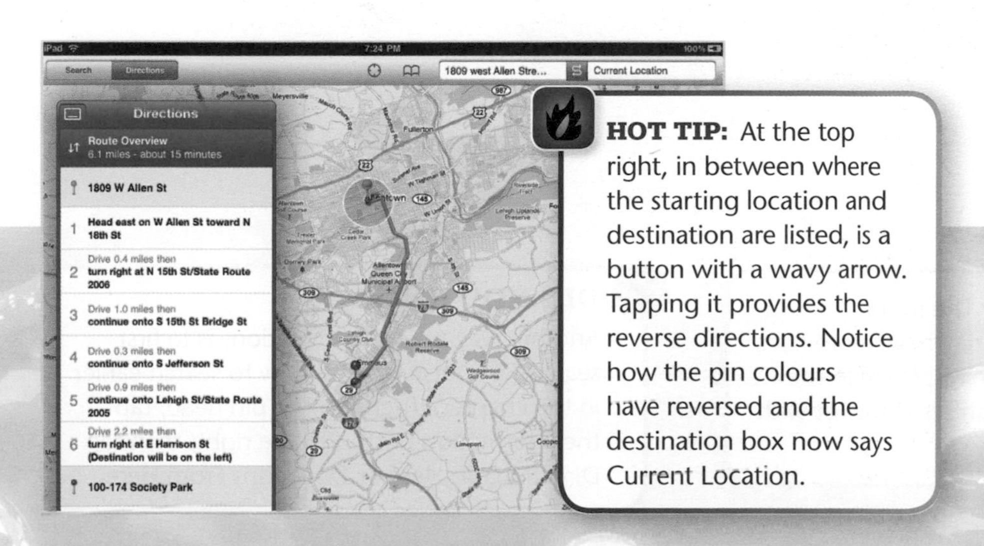

HOT TIP: At the top right, in between where the starting location and destination are listed, is a button with a wavy arrow. Tapping it provides the reverse directions. Notice how the pin colours have reversed and the destination box now says Current Location.

Directions between two locations

You can get directions between locations when neither location is your current location.

Tap the Directions button in the upper left. To the right are two boxes – for the start and end locations. Enter locations in each or select from the Recents list. Then tap the Search key on the keyboard. This example shows directions from Southampton to Exeter.

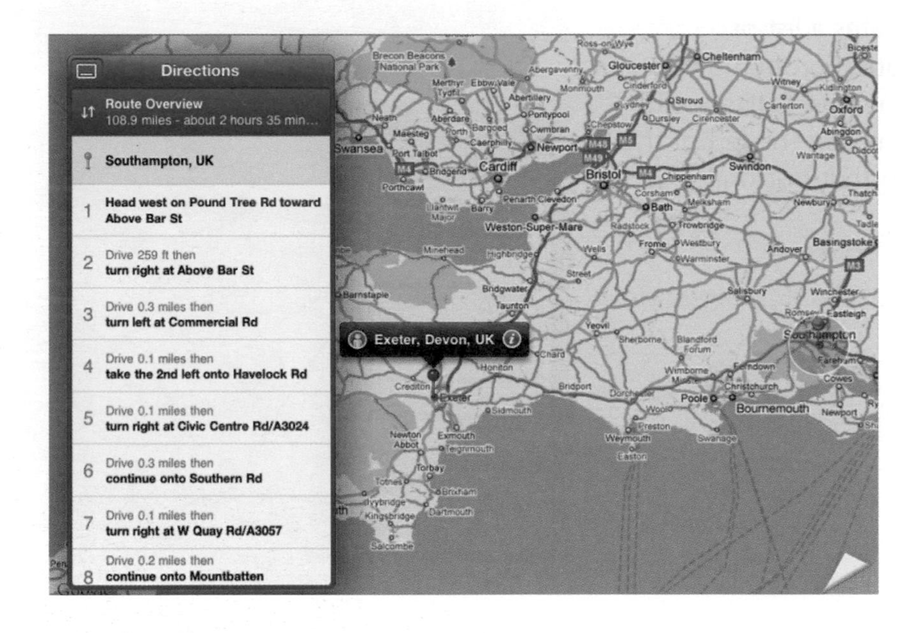

HOT TIP: The list of directions may have more lines than can be displayed in the box. You can scroll the list with your finger.

DID YOU KNOW?

Another way to gather directions is to first search for a location (see how to search earlier in the chapter), then tap the pin head, tap the information button to the right, then tap Directions To Here or Directions From Here.

Add an address to an existing contact

You may have a contact for which the address has never been entered. You can do so from the map.

1. Search for the address or drop a pin at the address (either way provides a pin).
2. Tap the pin, then tap the information button to the right. A box opens with information.
3. Tap Add to Contacts. You will be given a choice of how to apply the address.
4. Tap Add to Existing Contact.
5. The list of contacts appears. Tap the name of the contact that the address is for.

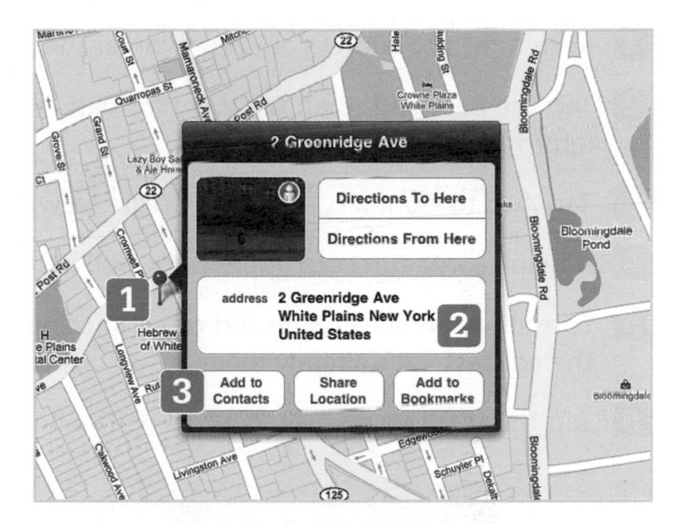

HOT TIP: You can add the same address to more than one contact.

Create a new contact from the map

As with adding an address to an existing contact, you can also create a new contact from the map.

1. Search for the address or drop a pin at the address.
2. Tap the pin head, then tap the information button on the right. A box opens with information.
3. Tap Add to Contacts, then tap Create New Contact.
4. A blank contact record appears, as well as the virtual keyboard.
5. Enter the contact's name and other information. However, you don't need to fill in the address – it's already there.
6. Tap the small Done button when you've finished.

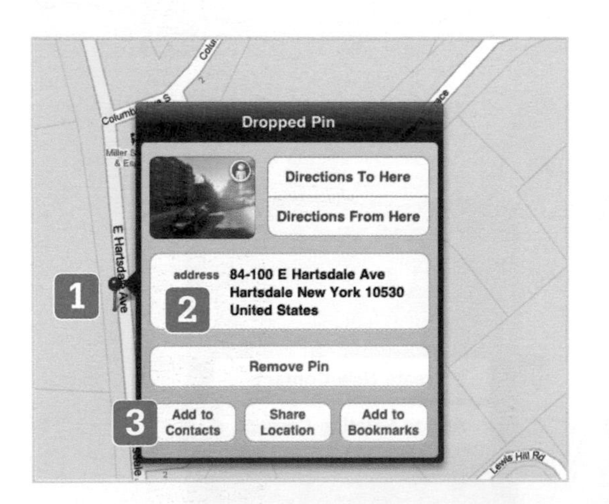

? DID YOU KNOW?

If you are in Contacts, you can tap on a contact's address and it will be shown on the map, with a pin with the contact's name.

Share a location

When you have an address you wish to forward to someone, the iPad is one step ahead and makes it easy.

1. From a pin, tap the information button to the right (tap the pin head first if necessary).
2. One of the buttons in the information box is Share Location. Tap this button.
3. An email message is created with the address and other information inserted into the body of the message.
4. Fill in the email recipient and tap the Send button.

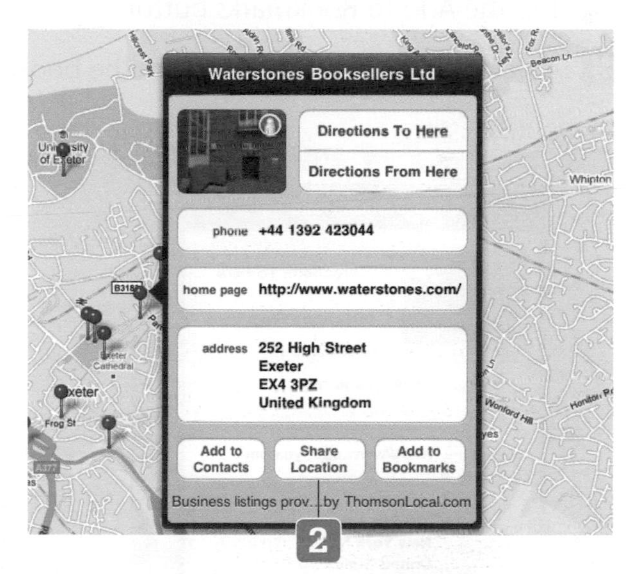

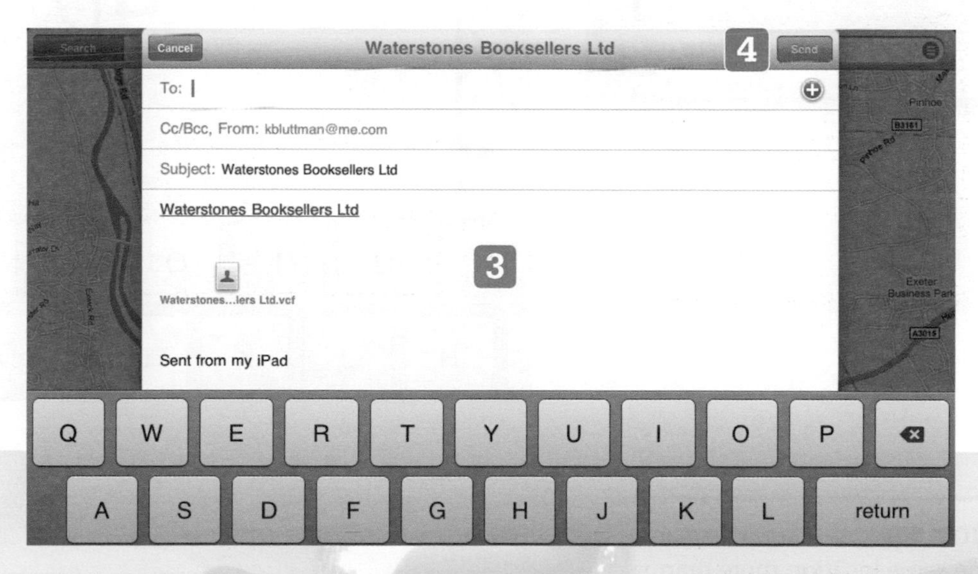

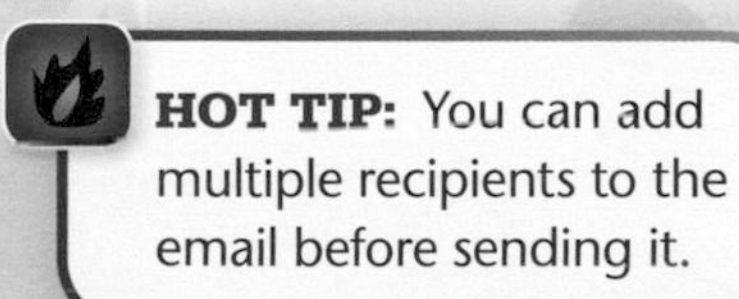

HOT TIP: You can add multiple recipients to the email before sending it.

Bookmark a location

Bookmarking a location makes it easy to find in the future.

1. Open the information box from a pinned location by tapping the information button in the pin heading.
2. Tap the Add to Bookmarks button.
3. A box opens to edit the name of the bookmark. Tap Save when finished.

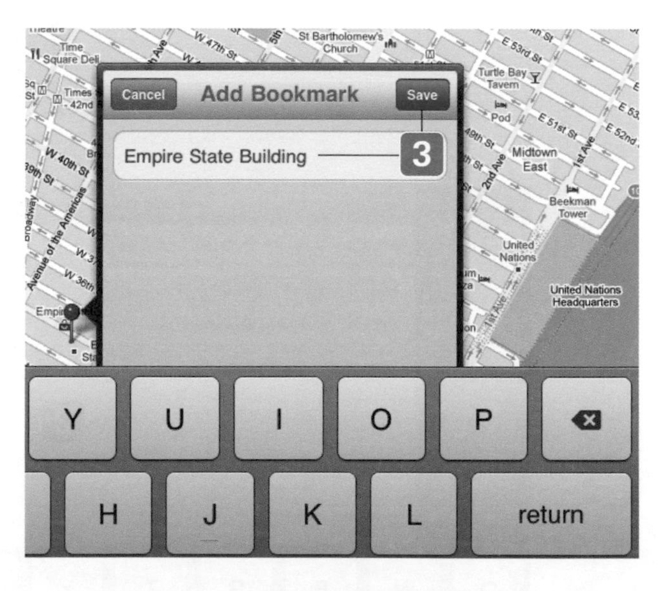

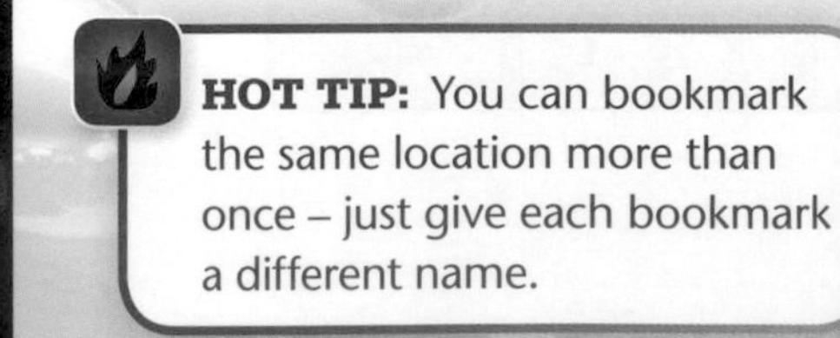

HOT TIP: You can bookmark the same location more than once – just give each bookmark a different name.

Find a location from a bookmark

Once a location has been bookmarked, it's easy to get the map to display it by using the list of bookmarks.

1. At the top of the map is the Bookmarks button. Tap it to display bookmarked locations.

2. Tap the desired bookmarked location. The map will display the location.

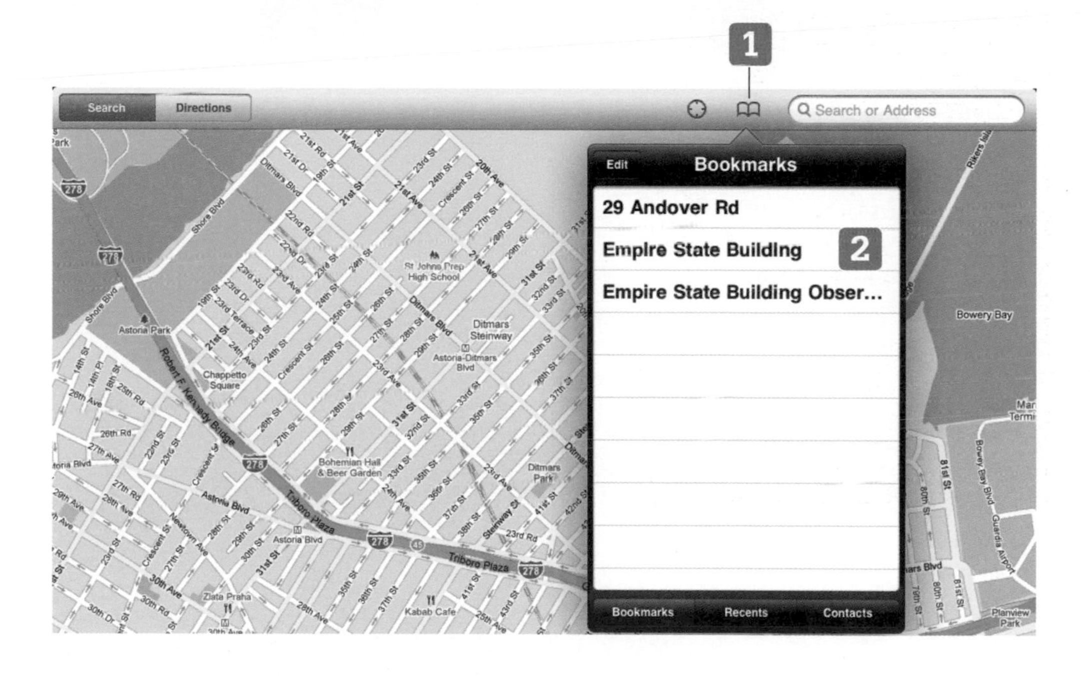

ALERT: Tapping the Bookmarks button displays a list, but it may not initially be the bookmarks. Along the bottom of the list are three buttons: Bookmarks, Recents and Contacts. Tapping any of these displays the associated list.

Drop a pin to mark a location

Pins are used as visual indicators of locations. At times you may see many pins, for instance if you searched for all pubs in the area. The task here is to mark a single location with a pin. All you need is a finger.

Tap and hold your finger down on the map. A pin will drop into the location.

DID YOU KNOW?

The title of the pin is simply Dropped Pin. This is because the pin was not placed as the result of a search or through a contact's address.

Remove a pin

Removing a pin is usually a tap away, but sometimes not.

1. From a dropped pin, tap the information button to the right. The information box opens. One of the choices is Remove Pin.
2. Tap Remove Pin. The pin is removed from the map.
3. In the case of a pin that appeared from a search or a bookmark, the Remove Pin button is not available. However, notice that the name is in the search box.
4. To remove this type of pin, tap into the search box. Note there is a letter x in the right side of the search box.
5. Tap the x, then tap on the map. The pin is removed.

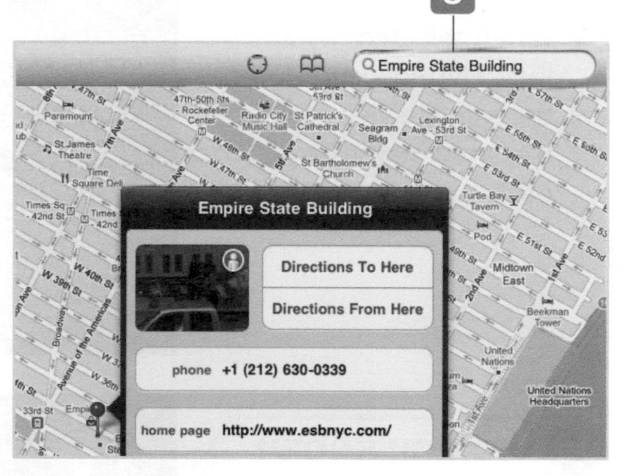

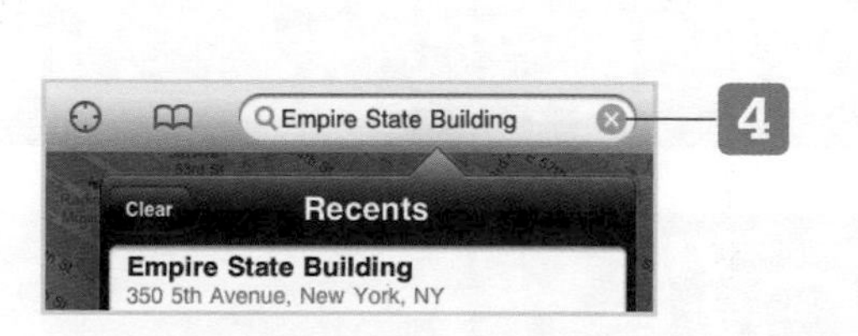

HOT TIP: Even though a bookmark's pin has been removed, the location has not been removed from the Bookmarks list. You can place the pin again by tapping the location in Bookmarks.

Explore different map types

There are five different ways to view a map: Classic, Satellite, Hybrid, Terrain and Street View. Each of these is interesting or useful for different needs. The Classic view is the most familiar and has been shown throughout this chapter. Here is how to use the other map types.

1. Tap the lower right corner of the map. You may notice that it looks like a piece of paper being turned. When you tap there, the map folds over to reveal some settings.

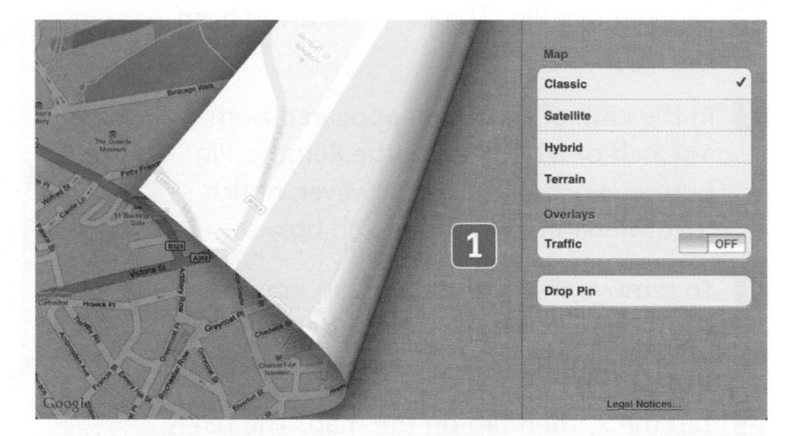

2. Tap Satellite and the map changes to a literal magnified view from a satellite above the Earth.

3. When selected (by a tap), Hybrid view shows the satellite view with the street names and other markers overlayed.

? DID YOU KNOW?

There are areas of the Earth for which Satellite view will not work. These areas are private – whether military or of an unfriendly nation, etc.

4. Terrain view is most noticeable in a mountainous area, such as the Rocky Mountains in the western United States, shown here.

5. Street View has been shown earlier in the chapter, however here is another example. To get to Street View, you need to drop a pin (or make one appear from a bookmark or a search). In the heading over the pin, on the left, is a red button. Tapping this button brings up Street View for the pinned location. Here, for example, is the Street View for Big Ben.

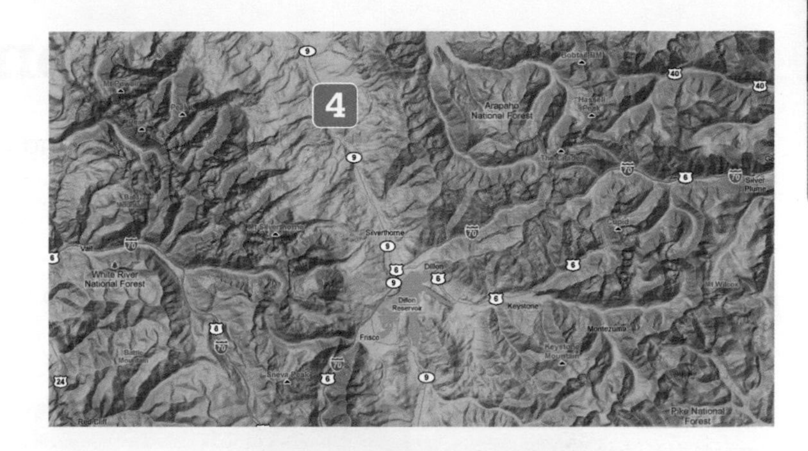

HOT TIP: Where's the clock? Street View shows ground level. However, with a little manoeuvring with your finger, you can 'look around' and even 'look up', as shown here.

Show traffic conditions

This feature really shows the power that technology brings us. Showing traffic conditions means providing the conditions 'right now' – a current, live view of how traffic is flowing.

1 Tap the corner of the map to reveal the settings. Tap the Traffic button to turn the feature on.

2 Tap the map.

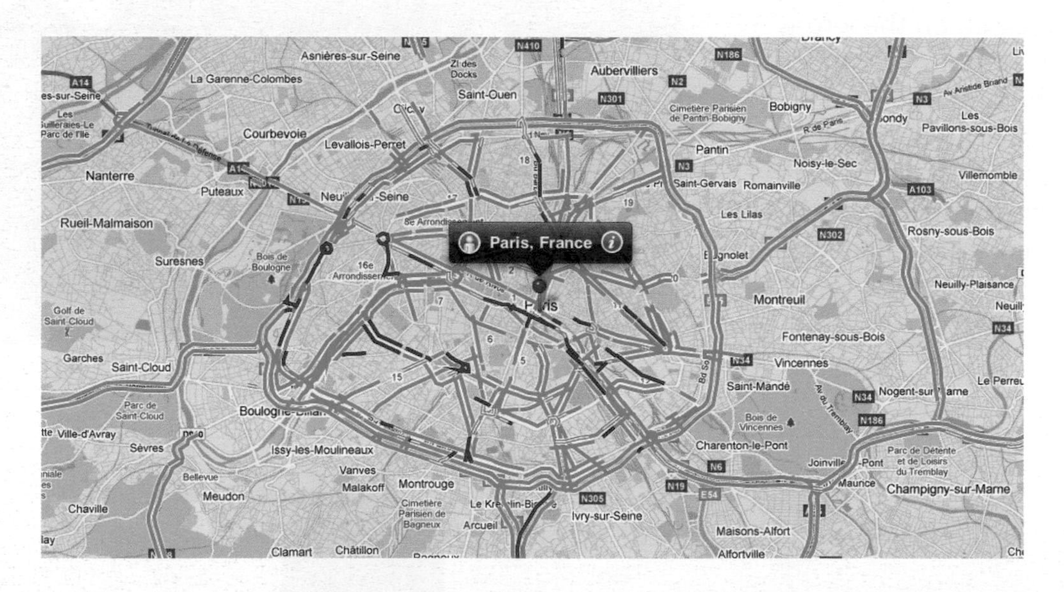

3 The traffic is shown with a colour-coded system. In order of good to bad is green, yellow and red.

ALERT: The traffic conditions are not available in all locations.

11 Caring for your contacts

Introduction

Where would we be without networking? Having a list of friends, family, associates, people we do business with and so on is essential to sharing news, information and everything else under the sun. The iPad comes with standard contact list functionality and it is easy to use. So, let's get started.

Add a new contact

The more contacts you have, the better off you'll be – as long as you can keep track of them. Contacts helps you do that by keeping the contacts in alphabetic order. Here's how to add a new contact.

1. On the Home screen, tap the Contacts icon.
2. The list of contacts opens. On the left are the alphabetical headings and on the right is the detail for a selected contact. To add a new contact, tap the plus (+) sign at the bottom of the left side.
3. A blank entry for a new contact appears, along with the virtual keyboard (not shown here). There are numerous fields you can fill in – name, address, email and more.
4. At the bottom is a green plus sign. Tapping it brings up more fields, such as job title and birthday.
5. When all the desired fields have entries, tap the small Done button at the top right of the contact record.

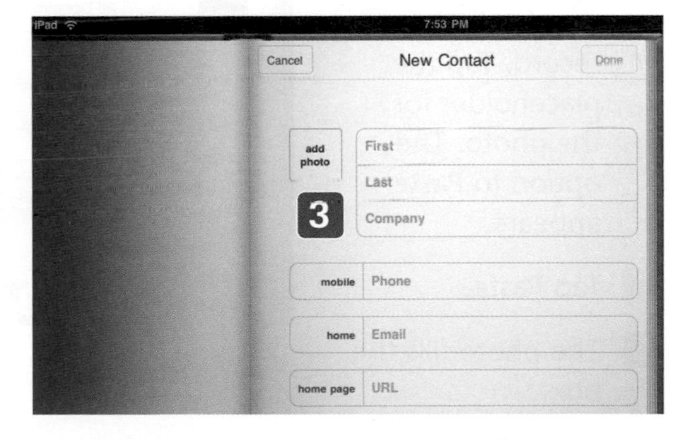

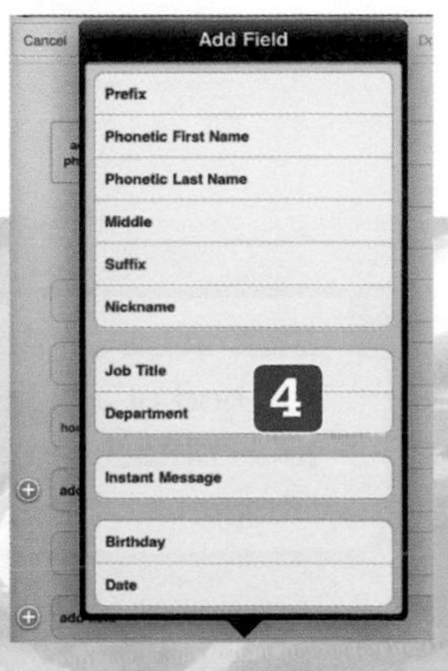

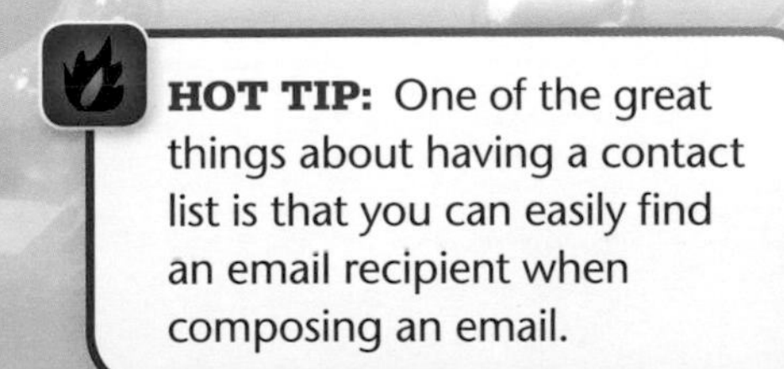

HOT TIP: One of the great things about having a contact list is that you can easily find an email recipient when composing an email.

Assign a photo to a contact

A picture is worth a thousand words, or at least a few dozen. Seeing what a contact looks like is quite helpful for remembering who the contact is. So if you have a picture to assign to the contact, here is one way to do it.

1. Find the contact's photo in the iPad. In this example, the photo is embedded in the body of an email message. Tapping and holding your finger on the photo presents an option to copy the picture.
2. Tap Copy. Press the Home button, then tap the Contacts icon.
3. Tap the contact's name on the left side of Contacts. This fills the right side with the detailed record. Tap the placeholder for the photo. The option to Paste appears.
4. Tap Paste.
5. The photo fills the box.

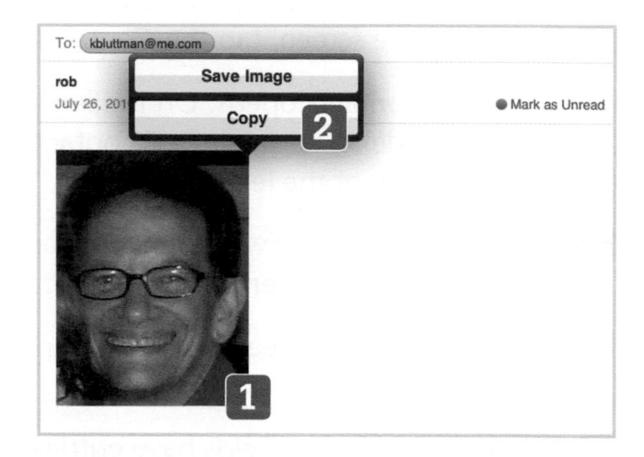

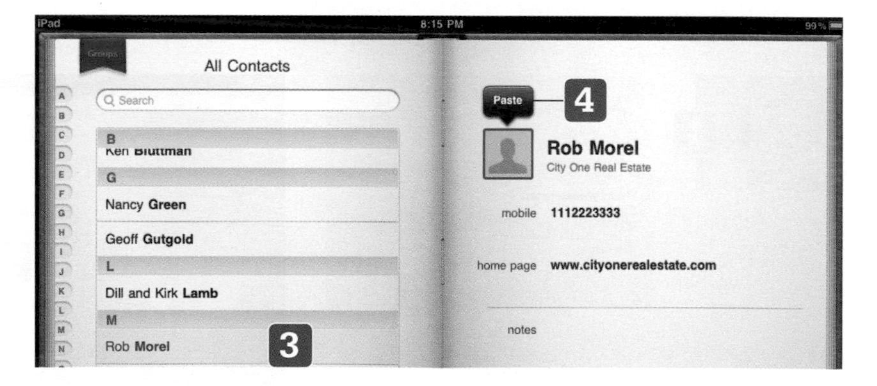

SEE ALSO: An alternative method of assigning a photo to a contact is shown in Chapter 6.

Search Contacts

If and when you have many contacts, you might find it helpful to search through the list.

1. On the left side of Contacts, near the top, is a search box.
2. Tap the search box so it is ready to accept an entry. The virtual keyboard appears. As you type in a name or other search term, the list of contacts filters to match what you have entered.
3. In the filtered list, tap the contact you need.

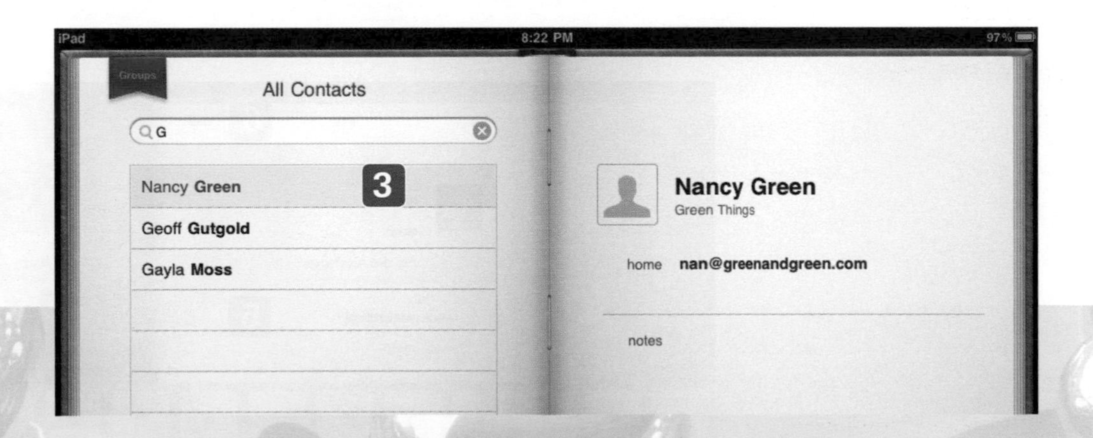

Edit a contact

People move, change jobs, get married, so of course you need a way to edit their contact record.

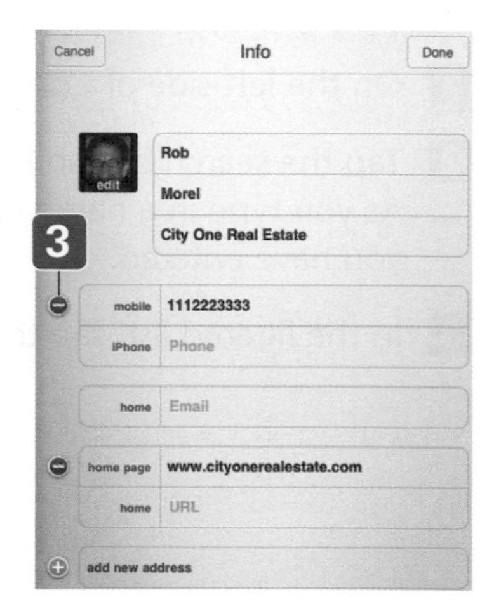

1. Select the contact on the left side of Contacts.
2. On the right side, at the bottom, is an Edit button. Tap the button.
3. The contact record becomes editable. Fields that are filled in have a red circle with a horizontal white line.
4. When a red circle is tapped, the white line becomes vertical and a Delete button appears. Tap the Delete button only if that is what you intend to do.
5. If you want to change information or add new information, tap into the desired field. The virtual keyboard appears. Make your changes and/or edits.
6. When you've finished, tap the small Done button at the top right of the contact's record.

Delete a contact

Deleting a contact is just a tap away.

1. For the contact to be deleted, tap the Edit button.
2. At the bottom of the record is a Delete Contact button. If you do not see it, scroll down.
3. Tap the Delete Contact button.
4. A confirmation box appears, from which you can proceed or cancel the delete.

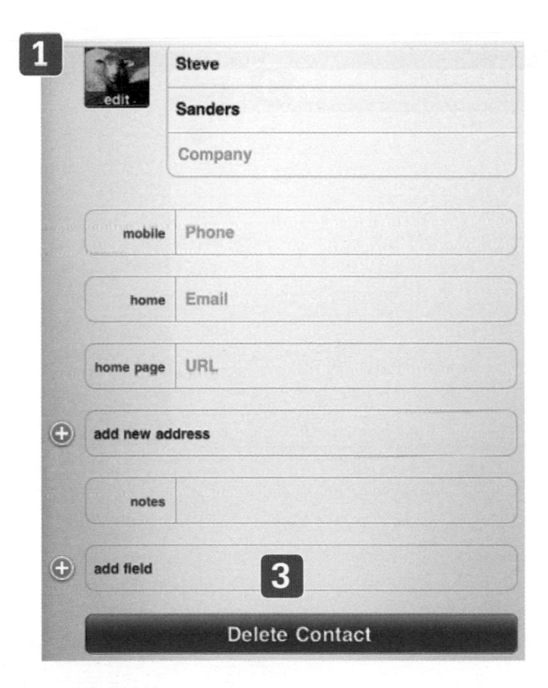

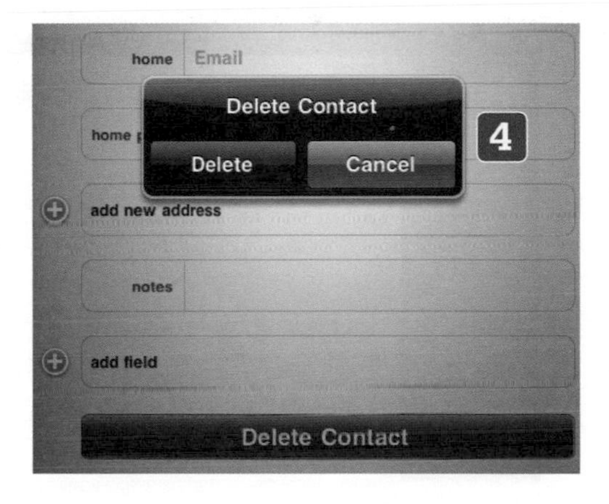

HOT TIP: What if you delete someone and realise later that you need their information? If you think you may need a contact at some point in the future, then instead of deleting, you can edit their name so that it starts with the letter x. Then at least people you no longer need to know about right now are all grouped together.

Share a contact

This feature makes forwarding someone's contact information a breeze.

1. With the desired contact selected – and appearing on the right of Contacts – tap the Share button found near the bottom.
2. A new email message is created with the contact's information attached as a VCF file.
3. Fill in the email, including who to send it to, and tap the small Send button at the top right of the email message.

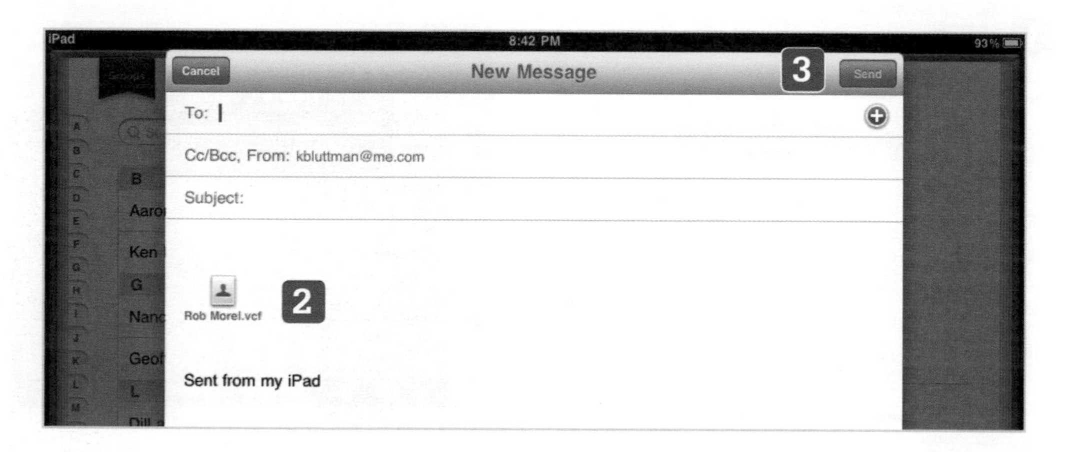

WHAT DOES THIS MEAN?

VCF file: A commonly used file format for sharing contact information among different types of address book or contact applications.

Add a contact from an email message

When someone emails a VCF card in an email, you can easily add the person to your contact list.

1. In the email, tap and hold your finger on the VCF icon until a box appears with detailed information and options at the bottom.
2. Tap the Create New Contact button. A contact record opens in which you can add information.
3. Tap the small Done button when you've finished.

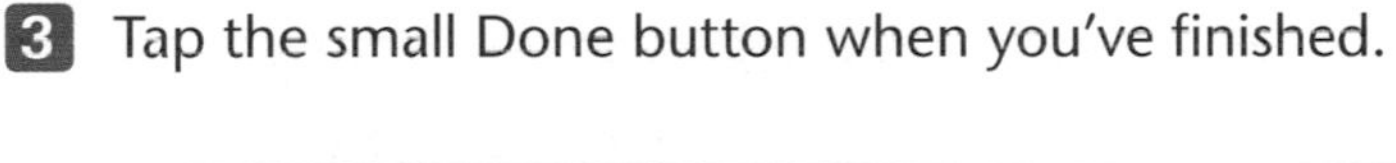

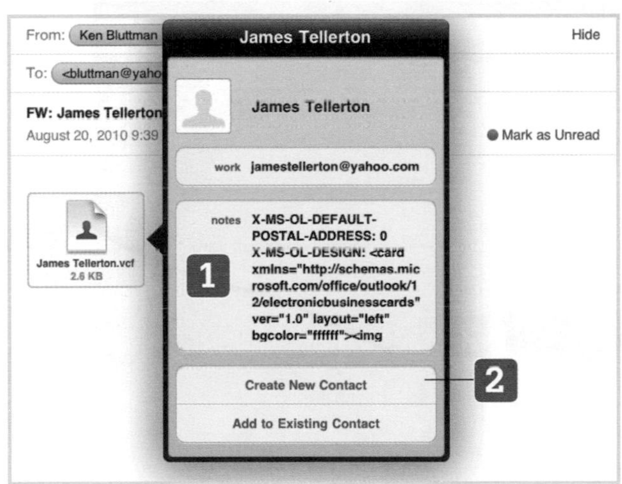

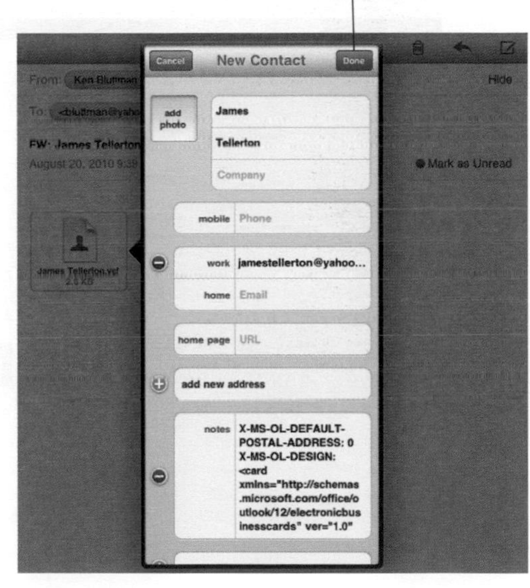

Locate a contact on the map

If you have an address entered in a contact's record, it is just a tap away to see where they are on the map.

1. Select a contact for whom the address has been entered. Tap the address.
2. The map opens and drops a pin at the address location.

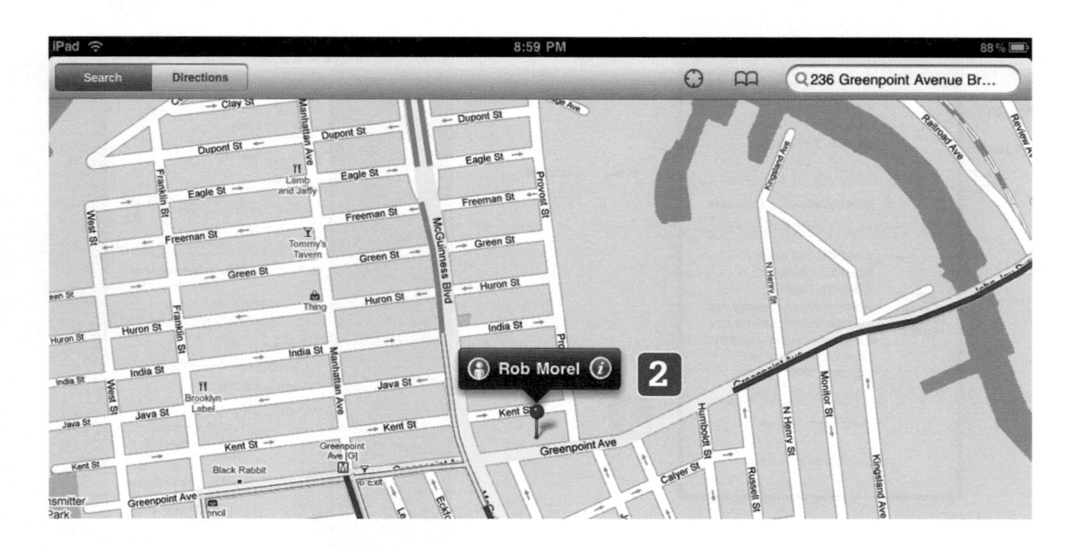

SEE ALSO: Chapter 10 shows how the contact's information can be seen directly from the map.

12 Staying organised with Calendar

Introduction

With our busy lives, it seems we don't have enough time for everything, so we squeeze in what we can. But one missed appointment or other commitment could wreak havoc.

The iPad has Calendar, a core app. It is like an appointment book – you can view items in different ways. It's easy to edit entries and you can even get the iPad to buzz you with a reminder that a scheduled activity is beginning soon.

Start Calendar

The icon for Calendar is interesting as it always shows the current date.

Tap the Calendar icon. Calendar will open and display the view from the last time the app was used.

Explore the different Calendar views

You can view the calendar of a single day, a week, the month or as a list of this week's events. Along the top of Calendar are buttons – Day, Week, Month and List.

1. Tap the desired view. Here is the Day view. Scheduled items are seen in blue. In the middle of the daily times is a thin bar with a red end point on the left. This shows the current time.
2. Along the bottom is a timeline. The currently displayed date (it doesn't have to be the current date) is highlighted in blue. You can drag along the timeline with your finger to get to a different date.

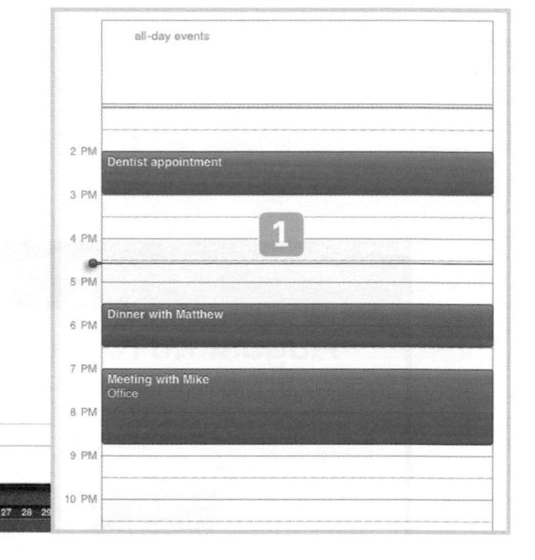

3. Tap a different view. Here, for example, is the display when the Week button is tapped.

3 Tapping Month provides a full month's view. The timeline on the bottom now shows months instead of days, making it easy to view different months.

4 Tapping the List button shows the week's appointments on the left. Tapping any item on the left will cause the right side to fill with that day's schedule.

HOT TIP: Tapping a scheduled item on the right displays a detailed box from which you can make edits or delete the scheduled item.

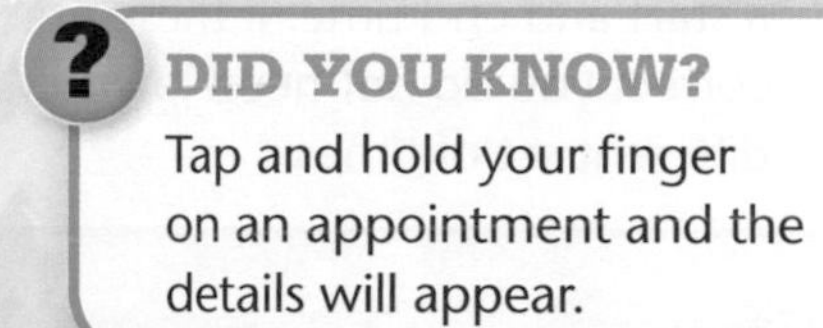

DID YOU KNOW?
Tap and hold your finger on an appointment and the details will appear.

Add an event

Adding an event follows the same steps no matter which view is present when you start. An event has:

- a title
- a location
- a start time
- an end time
- a selection to make it a repeating event
- a selection to set an alert to remind you the event is going to start
- a place to add a note about the event.

The details about an event are entered using the Add Event box.

1. Tap the plus sign in the lower right corner.
2. The Add Event box appears along with the virtual keyboard.
3. Enter a title and, optionally, a location. Not all events have a particular location.
4. To enter the start and end times, tap in the time box (where it says Starts and Ends).

HOT TIP: Calendar will suggest a start and end time. If these are correct you do not need to enter a different set of times.

5 The Start & End box opens. Setting the time with this box is done by pushing up or down on the date, the hour, the minute and whether it's AM or PM. As you scroll up or down with your finger on any of these four date/time attributes, you cycle through a list. Stop when the correct entry is in the middle. Notice that this first-time entry is the start time, since Starts is highlighted.

6 Set the end time. First, though, notice that the box has a suggested end time – of one hour later. If this is correct, just leave it as it is. If not, tap Ends near the top, then use the date/time selectors to dial in the end time, in this case of 9:00 PM.

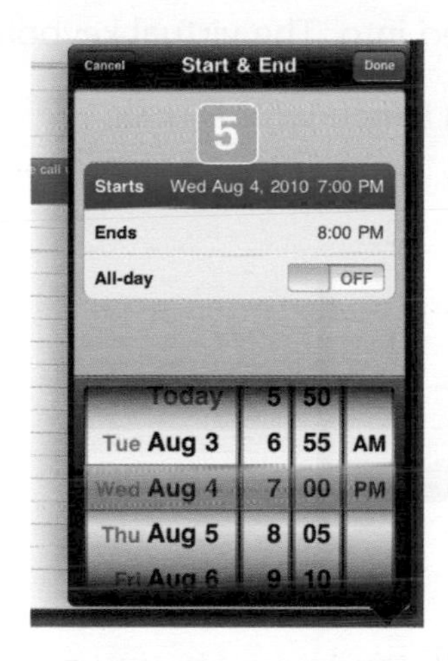

7 When you've finished, tap the Done button. The Add Event box is displayed again, now with the correct start and end times.

8 Repeat and Alert are discussed later in the chapter. For now, as an option, scroll down until you see where you can add a note. You can tap into the note box and enter any comments.

9 Tap the Done button when you've finished setting up the event. It is added to the calendar.

HOT TIP: The minutes selection is in 5-minute intervals. This should provide the granularity needed for setting an event's time.

Edit an event

You can change the title, date, time or any other facet of a scheduled item.

As an example, when looking at the scheduled entries, 'Lunch with Bill' should say 'Dinner with Bill'.

1. Tap the scheduled event. The Edit Event box appears.
2. For this example, the title box is tapped into. The virtual keyboard appears.
3. The editing change is made, replacing Lunch with Dinner.
4. Tap Done when you've finished.

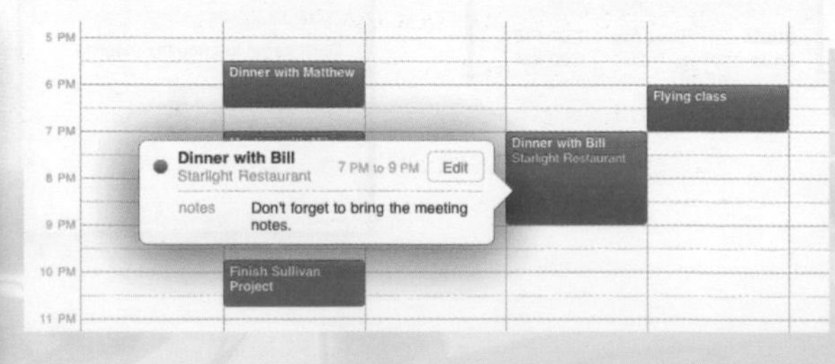

DID YOU KNOW?

If the calendar is in Week or Month view when starting an edit, tapping the event presents a small extended box that shows the name and time of the event. An Edit button also appears. Tapping the Edit button displays the full Edit Event box.

Delete an event

Schedules often change and events get cancelled. In this case you would probably like to delete the entry.

1. Tap the event to open the Edit Event box.
2. Tap Delete Event.
3. A confirmation appears. Tap Delete Event once again. The event is removed from the calendar.

HOT TIP: When deleting a repeating event, you have a choice to delete the current event (from the date you are on when starting the delete process) or to delete the full repeating series.

Set an event to repeat

Some events occur on a regular basis – once a week or at some other interval. Calendar has a method for setting up a repeating event.

1. Set up the title, optional location and start and end times as described earlier in the chapter.
2. Tap Repeat. A list of repeat options appears.
3. Select the appropriate interval. Tap the Done button when you've finished.
4. The display reverts to the Add Event box. Now a new item appears in the box – End Repeat. Tap on End Repeat.
5. You can set a date that the repeating event should end or set it to repeat indefinitely. Enter or select the appropriate choice, then tap Done.
6. The display reverts to the Add Event box. Tap Done to close it.

HOT TIP: In any calendar view, the repeating event will be seen on its set interval date, indefinitely so, if you selected that there is no end date.

Set an alert to notify an event will be occurring

Having a calendar application is great for being organised. Yet, unless we are constantly looking at the scheduled items, an event can go by without notice. Therefore it's good practice to set alerts – audio and visual reminders that an event will be starting.

1. Set up an event. Leave the Add Event box open.
2. Tap the Alert button. A list of choices appears.
3. Make your choice and tap Done. The Add Event box is displayed again. Tap Done to finish the entry.

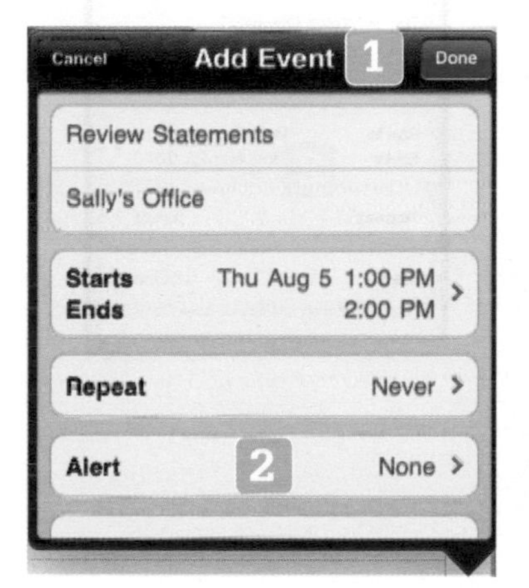

4. An option is to set a second alert. So, for example, you can be notified 15 minutes before an event and then again 5 minutes before the event.

When the time arrives for the alert, an audible soft alarm sound is heard and the screen displays a reminder.

HOT TIP: It is good use of the Alert function to set the second alert. Being reminded twice is sure to get your attention.

Set up an all-day event

Suppose you had to travel out of town or went on holiday or had some other matter to attend to that took up a day (or days)? In Calendar you can set this as an 'all-day event' – it takes just a single event entry and it's flagged to last all day.

1. While setting up an event, in the Start & End box, simply tap the All-day button to set it to On.
2. The Add Event box displays that Starts and Ends are the same date.
3. In Calendar, a single line at the top of the day displays the title of the all-day event.

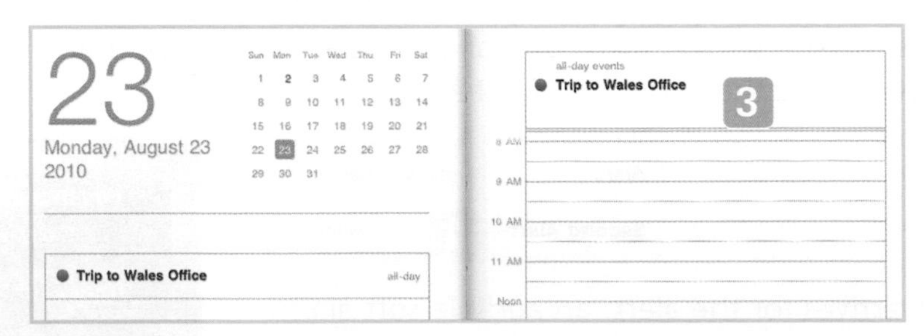

HOT TIP: In each type of view – Day, Week, Month or List – an all-day event appears in a different manner than non all-day events. For example, in Day view, it appears at the top of the day.

DID YOU KNOW?
If you have a sequence of all-day events, when setting up the event, set Ends to the last date of the sequence. Then, for example, you can set five days in a row as all-day events with just one entry.

Search Calendar

As with most iPad apps, there is a search feature. In the case of Calendar you might search for a person's name, a location or some keyword about an event.

1. In the upper right is the search box. Tap into the box. The virtual keyboard appears.
2. Enter a search term. A list will appear under the search box with results of the search.
3. Tap an event returned from the search to display the event.

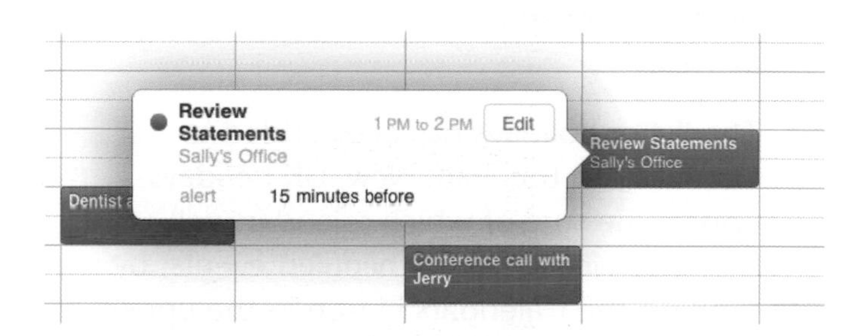

Subscribe to a calendar

Some online services provide lists of dates – holidays, historical and so on – that can be inserted into Calendar. The information from a list shows up on any associated dates.

1. Use Safari to visit www.icalshare.com.

2. Search for a useful calendar. Here, a search has turned up a list of UK holidays.

3. Tap the Subscribe to Calendar button. A confirmation prompt may appear as well.

4. The list of holidays has been added to Calendar on the iPad. Now, UK holidays appear. Be sure of which calendars will show, as well as your scheduled events, by tapping the Calendars button in the upper left and making sure the desired calendars are selected to show. Be sure that On My iPad is selected so that your scheduled events appear.

13 Taking notes

Introduction

The ability to quickly jot down your ideas or make a to-do list is helpful. Thoughts come and go and sometimes slip by if we don't put them down on paper. Or in the case of the iPad, put them down on an electronic notepad.

The Notes app works just like a notepad – sheets of paper glued together into a pad of paper. A Note is really more like a piece of paper on which any amount of text can be entered. Although it's all electronic, you can leaf through the sheets and find just the set of notes you are looking for. Of course, the search feature does wonders in this area as well.

Review a note

To see any of the existing notes you have entered is quite easy.

1. On the Home screen, tap the Notes icon.
2. On the left is a title summary of the notes, by name. On the right is the content of the note. Tap a note title on the left and the right shows the detail.

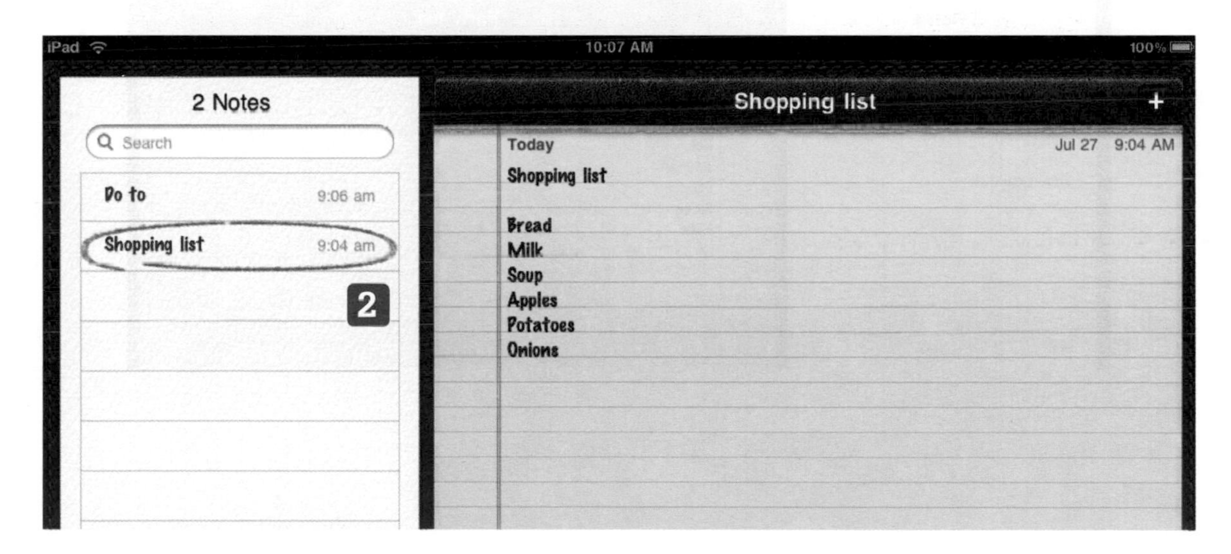

Add a new note

The iPad can hold an endless number of notes. There is no doubt some practical limit based on how much memory is available, but you will be hard pressed to ever get near that limit. So add as many new notes as you need. To add a note tap the plus sign in the upper right corner and a new note is ready for entry.

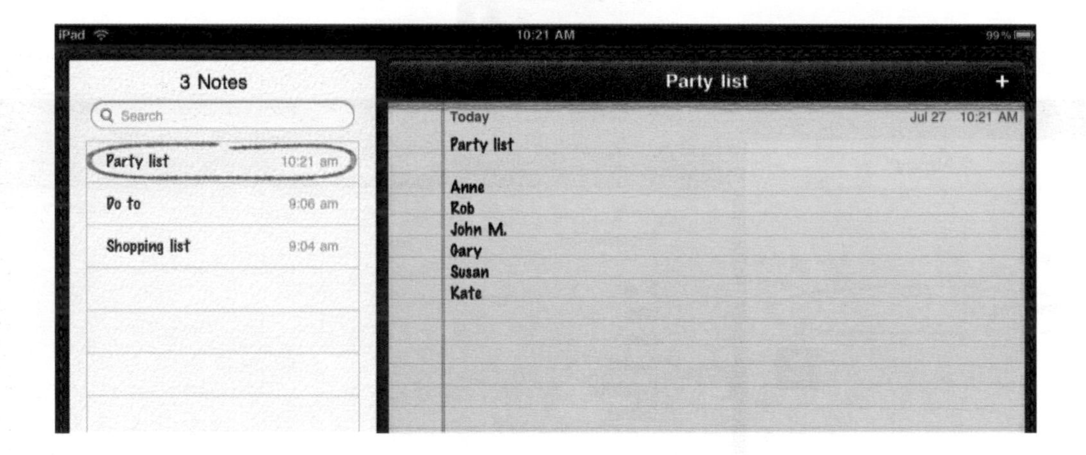

HOT TIP: The title of the note is created from the first line of entry of the new note. This can be seen here as a party list is assembled and the title on the left is named from the first line of the note.

Edit a note

Notes are essentially editable without any need to first enable them to accept changes. Just simply tap on the line to edit and delete and/or add characters with the virtual keyboard.

1. Tap on a line in the content of a note.
2. The virtual keyboard appears and you make any necessary changes. Here, Gary has been changed to Gary and Lisa.
3. Tap on any note title on the left side to complete the edit – the virtual keyboard disappears.

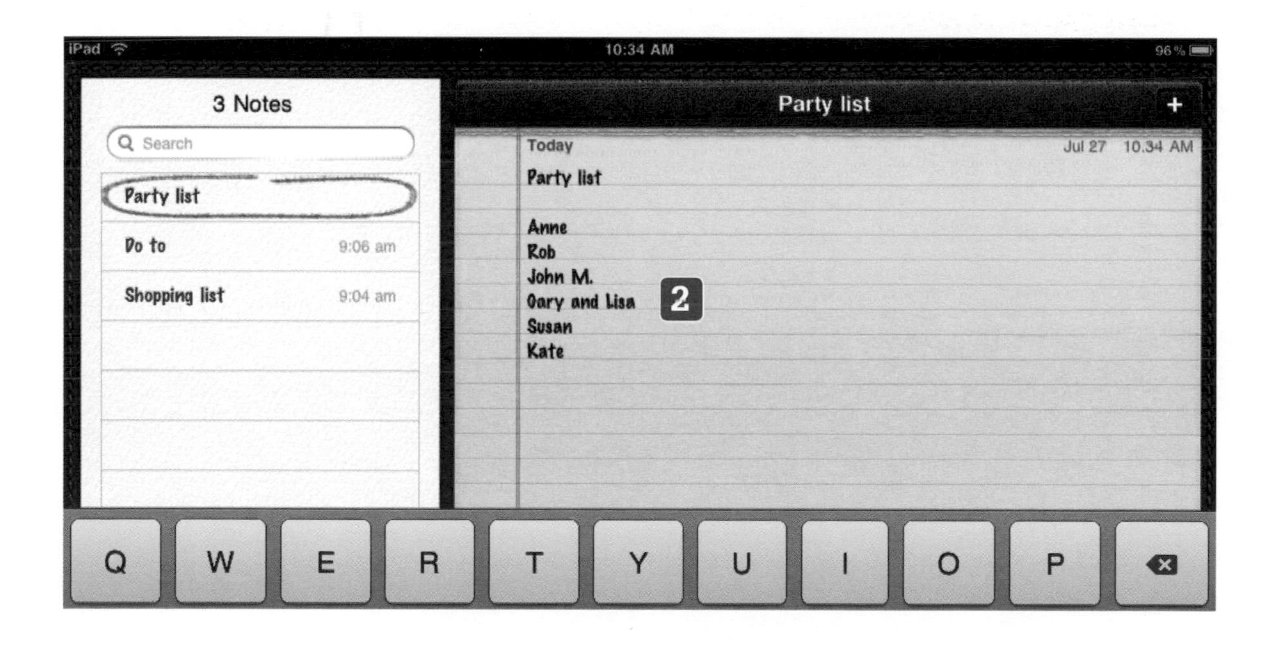

Delete a note

As with many of the note operations, deleting a note is quite easy to do.

With the note visible on the right, tap the trash icon near the bottom. The note is removed.

Email a note

Having a note stored in the iPad is great – until and unless you have to print it or send it to someone. Email to the rescue!

1. With the note visible on the right, tap the email icon (looks like an envelope).
2. An email message opens up with the contents of the note put into the body of the email. Just enter a recipient and send the email.

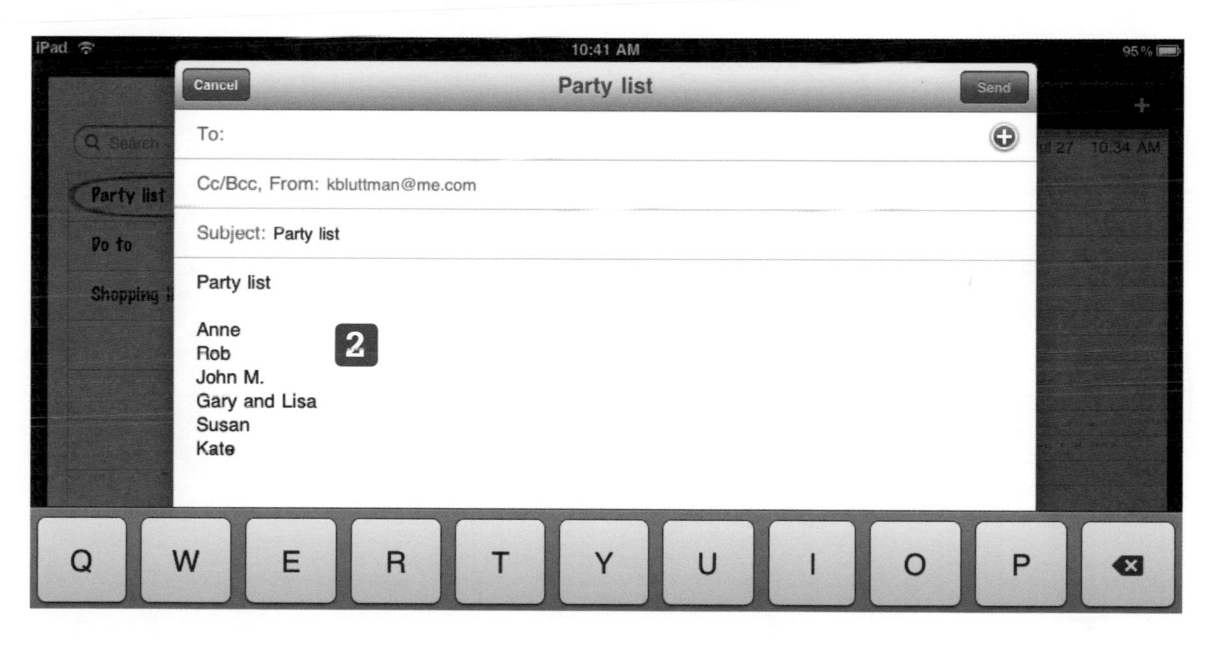

Browse through notes

Although you can type on the note titles on the left and then view the contents of each on the right, there is an easy way to quickly view the contents of multiple notes, sequentially.

On the right, near the bottom are forward and back buttons (respectively on the right and the left). They look like arrows. Using these you can move forwards or backwards through all the notes.

Search through notes

When you need to find an item that is in one of your notes but you can't recall which note it is, then you can search for it.

1. On the left, at the top, is a search box. Tap in it. The virtual keyboard appears.
2. Type in a search term. As you type, the list of notes filters to those which have contents that contain what you have entered.

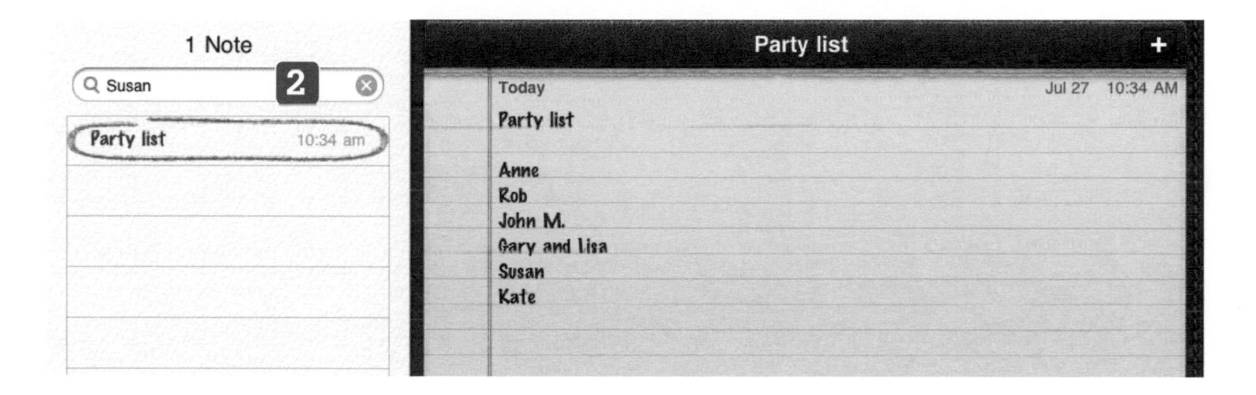

HOT TIP: To return to the full list of notes, clear out the search box by tapping the little x inside the box, towards the right.

14 Accessibility

Introduction

Apple has done a great job including accessibility features for the iPad. These features are specifically for those with disabilities, such as vision impairment, hearing impairment and limited physical abilities. When implemented, these features tend to change how to use the iPad, to a degree. It takes some getting used to.

One of the major features is VoiceOver. This instructs the iPad to read what is on the screen. There are various ways to set this to work. Another feature is Zoom, to make everything larger. These features open doors for people with disabilities to help them get the best use out of the iPad. There are even some benefits for those without disabilities. For example, if a person is learning a new language, they can turn on the text reading, and hear the foreign words.

Turn on VoiceOver

VoiceOver is a feature of the iPad that enables the iPad to read to you. It will read screen names, button captions, text such as that from an email or other source (document, book, etc.). VoiceOver is a help for those with vision impairment and other disabilities in which an audible voice is necessary to work with the iPad. When VoiceOver is on, the finger gestures change. This allows the iPad to make use of single taps and double taps and also the three-finger swipe.

The accessibility features are controlled in Settings.

1. Tap the Settings icon. Then tap the General tab on the left. A single tab on the right, labelled Accessibility, is to be tapped. You may need to scroll down to see it.
2. Tap VoiceOver. The right side of the screen displays various settings. The first one is VoiceOver.

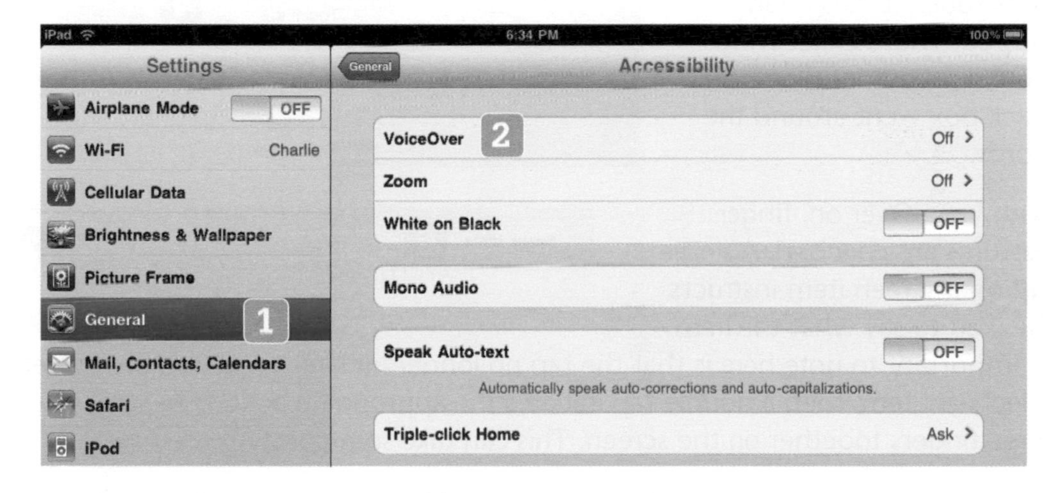

ALERT: Don't be startled when you turn on VoiceOver and the iPad begins speaking.

HOT TIP: With VoiceOver on, tap an item once to select it, then double tap it to perform its function (such as an icon opening an app or a button performing an action).

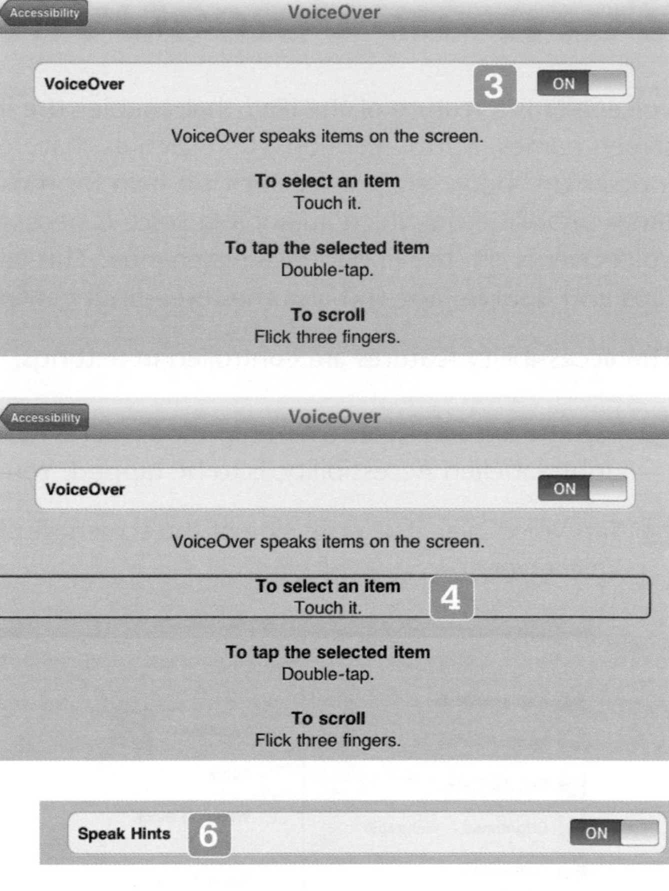

3. Options appear. The top one is simply an overall on/off setting. Tap the On/Off button to turn it on.

4. Even though you are still in Settings, VoiceOver is on and is working immediately. Even as you touch further options, the iPad verbally states what you tap on the screen. When you tap something, a black border goes around it and the voice reads the words. Here, for example, 'To select an item Touch it' has been tapped. Those exact words were read out loud and the black box went around the words.

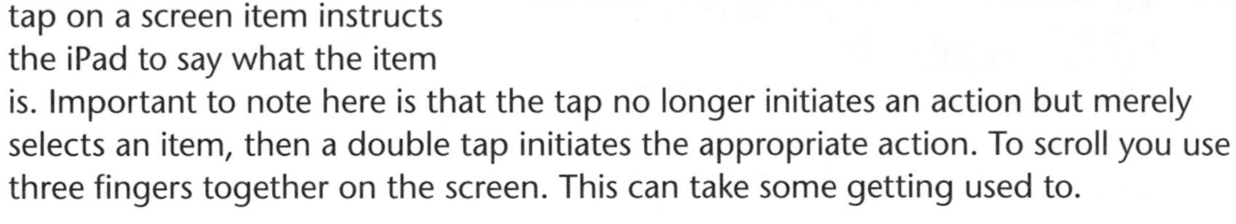

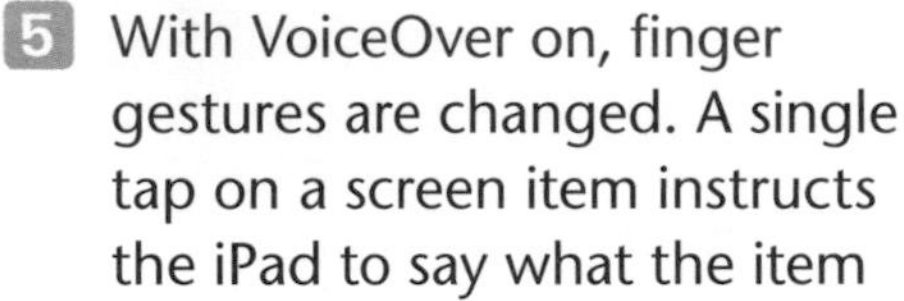

5. With VoiceOver on, finger gestures are changed. A single tap on a screen item instructs the iPad to say what the item is. Important to note here is that the tap no longer initiates an action but merely selects an item, then a double tap initiates the appropriate action. To scroll you use three fingers together on the screen. This can take some getting used to.

6. Speak Hints is a setting that can be turned on or off at your discretion. When on, VoiceOver provides more information about an item, whether tapped or from being the first item on a new screen. Speak Hints does not always provide additional information – it depends on what the item is.

ALERT: VoiceOver can seem difficult to work the way you want it to. For example, if an iBook is open, you don't tap and double tap on the text if you want to hear the whole page read, you double tap on a blank place in the page. To stop the voice reading, tap somewhere on the text. There is no clear way to explain all the nuances of VoiceOver. Using it is the best way to learn how to make it work in the way to best suit your needs.

Change the speaking rate

You can control the speed at which the voice talks. A setting of around 20 per cent is roughly the speed of normal speech. One caveat with changing the speaking rate is that it is quite difficult to change Speaking Rate while VoiceOver is on.

1. Turn VoiceOver off if necessary. If it is on, first tap the VoiceOver On/Off button, then double tap it.
2. Adjust the Speaking Rate using the slider.
3. Turn VoiceOver back on. You immediately hear the updated voice speed. Re-adjust if necessary by repeating the instructions in this task.

HOT TIP: It is easier to adjust the speaking rate when speaking (VoiceOver) is off.

Zoom

The Zoom feature provides a way to magnify the screen. When on, it is controllable using three fingers together on the screen.

1. Tap Settings, tap General on the left, then tap Accessibility on the right.
2. Tap the Zoom button. A further screen provides the On/Off button for Zoom, along with instructions on how to use three fingers to control the Zoom feature.
3. Tap the On/Off button to turn Zoom on. Immediately the screen is magnified.
4. Tapping with three fingers together works as a toggle for the Zoom feature. If the screen is magnified, a tap with three fingers will bring it back to normal view. If in normal view, a tap with three fingers will magnify the screen.
5. When the screen is magnified, you can place three fingers on the screen and use them to scroll the screen. This is a nice feature because when the screen is magnified, there is less showing and scrolling is a way to pull what is off screen into the viewing area.

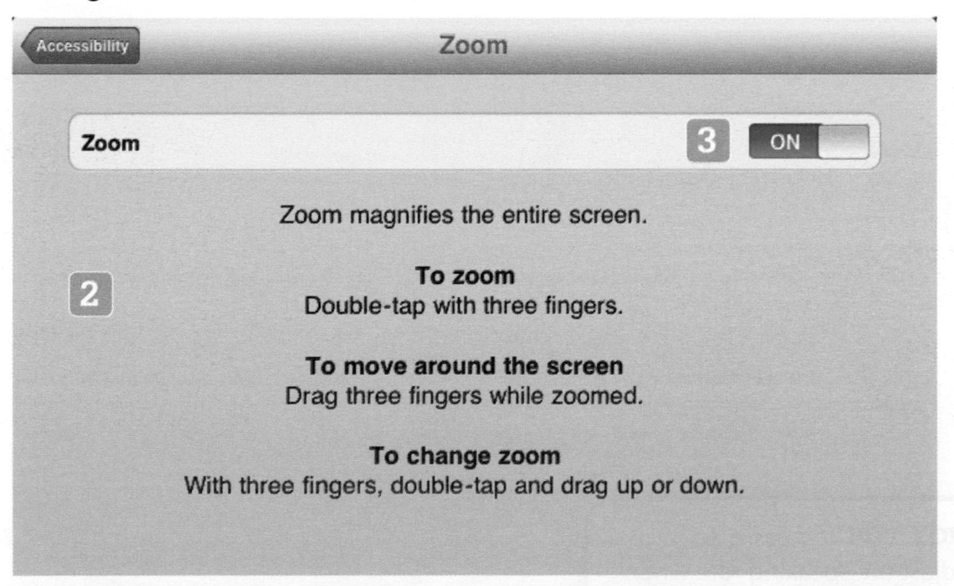

HOT TIP: A good approach to using Zoom is to double tap with three fingers to reduce the magnification back to normal, scroll around (or access an app, etc.) and then double tap again to Zoom.

White on Black

This is a single switch of the screen's colour scheme. Instead of a white background, it changes to black. Text, icons and other items that are on the screen change colours to make a strong contrast against the background. Text is white while the screen is black.

1. Tap Settings, tap General on the left, then tap Accessibility on the right.
2. Tap the White on Black On/Off button to turn the feature on.

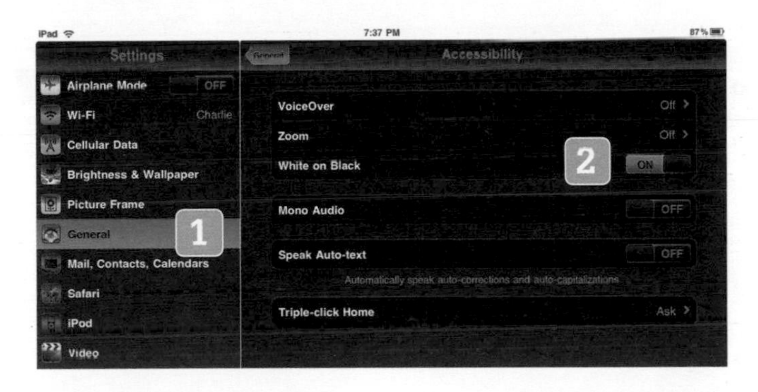

DID YOU KNOW?
Even photos are inverted. Compare these two versions of the same photograph.

Mono Audio

By default, audio is stereo. However, taking into account people with hearing issues, there is a setting to set the audio output to mono. This would benefit a person with hearing in only one ear, for example.

1 Tap Settings, tap General on the left, then tap Accessibility on the right.

2 Tap the Mono Audio On/Off button to turn the feature on.

DID YOU KNOW?
Audio played in stereo has different parts of the sound played through the left and right speakers that together provide the full sound. Mono sends all the audio to both the left and the right – therefore, listening to just one side of mono output provides the full sound.

HOT TIP: The mono output is most noticeable when headphones are worn.

How the Home button responds to a double click or a triple click

One feature that is not obvious at first is that the Home button can be pressed more than once in succession. If the iPod is playing a podcast, music or other audio, for instance, pressing the Home button twice in quick succession displays a small box to control the audio.

The real accessibility feature associated with the Home button is when you press it three times in quick succession. The iPad provides a choice of what the behaviour should be when the Home button is pressed three times.

1. Tap Settings, tap General on the left, then tap Accessibility on the right.
2. Tap Triple-click the Home Button. This leads to the list of options. The choices are:
   - Off – a triple press does nothing.
   - Toggle VoiceOver – VoiceOver is turned on or off.
   - Toggle White on Black – the screen colour inversion feature is turned on or off.
   - Ask – this instructs the iPad to present the options at the time of the triple press.

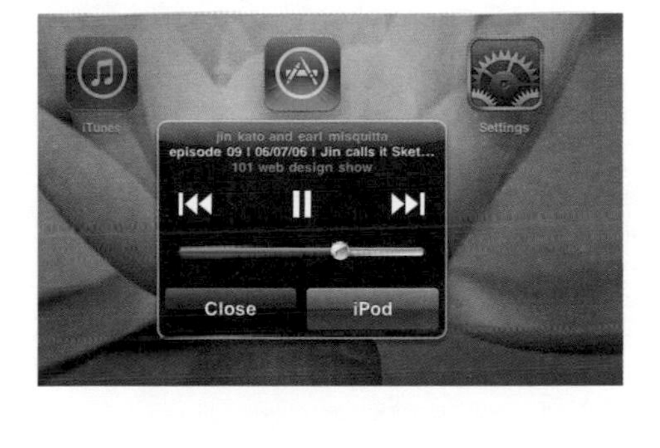

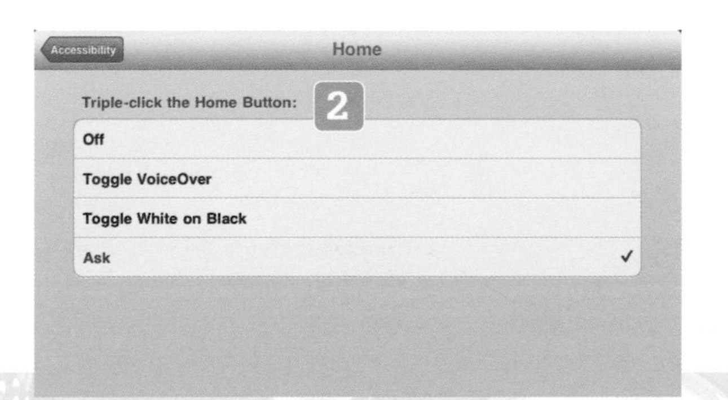

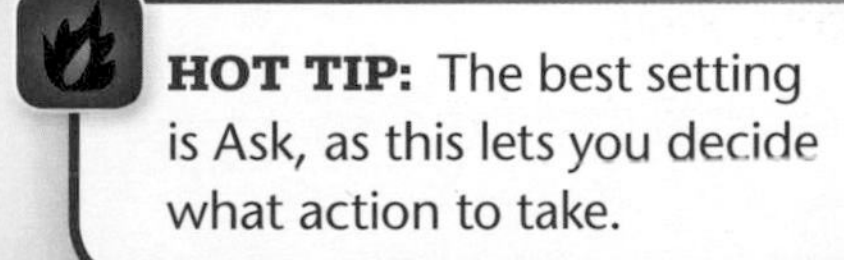

HOT TIP: The best setting is Ask, as this lets you decide what action to take.

How the Home button responds to a double click or a triple click

[illegible]

[illegible]

[illegible]

HOT TIP: [illegible]

15 More about Settings

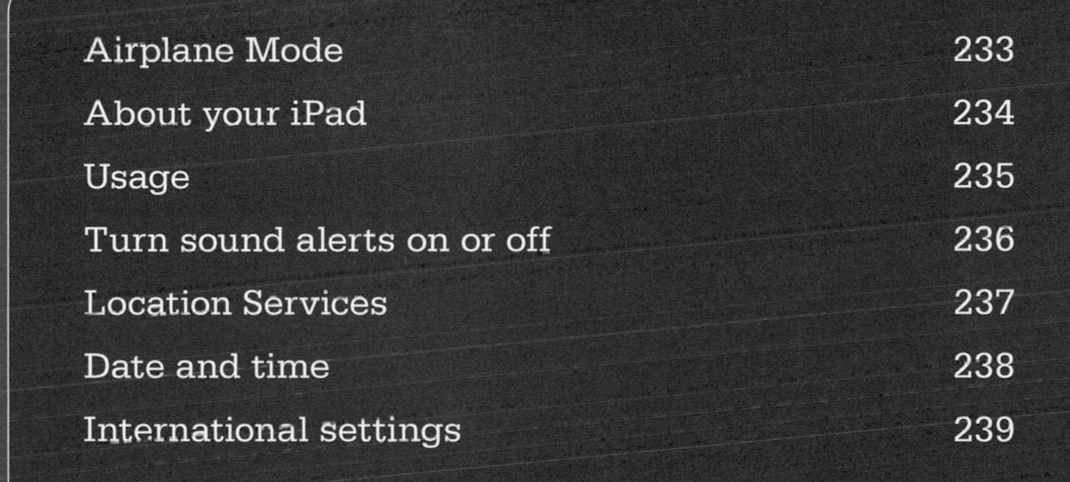

Introduction

Settings is a major component of the iPad. In Settings, you control the behaviour of various apps and the iPad itself. Also in Settings you can find out information about the iPad – for example, how much memory is available.

Throughout the book, Settings has been discussed in relation to the subject matter of a particular chapter. In this chapter we look at aspects of Settings that have not been covered earlier in the book.

Airplane Mode

When travelling on a commercial flight, wireless systems are usually not allowed to be on. The iPad has wireless ability in order to use 3G, Wi-Fi and Bluetooth services. Switching on Airplane Mode instantly turns off the assortment of wireless services.

Tap Settings. Tap the Airplane Mode button to toggle it on or off. When it is on, a small picture of an aircraft is visible in the upper left corner of the screen.

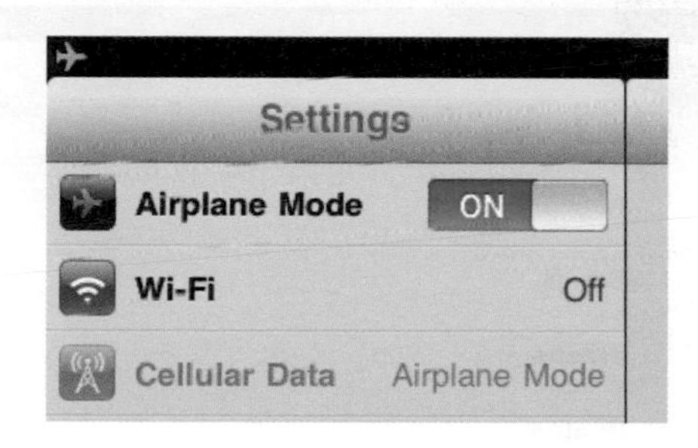

DID YOU KNOW?
Unlike most options in Settings, Airplane Mode has a simple On/Off button on the left side of the screen. There is nothing that appears on the right side that offers anything else to make selections. Airplane Mode quite simply is a yes or no choice.

ALERT: Airplane Mode is a setting available on the 3G/Wi-Fi versions of the iPad. If you do not have an iPad with these features, you will not see a setting for Airplane Mode.

About your iPad

There is a wealth of information available about your iPad. You can instantly see how many photographs, videos or songs are in the memory or how much overall memory (capacity) is left.

Tap Settings. Then tap General on the left. The first item on the right is About. Tap About. This leads to a further screen with the information.

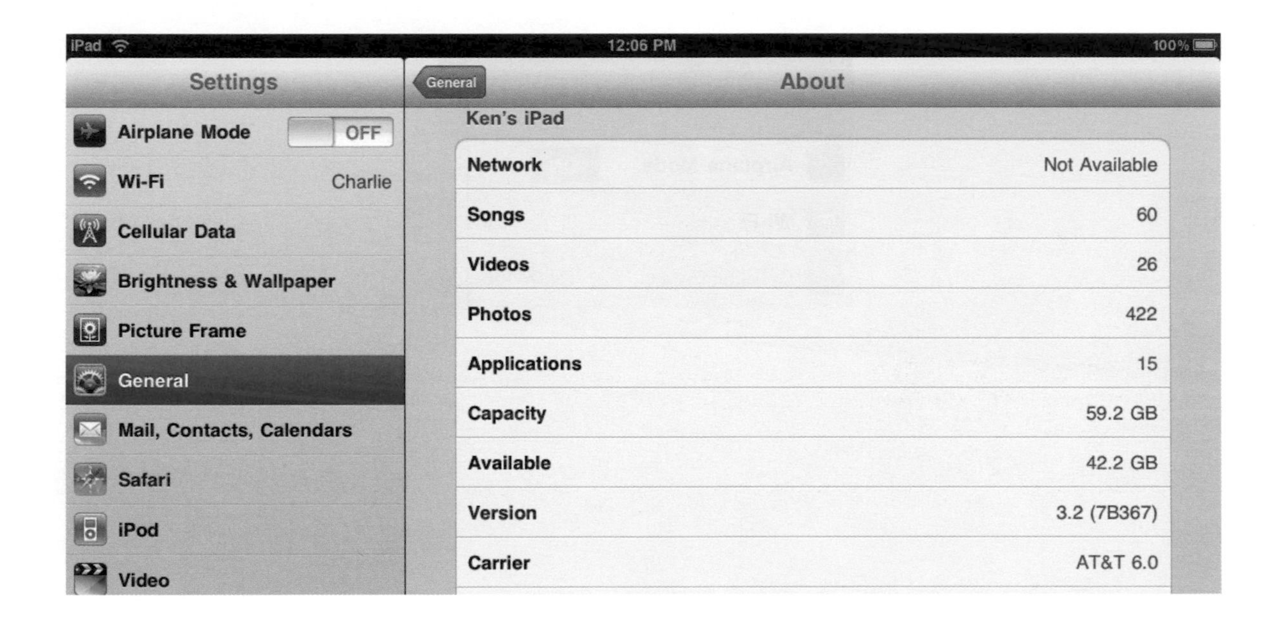

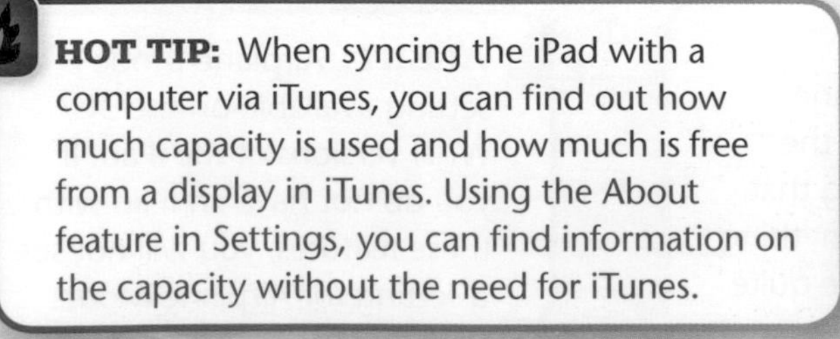

HOT TIP: When syncing the iPad with a computer via iTunes, you can find out how much capacity is used and how much is free from a display in iTunes. Using the About feature in Settings, you can find information on the capacity without the need for iTunes.

Usage

This setting pertains only to those with 3G service. You can find out how much data has been sent and received. If you are on a plan that has a data usage limit, you can track your usage.

Tap Settings. Tap General on the left. Tap Usage on the right. A further screen opens.

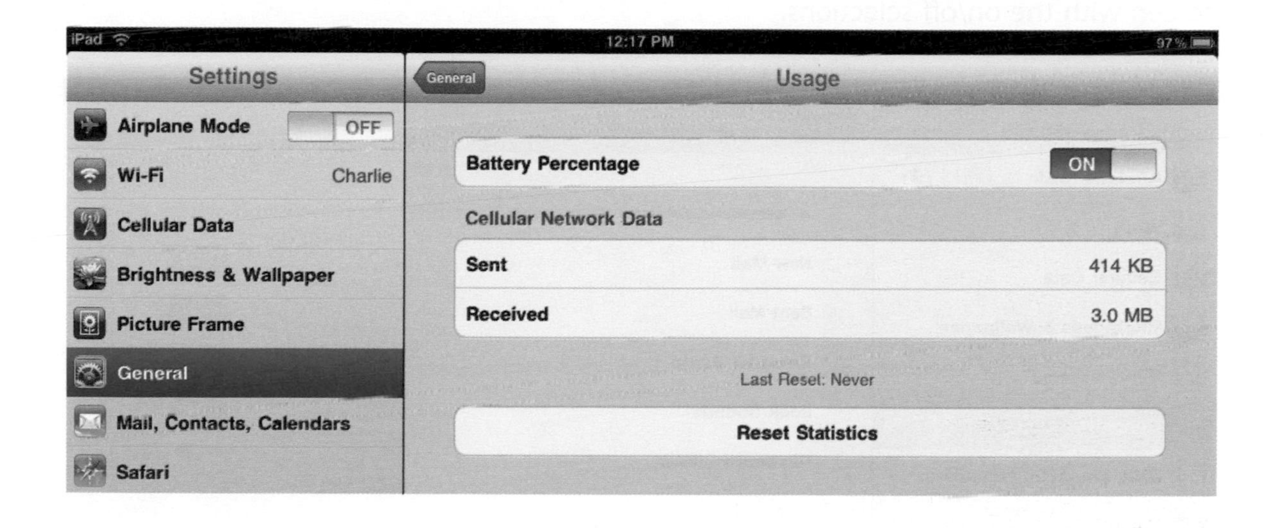

ALERT: The amount of data sent and received is shown, but there is no indication of the time period. Keep track of this yourself – at the bottom is a button to Reset Statistics. Tap this at the beginning of each billing period to reset the sent and received amounts to zero.

Turn sound alerts on or off

When certain actions occur, such as mail is sent or when you press a key on the keyboard, a sound is heard. That is, you have a choice whether a sound is heard or not. There are five actions you can set for sound on or off: New Mail, Send Mail, Calendar Alerts, Lock Sounds and Keyboard Clicks. Each of these has an On/Off button.

Tap Settings. Tap General on the left. On the right, tap Sounds. This leads to a further screen with the on/off selections.

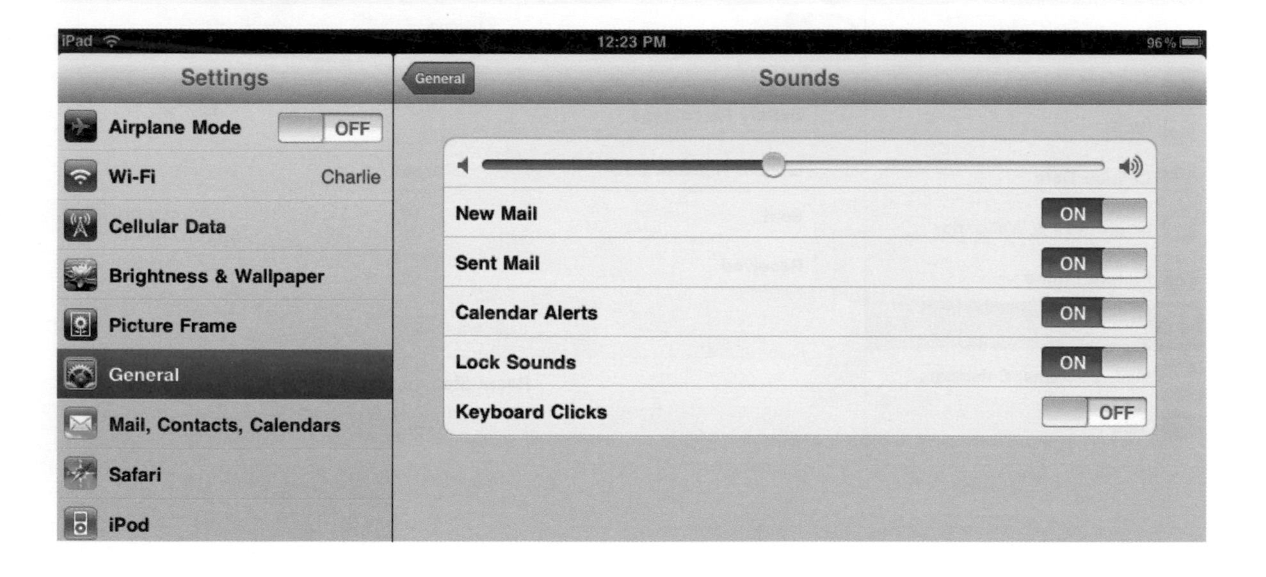

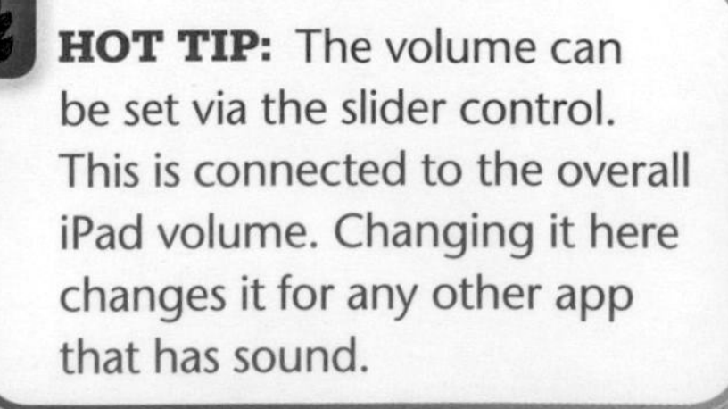

HOT TIP: The volume can be set via the slider control. This is connected to the overall iPad volume. Changing it here changes it for any other app that has sound.

Location Services

With the map app, and plenty of third-party apps, letting your location be known provides features that otherwise would not be available. For example, in Maps is the tracking button for pinpointing your location on the map. That is possible only when Location Services is set to on.

Tap Settings. Tap General on the left. On the right is a simple On/Off button to turn Location Services on or off. Set it to your preference. It is a good idea to leave it on – to make the most of the apps that use it.

HOT TIP: Location Services works only with 3G/Wi-Fi-enabled iPads.

Date and time

When 3G or Wi-Fi is enabled, the iPad can determine the date and time on its own. Without internet connectivity, you will need to set the correct date and time.

1. Tap Settings. Tap General on the left. Tap Date & Time on the right. A screen with options opens.
2. If Set Automatically is on and you have internet connectivity, there is nothing you have to do.
3. However, if/when you set Set Automatically to off (by tapping the On/Off button), further options appear.
4. If necessary, tap Time Zone to select the correct zone. Tapping this leads to a screen where you type in your location (city, etc.).
5. Tap Set Date & Time to display the box in which you dial in the correct date and time. The dialling-type switches display what is necessary to change either the date or time. This is determined by a tap on either the date or the time just above it.

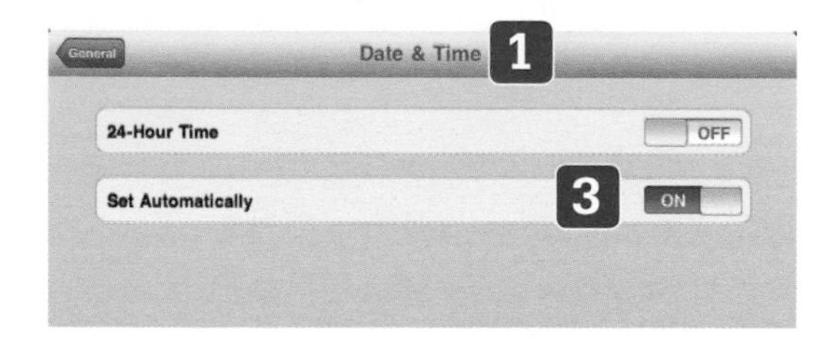

International settings

The iPad provides several nationalities with regard to language, keyboard and region. The choices within these categories may differ as selections are made. For example, selecting French for the language changes the choices within the Region setting.

1. Tap Settings. Tap General on the left. Tap International on the right. A new screen appears.
2. Tap Language. A new box opens with language selections. If you select one, the iPad will take a moment to reset itself. It may appear to turn off, but it ends up in Sleep mode. Just press the Home button for the screen to come back – only notice that some items are now in the selected language.
3. Tapping Keyboards displays any previously selected keyboards, along with an option to select from a further list.

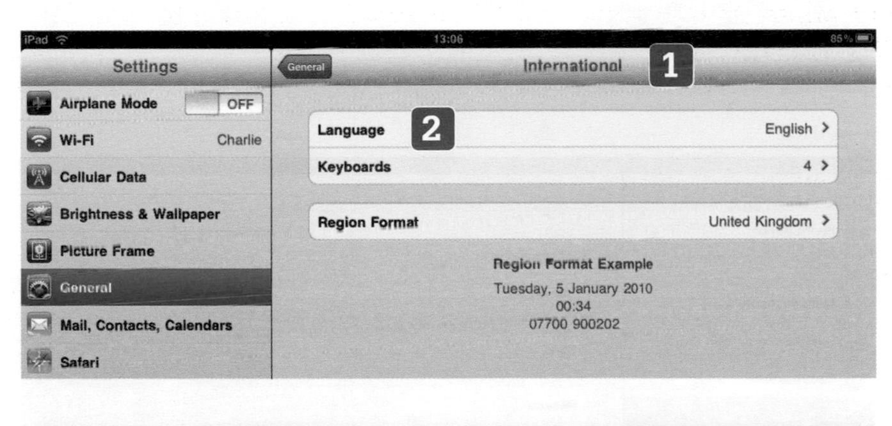

4 Region presents a list of dozens of selections. Those with arrows on the right lead to further selections within the region.

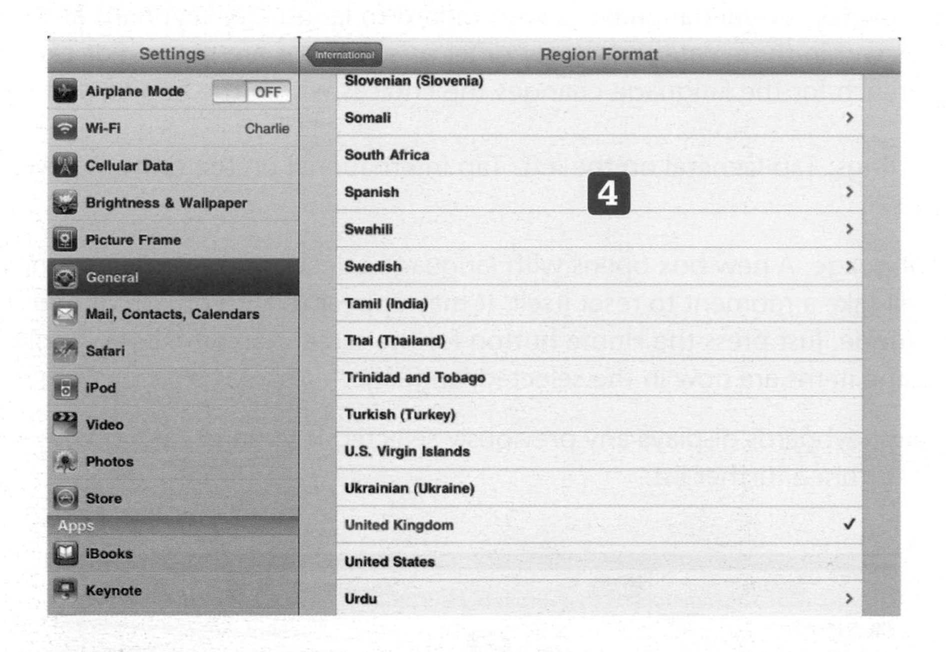

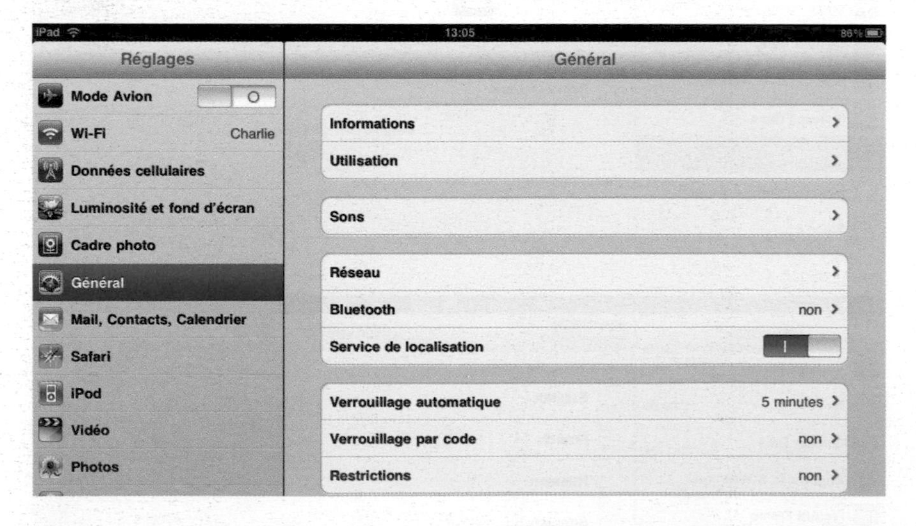

ALERT: Once you change the language, if you are not familiar with it you may have a difficult time getting the iPad back to working in English, as much of what you see will be in the language you have selected. Here is an example of what you see when French is selected. Note that not all of the screen items are in French, but perhaps enough are to confuse you if you don't know any French.

Top 10 iPad problems solved

Problem 1: The iPad is not responding

This is the equivalent of a crashed computer. No response from the device. At least the hope here is that you get it to respond to an attempt to turn it off. Then you can turn it back on and it should be free of whatever bogged it down.

1. Turn off the iPad by holding down the On/Off, Sleep/Wake button until the screen shows the red slider switch to complete the shutdown.
2. With your finger, move the slider on the screen to complete the shutdown.
3. Wait a few minutes, then hold down the On/Off, Sleep/Wake button until you see the Apple logo. The unit is turning back on.

HOT TIP: It is possible that holding down the On/Off, Sleep/Wake button until the red slider appears but *not* finishing the shutoff may work. After a few moments the red slider disappears, or tap the Cancel button if you see one. See whether the iPad works now – you might have to press the Home button first.

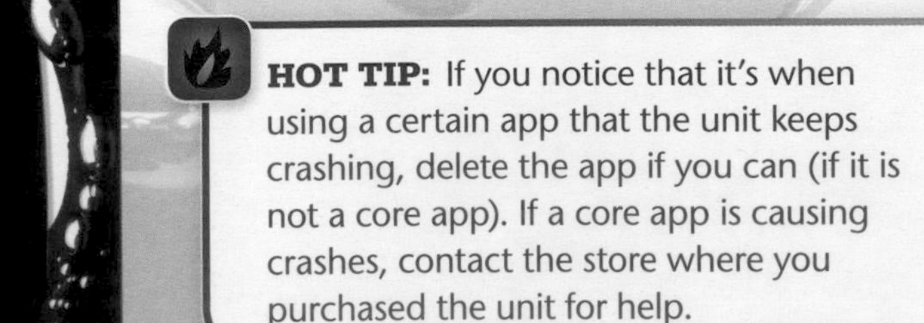

HOT TIP: If you notice that it's when using a certain app that the unit keeps crashing, delete the app if you can (if it is not a core app). If a core app is causing crashes, contact the store where you purchased the unit for help.

DID YOU KNOW?
It's a good idea to occasionally shut down the iPad anyway, even if there are no performance problems.

Problem 2: The iPad is not responding at all – not even to restart it

This occurrence is rare and hopefully you will never come across it. However, if the iPad is completely unresponsive, to the point that you can't even turn it off, then a system reset is needed. This method does not necessarily lose your data; however, syncing with the computer after the reset will put apps and media back onto the iPad.

1. Simultaneously press and hold down the On/Off, Sleep/Wake button and the Home button. Hold them down for several seconds until you see the Apple logo on the screen. Then let go of the buttons.
2. Wait a few moments until the logo disappears. The iPad should now be ready to go.

Problem 3: I need to erase all my data and files

Perhaps you are giving away your iPad. First you may want to erase all your data.

1. Tap Settings. On the left, tap General. On the right, at the bottom, is a button captioned Reset. You may have to scroll down to see it.
2. Tap the Reset button. A further screen is displayed in which you can select how to reset the iPad.
3. Tap Erase All Content and Settings. Confirm if prompted.

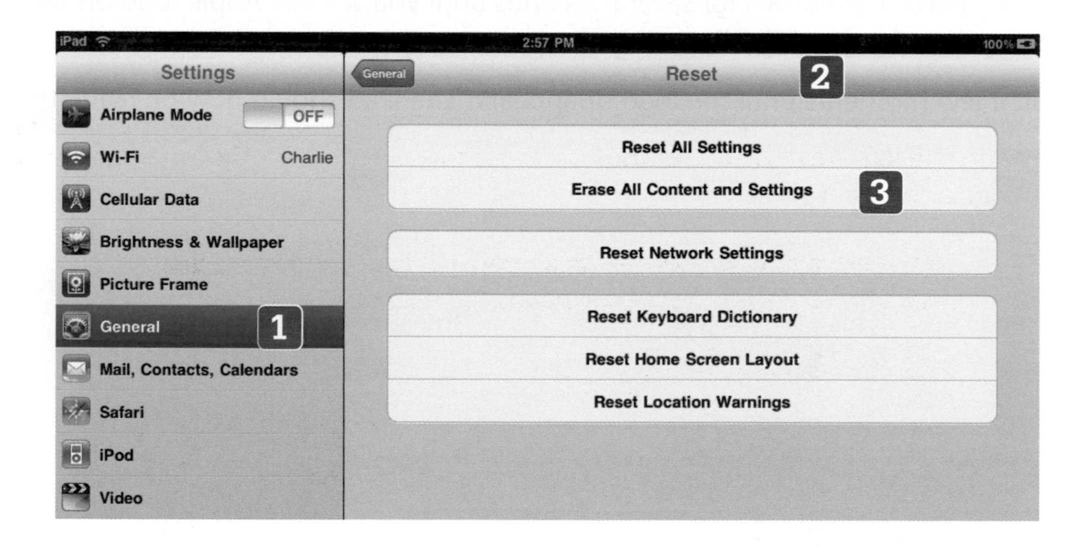

ALERT: This is an action you cannot undo – and you will not be able to find your contacts, appointments and other data that you entered. Make sure you don't need this information or have it backed up elsewhere.

HOT TIP: The other Reset options clear just portions of the iPad, as indicated by the captions.

Problem 4: I can't connect to the internet

Not having an internet connection when you expect it to be available can be frustrating, not to mention that it may prevent you from working. There are a few things to check.

1. Tap Settings. See whether Airplane Mode is on. If so, tap the On/Off button to turn it off.

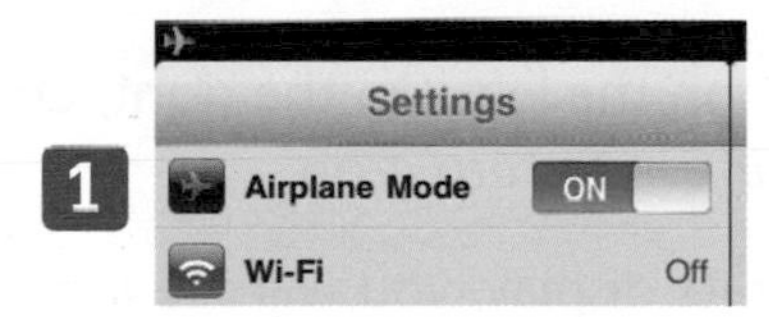

2. If you are using Wi-Fi, make sure you are in a hot spot. Also, tap Settings, then tap Wi-Fi on the left. Review the settings on the right. See that Wi-Fi is on and that you are connected with a network.

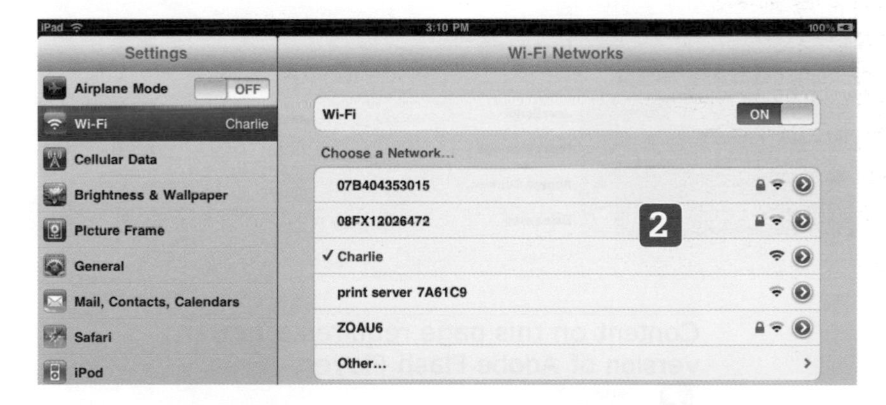

3. If you are using 3G, check the signal strength by looking at the number of bars. You might be in a location that has poor 3G coverage. If so, you will need to change locations until you have better reception.

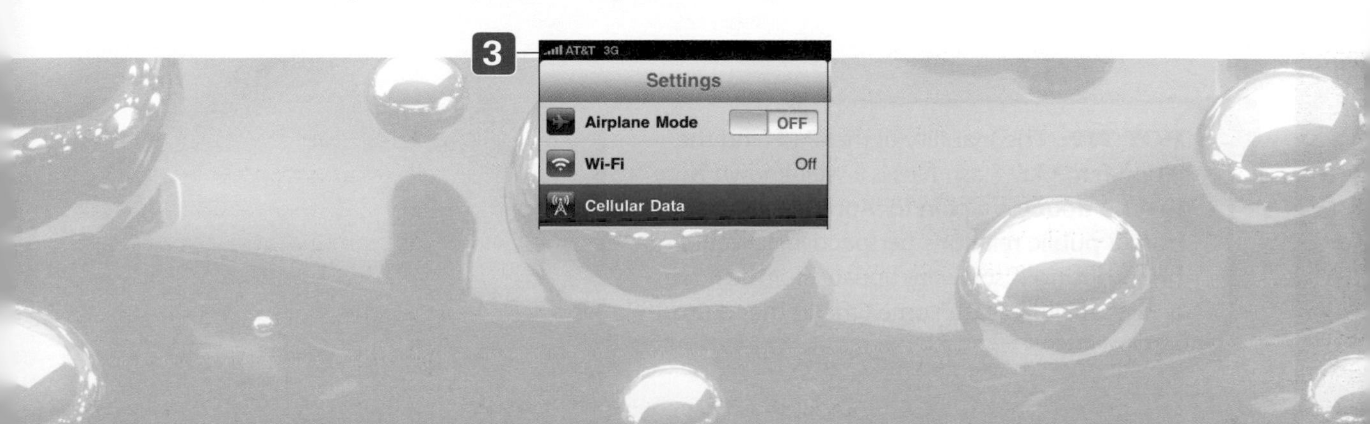

Problem 5: Some websites I visit are not working the way they should

There are two probable causes for this issue. One is JavaScript, the other is that you are trying to view a site that uses Flash. Flash is a technology used for visual work on websites. The Safari web browser on the iPad cannot display anything created with Flash.

1. Tap Settings. Then tap Safari on the left. On the right, check that JavaScript is set to On. If not, tap the On/Off button to turn it on.
2. If the site has Flash as part of its display, you will see a message asking that you download the latest Flash player. However, attempting to do so just ends up with another message that Flash is not allowed on the iPad.

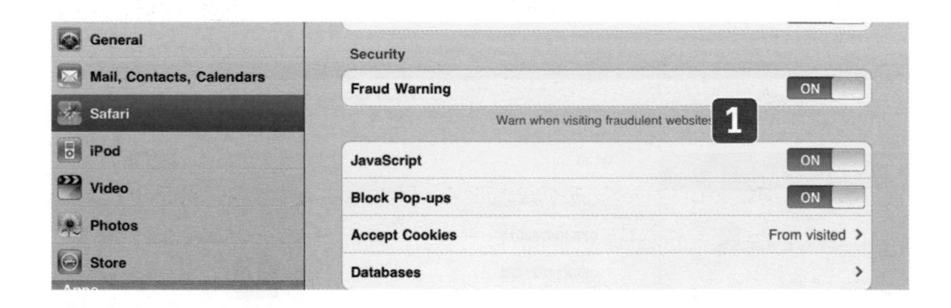

Content on this page requires a newer version of Adobe Flash Player.

Get ADOBE® FLASH® PLAYER

HOT TIP: The inability of the iPad (and the iPhone) to play Flash files is a well-known issue that no doubt is a pain for Apple to manage from a public relations perspective. It would not be surprising if software updates for the iPad and iPod allow Flash some time in the future.

Problem 6: The iPad displays the wrong time

When the iPad displays the wrong time the likely culprit is that the time setting is set for the wrong location.

1. Tap Settings, then tap General on the left. On the right, tap Date & Time. A further screen appears.
2. If Set Automatically is set to On, set it to Off by tapping the On/Off button.
3. Tap the Time Zone button and change the time zone to your location.

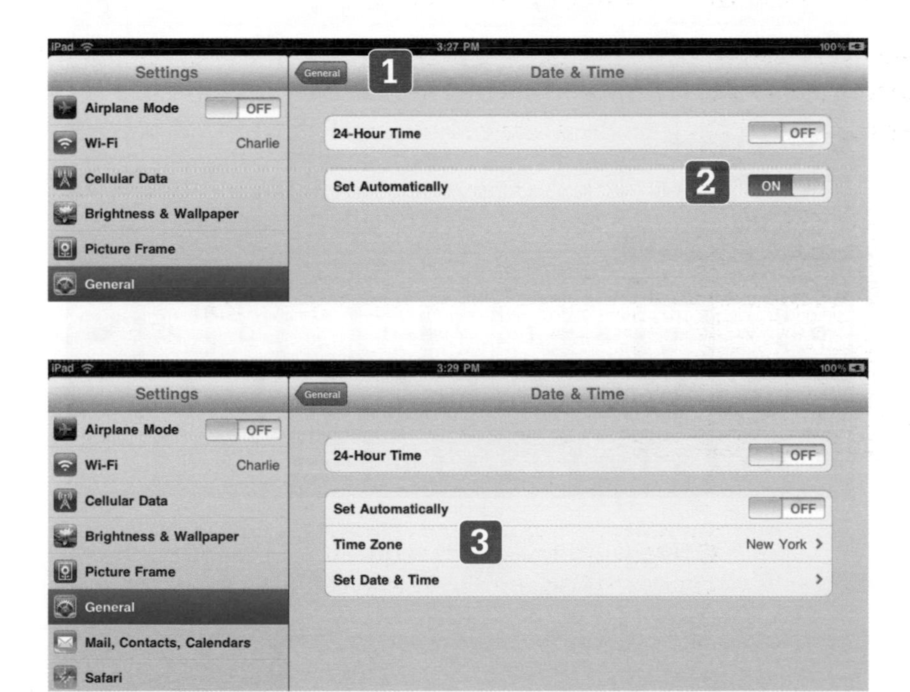

HOT TIP: When Set Automatically is set to On, it is not likely that the time is off, unless the battery ran out and the internal clock stopped, or you have been out of a hot spot or without 3G turned on for a significant time.

Problem 7: All emails I send say 'Sent from my iPad'

It is common for an email program to provide a setting for the 'signature' line. The iPad has this feature and it comes with the default 'Sent from my iPad'. This means that all emails that are sent will show this to the recipient. You can change it or delete it.

Tap Settings, then tap Mail, Contacts, Calendars. On the right is a button captioned Signature. Tap the button. An edit screen opens in which you can change it.

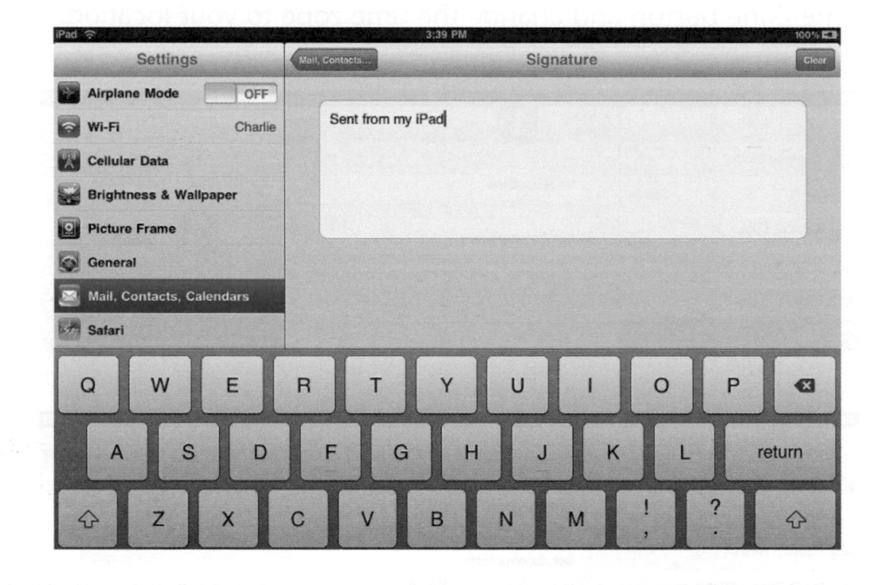

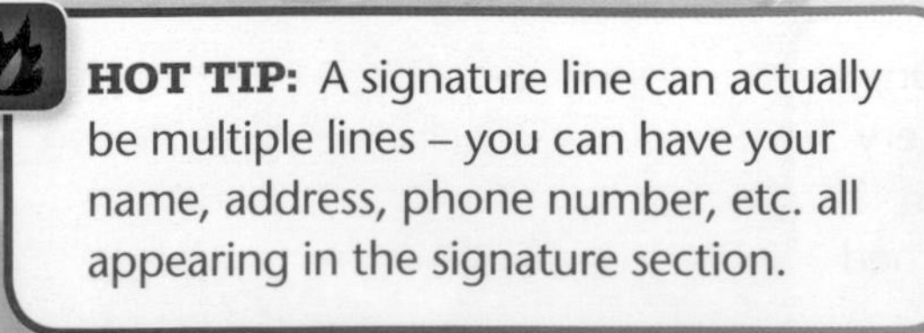

HOT TIP: A signature line can actually be multiple lines – you can have your name, address, phone number, etc. all appearing in the signature section.

Problem 8: My contacts are sorted by first name instead of last name

This is a matter of preference. Some people like to sort by first name, others like to sort by last name. Here is a picture showing a first-name sort.

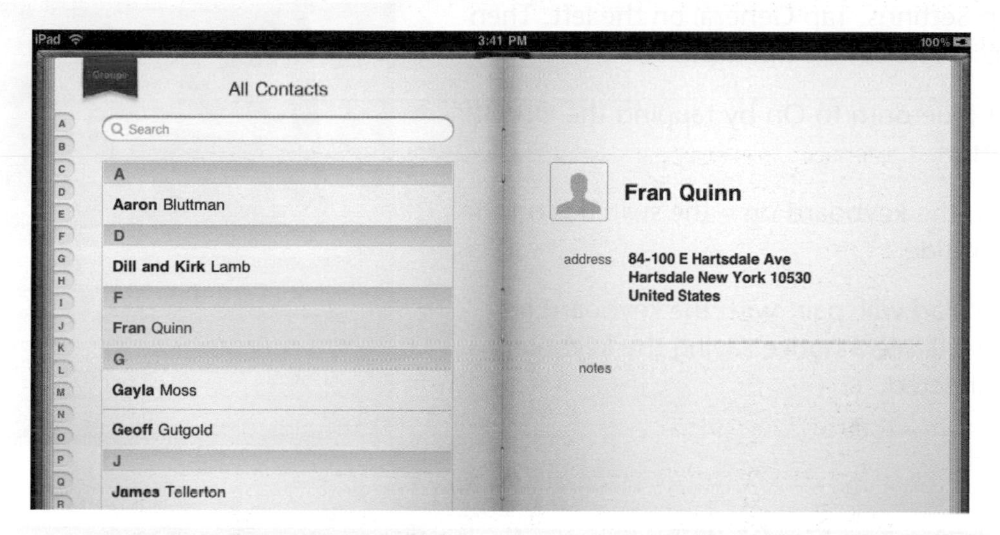

Tap Settings then tap Mail, Contacts, Calendars. On the right is a button captioned Display Order. Tap the button. A screen opens in which you select the display order by tapping on one of the choices.

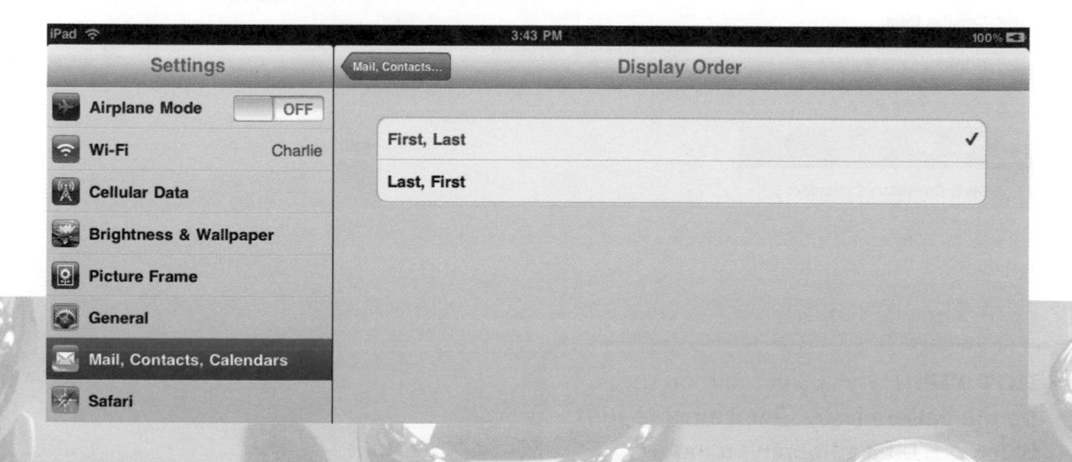

Problem 9: The virtual keyboard is difficult to use

As handy as it is, typing on a keyboard that appears on the screen just doesn't measure up to using a physical keyboard. A fix for this is to purchase Apple's wireless keyboard and use it with the iPad via Bluetooth technology.

1. Tap Settings. Tap General on the left. Then tap Bluetooth on the right.
2. Set Bluetooth to On by tapping the On/Off button.
3. Turn the keyboard on – the switch is on the right side.
4. The iPad will 'pair' with the keyboard and you will see a notice saying the keyboard is connected.

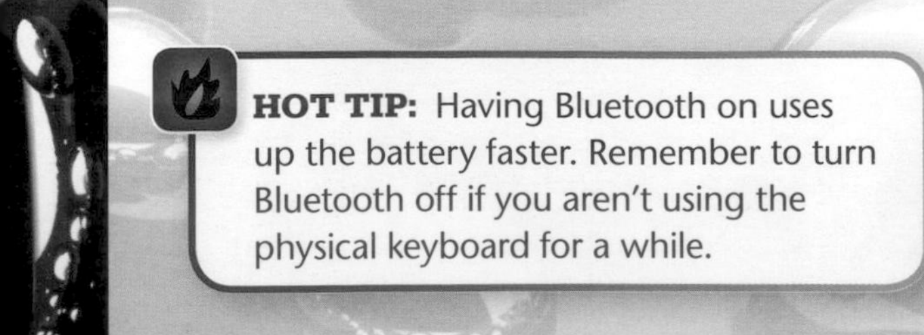

HOT TIP: Having Bluetooth on uses up the battery faster. Remember to turn Bluetooth off if you aren't using the physical keyboard for a while.

Problem 10: I erased an app (or audio, video) by mistake

To err is human. To erase an iPad app is forgivable and, thankfully, recoverable.

1. Sync with the computer by connecting the iPad to the computer. iTunes runs the sync.
2. The app will reappear on the iPad (assuming that during a previous sync a copy ended up on the computer).